DYSTOPIA'S PROVOCATEURS

DYSTOPIA'S PROVOCATEURS

Peasants, State, and Informality in the Polish-German Borderlands

Edyta Materka

Indiana University Press

Bloomington and Indianapolis

This book is a publication of

Indiana University Press
Office of Scholarly Publishing
Herman B Wells Library 350
1320 East 10th Street
Bloomington, Indiana 47405 USA

iupress.indiana.edu

The paper used in this publication meets the minimum requirements of the American National Standard for Information Sciences—Permanence of Paper for Printed Library Materials, ANSI
Z39.48-1992.

Manufactured in the United States of America

Cataloging information is available from the Library of Congress.

ISBN 978-0-253-02887-7 (cloth)
ISBN 978-0-253-02896-9 (paperback)
ISBN 978-0-253-02909-6 (ebook)

1 2 3 4 5   22 21 20 19 18 17

In memory of Czesław and Zofia

Nothing was your own except the few cubic centimetres inside your skull.

—George Orwell, *1984*

Contents

Acknowledgments

ONE OF THE last memories my father, Czesław, shared with me was of his lonely childhood growing up in a hay-thatched farmhouse surrounded by a bombarded agrarian landscape on the Polish-German borderlands after World War II. Abandoned by his family who had moved to a nearby city, he lived with his grandparents, who still suffered from illnesses contracted in Nazi concentration camps. He escaped his dystopian reality through the portals of adventure and history books. A week after he passed away, I began my doctoral studies at the London School of Economics and Political Science, where I would embark on a journey back to my village, searching for physical and memory fragments of that past as a means to reconnect with my father. This book is the product of a decade-long ethnographic exploration of the soul; namely, how ordinary people devised extraordinary ways to survive their private and societal dystopias.

Writing a postwar history of colonization on disputed territories is no easy task. I am indebted to those villagers who opened their doors and hearts not only to me but also to the very idea of historical investigation. They remain invisible behind pseudonyms for their own protection. I am deeply indebted to my late maternal grandmother Zofia who was the main gatekeeper during fieldwork, who believed in the project when others chose to "forget" history, and who always fought for the truth, especially during interviews with former socialist officials and elites. It was her childhood dream to become a geographer and I hope that our historical exploration of these borderlands together gave her some satisfaction of having made a contribution to the field. My mother, Bogusława, also connected me to her socialist-era networks, helped decipher the archives and interviews, and protected me from those who questioned my allegiances to the borderlands. My sister Małgorzata also helped document the German tombstones around the village. This book is the product of an intergenerational effort by village women—a demographic that has traditionally been the subject of many academic explorations but has itself been on the sidelines of "writing" history in a traditionally male-dominated field. Written in between the deaths of Czesław and Zofia, a chapter in my life when I sought survival strategies to deal with my own dystopia of trauma and loss, this book is now ready to take on a life of its own, and maybe even become a portal to individuals in search of agency or an escape from personal purgatories.

I am also grateful to those scholars who trusted my investigative instincts and recognized the import of writing a history of an invisible practice that could not be easily supported by laws, newspapers, or other conventional resources that bolster narratives in historical ethnography. Sharad Chari of the Department of Geography at University of California, Berkeley, and Gareth A. Jones of the Department of Geography and Environment at the London School of Economics and Political Science have provided years of mentorship and support well beyond the doctoral years. Frances Pine, of the Department of Anthropology at Goldsmiths, University of London, and Keith Halfacree, of the Department of Geography at Swansea University, served on my viva committee and encouraged me to revise my dissertation for publication. Alena Ledeneva, at the University College London School of Slavonic and East European Studies, who trailblazed the study of *blat* in Russia, reviewed this manuscript and boldly supported it through publication. An anonymous reviewer provided keen and incisive comments that helped me tackle structural issues I had avoided for too long. Editors Raina Nadine Polivka, Janice Frisch, and Jennika Baines at Indiana University Press were my compass in the wilderness of book publishing.

Fieldwork was funded by a full MPhil/PhD scholarship from the London School of Economics and Political Science, a John Coffin Trust Grant from the University of London, and the Polonia Aid Foundation Trust Grant. The writing process was funded by a Dissertation Writing Fellowship in East European Studies from the American Council of Learned Societies and the Harriet Irsay Scholarship from the American Institute of Polish Culture. My first fieldwork trip to Bursztyn in 2006 was funded by the Jerome and Lorraine Aresty Undergraduate Research Scholarship and supported by Gordon Schochet, Frank Popper, and Briavel Holcomb from Rutgers University's Edward J. Bloustein School of Planning and Public Policy. All views are my own and do not represent the positions of any of the organizations that provided funding.

I wrote most of this book as a postdoctoral fellow at Harvard University's Davis Center for Russian and Eurasian Studies. My brilliant colleagues Elena Ion, Elizabeth Ransome, Daria Bocharnikova, Krista Goff, and Rachel Koroloff provided much-needed collegiality and laughter during this uncertain time. I also benefited from Christina Thompson's book-publishing seminar at Harvard, where I had the fortune of meeting scholars in the same professional stage in life and sharing my work with them. The Harriman Institute and East Central European Center at Columbia University, both the Polish Academy of Social Sciences and Collegium Civitas in Warsaw, and the Center for Place, Culture, and Politics at the City University of New York gave me an academic home during various stages of the writing process. David Harvey's weekly seminar at CUNY was intellectually stimulating, for I was in the presence of devastatingly brilliant minds. I also wrote portions of the book as a writer-in-residence at the Milkwood International Residency in the Czech Republic, the Nes Artist Residency in Iceland, and the Vermont Studio Center in the United States. It was at the Vermont

Studio Center where I met novelist Kiran Desai, who told me I should become a writer. Her kind words have been my guiding light. During the manuscript revision, the good people at Pennylane Coffee in New York City saved a chair for me at the counter and nourished me with good food, coffee, and company.

A wonderful and talented group of professionals helped me pull the manuscript together. The staff at the National Museum in Warsaw, the Muzuem Ziemi Lubuskiej in Zielona Góra, Archiwum Państwowe w Koszalinie, the British Library, UCL Library at the School of Slavonic and East European Studies, the Harvard Map Collection, and the Herder Institut all helped me secure my resources and archives for this book. Katherine Faydash and Jay Harward at Newgen North America beautifully polished the manuscript and prepared it for publication. Molly Mullin, anthropologist and editorial consultant, tirelessly edited multiple versions of the manuscript and graciously shared her wisdom. Aliza Krefetz meticulously proofread the manuscript and translated the German terms both in the text and in the archives. I also want to express thanks to Michael Needham, at Humanities First, who edited an earlier version of the introduction; Jim Lance, at Cornell University, who provided valuable feedback on how to restructure the book; Daniel Huffman, at somethingaboutmaps, who patiently worked through many versions of the map; and Alexander Zholkovsky, at the University of Southern California, who allowed me to use his description of the Russian kombinator as "dystopia's provocateur" in the title. This book would have not been possible without the care and support of this entire team who joined me along this quest.

But most of all, I am most grateful to my partner, Neil Alejandro Anderson, who has been the invisible force behind this book throughout all of these years, who has given me love and laughs during the darkest times, cooked dinner during nail-biting deadlines, read through and edited dozens of drafts, financially supported the book during funding gaps, formatted more manuscript drafts than we could count, and most importantly, never doubted my abilities to fulfill my dream of becoming a writer even when I was hopelessly lost in the labyrinths of history, ethnography, theory, and personal tragedy. He always brought me back down to earth, helped me see the silver lining and believe in a new world of possibilities just over the horizon.

Note on Pronunciation and Translation

1. Polish is a Slavic language written in the Latin alphabet that includes the letters *ą, ć, ę, ł, ś, ź* and *ż*. All come after their Latin counterparts *a, c, e, l, s,* and *z*. Here is how to pronounce them:

ą = "ahn," as in the German word *Autobahn*
ć = "ch" as in *change*
ę = "en" sound in the middle of word and "eh" sound at the end of a word (e.g., *będę* is pronounced b*en*d*eh*)
ł = "w" as in *walk*
ś = "sh" as in *share*
ź = "j" as in the name *Jean*
ż = "zh" as in mira*ge*

2. All translations are my own. Polish was a second language for different ethnic minorities—Ukrainian, Belarusian, German, Kashubian, Lithuanian, and so on—who populated the Recovered Territories after World War II.

3. The term *kombinacja* has many colloquial variations and conjugations: *kombinacya, kombinować, kombinowanie, skombinować, wykombinować, skombinowane, kombinatsiia*. I use the noun form *kombinacja* for clarity purposes and only include the other conjugations if they were used in texts and quotes.

4. I anglicize the plural version of some terms like *kombinator, kułak,* and *kołchoźnik* by adding an *s* rather than their Polish conjugations, because this is easier for English speakers to read.

5. With the exception of Zofia, Czesław, and Bogusława, people's names have been changed to preserve their anonymity. I have kept the names of large cities like Warsaw, Łódź, Zgorzelec, and Słupsk but have changed the names of all villages and state farms. I have substituted these pseudonyms in brackets in the bibliography.

Acronyms

AK   Home Army
Armia Krajowa

AWRSP State Treasury Agricultural Property Agency
Agencja Własności Rolnej Skarbu Państwa

CDU   Christian Democratic Union of Germany
Christlich Demokratische Union Deutschlands

GRN   Commune State Council
Gminna Rada Narodowa

GS   "Peasants' Self-Help" Commune Cooperative
Gminna Spółdzielnia "Samopomoc Chłopska"

KP PZPR County Committee of the Polish United Workers' Party
Komitet Powiatowy Polskiej Zjednoczonej Partii Robotniczej

KR   Agricultural Circle
Kółko Rolnicze

KRN   State National Council
Krajowa Rada Narodowa

LWP   Polish People's Army
Ludowe Wojsko Polskie

MO   Citizens' Militia
Milicja Obywatelska

MZO   Ministry of Recovered Territories
Ministerstwo Ziem Odzyskanych

NATO   North Atlantic Treaty Organization

ORMO   Volunteer Reserve Militia
Ochotnicza Rezerwa Milicji Obywatelskiej

PGR   State Agricultural Farm
Państwowe Gospodarstwo Rolne

PKWN   Polish Committee of National Liberation
Polski Komitet Wyzwolenia Narodowego

PPR   Polish Workers' Party
Polska Partia Robotnicza

PRL   Polish People's Republic
Polska Rzeczpospolita Ludowa

PUR   State Repatriation Office
Państwowy Urząd Repatriacyjny

PZPR   Polish United Workers' Party
Polska Zjednoczona Partia Robotnicza

PZZ   Polish Western Union
Polski Związek Zachodni

RP   Republic of Poland
Rzeczpospolita Polska

RSP   Agricultural Production Cooperative
Rolnicza Spółdzielnia Produkcyjna

RWPG   Council for Mutual Economic Assistance
Rada Wzajemnej Pomocy Gospodarczej

SKR   Agricultural Circles Cooperative
Spółdzielnia Kółek Rolniczych

UB   Ministry of Public Security
Urząd Bezpieczeństwa

UNRRA   United Nations Relief and Rehabilitation Administration

ZLP   Polish Writers' Union
Związek Literatów Polskich

ZNMR   State Agricultural Machine Enterprise
Zakład Naprawczy Mechanizacji Rolnej

ZO   Recovered Territories
Ziemie Odzyskane

ZUS   Social Insurance Institution
Zakład Ubezpieczeń Społecznych

DYSTOPIA'S PROVOCATEURS

Map of postwar territorial changes, 1945. Courtesy Daniel P. Huffman.

Introduction

Toward the end of World War II, the Soviet Union's annexation of eastern Poland and Poland's annexation of eastern Germany precipitated one of the largest demographic upheavals in European history. The Soviet-backed Polish government expelled millions of Germans west of the new Polish-German border and replaced them with millions of ethnic Poles from south and central Poland, along with "repatriated Poles," a group comprising Ukrainians, Lithuanians, Belarusians, Kashubians, Jewish Holocaust survivors, and other ethnic minorities from Poland's lost east and newly acquired German lands.[1] The Polish government called this new western frontier the "Recovered Territories" (Ziemie Odzyskane)—a Polish homeland that had been lost to German colonialism for a millennium.

What these Slavic settlers would "recover," however, was unclear. Some propaganda posters depicted the German lands as an El Dorado, filled with jewelry, Singer sewing machines, porcelain, schnapps, and women waiting to be claimed as reparations for Nazi atrocities. Others depicted cheerful peasants marching arm in arm on a socialist mission to carry out the government's agrarian reform by systematically ousting German property owners from large landed estates and redistributing the land to Polish settlers. Fabricating the wildly successful imaginary of these territories as Poland's recovered western homeland gave the provisional communist authorities in Lublin and Warsaw the political capital with which to Polonize these Nazi lands and transform them into a socialist space with a Soviet-style command economy.

From the genesis of socialism to its disintegration in these lands, the Slavic settlers adopted a strategy called *kombinacja*, which allowed them to negotiate power and preserve a modicum of agency even as the claustrophobia-inducing fetters of oppression and marginalization constrained them. Kombinacja involves the artistic, innovative practice of bending legal or cultural rules to access commodities, labor, information, and power. As an informal strategy, it is a type of agency that reworks difficult economic, political, or cultural conditions. When used discursively, it becomes a culturally sanctioned way of aligning with certain ideas and activities and disconnecting oneself from others. It can be a powerful tool for building both social control and solidarity. Kombinacja is most often practiced by individuals who manipulate minor loopholes in their everyday lives, but when groups use it en masse in the public sphere and appropriate it as a dominant political discourse, it can ruin, and even substitute for, a state-regulated formal economy. Memories of informality provide a new historical narrative alongside the official state records and can help contextualize the conditions under which new worlds emerge and disintegrate on the local level.

Dystopia's Provocateurs traces villagers' rich memories of kombinacja to tell their stories of metamorphosis before, during, and after socialism in the Recovered Territories. It tracks how peasants, workers, and state elites (nomenklatura) alike have dabbled in the art of kombinacja to survive, and even benefit from, economic and political gridlock that has occurred under both socialism and capitalism. In doing so, it offers a broader understanding of how informality has been a site of ingenuity and inequality, innovation and suffering, across time and space. Contrary to informality studies that romanticize the practice of informality as a form of resistance against neoliberalism, this historical ethnography cautions that informality can be used to subvert and accommodate the state, to subjugate and crystallize hegemony, as those marginalized by power use it to control the conditions of their own subjection and those in positions of power use it to control the conditions of others' subjection.

Terra Incognita

There are as many definitions and histories of kombinacja as there are people in Poland. I define *kombinacja* as the improvisational process of reworking economic, political, or cultural norms for personal gain. A *kombinator* creatively bends the rules to appropriate a desired resource, like food, commodities, labor, information, or power, and then "combines" or conceals the act of appropriation without leaving a trace.[2] As "dystopia's provocateur," he or she expertly navigates the Orwellian "labyrinthine world of doublethink," performing magical tricks in a liminal dimension betwixt and between physical, political, economic, cultural, and religious boundaries, rendering them porous.[3] A kombinator is not an anarchist by definition, for he or she could equally be identified as God, a state, or an all-powerful process like industrialization that can reorder entire landscapes to consolidate hegemony. A kombinator can be a dictator or a peasant. Likewise, no one owns kombinacja; it is a "weapon of the weak" and a "weapon of the strong."[4] But it is not ambiguous; that is, in each context, there is bad and good kombinacja. It is a game.

Which strategies constitute exploitation, and which resistance, is in the eye of the beholder. Those disenfranchised by a perceived "bad" kombinacja that schemes to benefit from others' misery can also devise "good" kombinacja to rework or check it in a way that benefits "us." The judgment depends on many factors, including class, ethnicity, nationality, gender, politics, aesthetics, and proximity to state power. State officials and peasants could each see the other as the bad kombinator, even though they both commit similar kinds of kombinacja, like pilfering from state warehouses. Although as a practice it is open to all, the discourse of kombinacja reveals a field of struggle over power between competing actors. In a dog-eat-dog world, everyone sees their kombinacja as necessary and therefore justifiable.

Plagued by a millennium of wars, partitions, and border and regime changes, the Polish people have grown quite cynical about the utopian visions of dictatorships, the permanence of borders, and the finality of historical regimes. Peasants, in particular, many of whom have had no formal education in history, philosophy, or political economy, have developed kombinacja as part of their discourse to understand how processes like oppression and occupation take hold of everyday life. They have, in turn, forged socially sanctioned antiestablishment practices to adapt to drastically shifting powerscapes represented by "the establishment." Thus, the discourse of good and bad kombinacja itself adopts the positionality of the disenfranchised, who have been perpetually excluded from both resource pools and access to formal political platforms while being perpetually sapped of their resources, capital, labor, and privacy by each new order. Of course, the caveat is that anyone with a mental map of the state's spatial, symbolic, and institutional powerscapes could lay claim to that position. Local state elites overwhelmed by a peasant uprising could justify their tyranny by depicting themselves as disenfranchised, overworked villagers burdened by the monstrous pressures and responsibilities forced upon them by the higher echelons of the state.

Kombinacja's dual role as a tool of oppression and resistance has origins in Western philosophy and historical events. The term *kombinacja* comes from an archaic usage of the English term *combination*, or "freedom of association," a set of practices that fascinated nineteenth-century Enlightenment thinkers like John Stuart Mill, Adam Smith, and Karl Marx at the dawn of the Industrial Revolution in Great Britain. Before the advent of labor and trade unions, only employers ("masters") were allowed "to combine," or meet to agree on working conditions like wages, hours, and the use of apprentices; their goal was to ensure they did not compete for labor. Anti-combination laws, in contrast, prohibited "workers' combinations" from legally forming and fighting for their share in a quickly industrializing workplace. The revelation that the elites themselves combined against worker combinations shattered the perception of economic wealth as part of the natural order, exposing the organized machinations used by elites to subjugate workers. The drama over combination rights in Britain throughout the nineteenth century led to the birth of trade unions and to the modern state.

This notion that the elite "combined" against the workers by corrupting government with their economic interests, and that in turn, the workers could "combine" against the elites, enchanted the nineteenth-century Polish intelligentsia, many of whom were living in exile in France and Britain, watching their country struggle to survive under Russian, Prussian, and Austrian partitions. Poland had been erased from the geopolitical map. Reeling from a failed military insurrection against the Russian tsar in 1864, Polish novelists, the era's bards of nationalism, infused their literature with economic critiques of the "kombinacya" of foreign industrial capitalism that disenfranchised Polish workers. They suggested that Poles could counter those forces with their own kombinacja, through Luddism or by psychologically separating themselves from the foreign partition system. Imagination, creative thinking, and the forging of economic alternatives were all survival strategies that amounted to kombinacja against partition. Kombinacja helped ordinary people understand not only the processes working against them but also what they could do to combat those processes without any legal rights. Oppressed by the conditions that invasions of bad kombinacja had brought into existence, the Polish people would fight back using a kombinacja of their own. Resistance shifted from visible military uprisings to invisible, private self-determination. Embracing strategies of liminality became the organizing principle of an underground, nationalist resistance movement called organic work (*praca organiczna*). This may be one reason many Poles today simply define *kombinacja* as "thinking," or as deploying creative thought in the privacy of one's head to unfetter oneself from an oppressive situation.

Kombinacja took on a life of its own as new generations adapted it to their struggles. After the First World War and the reconstitution of Polish borders in 1918, gay and women's rights novelists in Poland battled the unnatural "bad" kombinacja of heterosexual norms that suppressed sexual self-determination, subversively inserting the term *kombinacja* in Polish literature as a sexual euphemism to normalize homosexuality by engaging readers in imagining homosexual acts—thereby expanding the sexual horizons of the Polish imagination. Later, after the outbreak of the Second World War, kombinacja leaped across literary genres, resurfacing in the oral histories of war and Holocaust survivors. Holocaust memoirs and fiction described how "bad" kombinators collaborated with Nazi guards to loot abandoned Jewish property while "good" kombinators black-marketeered across camp borders to acquire the extra piece of bread that helped them survive. Everyone used kombinacja to survive, but to some, kombinacja that colluded with Nazis to acquire goods was less ethical than kombinacja that subverted the Nazi regime, sometimes with the aim of acquiring those same goods. After the war, during the birth of socialism in Poland, this bifurcation took on class dynamics. Peasants who pilfered from state land to feed their private livestock, workers who installed state property into private homes for vodka, and communist party officials who moonlighted as black marketeers used kombinacja, but each saw the other as a detriment to the ideals of the socialist revolution. Since the collapse of the Soviet Union, postsocialist kombinators have included village officials, who channel European Union funds into former state farms for private gain, and the fallen proletarians, who act to secure quickly diminishing entitlements and economic niches in hopes of surviving neoliberalization. Elites use kombinacja to obtain the trappings of a Western, middle-class lifestyle, while the poor use it to keep from falling into the abyss of poverty and eastern "backwardness." Historical inquiry into kombinacja reveals its contextual treatment of time: stories and memories of kombinacja in the literature do not culminate in public spectacles of resistance between two opposing forces. Instead, they take place in the realm of timeless and invisible struggles that migrate across generations, identities, and borders. How is kombinacja socially reproduced, and how does it migrate to new sites? What does it mean to transform into a kombinator, and how does that transformation occur?

This historical ethnography intercepts kombinacja in the Polish-German borderlands after the Second World War. It attempts the impossible: to give the kombinators a history and to give form to their polysemic ideology. It investigates kombinacja along a trio of dimensions: as a practice of assembling scarce resources in the face of ideological constraints; as an ambivalent discourse about individuals, community, the state, and history; and as a flexible, context-dependent method of narrating history and societies in transition. Communist authorities in Warsaw had carte blanche to Polonize and Sovietize the newly absorbed German lands with an uprooted, diverse population of Poles, Ukrainians, Belarusians, Kashubians, Germans, Silesians, Lithuanians, Latvians, Greeks, Mazurians, and Jewish Holocaust survivors. People of diverse ethnicities, linguistic groups, political leanings, and religious backgrounds adopted kombinacja vis-à-vis the Polonization of the German lands and the genesis of a modern state in the borderlands. How did a diverse group of settlers embrace the art of kombinacja? How did they transform into kombinators? Could the practice of kombinacja have been a marker of a new, modern, Polish-Soviet identity in the borderlands?

To be perfectly honest, I did not set out in search of kombinacja when I started my fieldwork. At the time, I was concerned with questions regarding the checkerboard effect of Soviet collectivization, namely, why some villages had collectivized while their neighbors retained a more or less private agricultural structure, and how uneven Soviet development trajectories continued to affect capitalist transformation in these villages. To this end, I undertook multiple fieldwork trips between 2009 and 2014 to my village of Bursztyn in the northern part of the Recovered Territories, where my maternal grandparents settled on a German farm in 1946, where my parents lived under socialism, and where I was raised in the 1980s. Over the course of these trips, I interviewed sixty members of the first generation of settlers in the village.[5] When I interviewed Fidelis, a former Communist Party activist who had spread the gospel of Soviet collectivization to the settlers in the 1950s, he recalled that villagers used kombinacja for the express purpose of evading collectivization. The borderlands, as peripheral and contested spaces, enabled and helped to cloak the practices of kombinacja.

Although I knew about kombinacja through early socialization into the practice and discourse, I had never thought of it as a process that could have given the borderlands their "aesthetic" checkerboard identity, or for that matter, as a deterrent to entire development policies. I did not know it could be such an effective tool. However, when I returned to my interviews and retraced the contexts in which villagers had used the word *kombinacja*, I realized that this was the history people had been trying to tell me all along; of the terrible and dark ways the state and its elites had schemed against them, and of the ingenious and often funny strategies they had used in response to dupe the state. Since then, I have sought to understand not only how kombinacja migrated across space and to new groups of people but also the consequences this kind of informality has had for many types of development in the borderlands.

Memories of informality offer a fascinating historical account of transformation, but their pluralism makes it difficult to situate them in a linear historical narrative with dates, events, and major characters. Nonetheless, these memories exist, and together they present a particular kind of historical narrative. Villagers' memories of kombinacja soared through time and space, spanning wartime Nazi occupation, the arrival of Stalinism in the village, the various stages of socialism, the collapse of the Soviet Union, and the postsocialist transition into capitalism. Bursztynians saw history on a broad scale; events that occurred centuries ago are very much relevant in the present. They shared stories of survival and suffering, stories that told of being excluded from resources, time and time again, by system after system. Reconstructing their memories of kombinacja, I uncovered horrific human rights abuses and the stubborn resilience of feudal institutions in the postwar period that were, like kombinacja itself, scarcely mentioned in the state archives or in any historical record. Sometimes, it was unclear which system the villagers were talking about—capitalism or socialism, wartime or postwar—but perhaps this blurring of history was a symptom of their cynicism toward any regime that promised change. I began to see memories of kombinacja as a distinct historical archive that drew its legitimacy not from "law" or "political economy" or "facts," but from the resonance between works of literature and "past" lives and events. Villagers legitimized their kombinacja stories under socialism, for example, by relating them to similar kombinacja contexts that they had experienced in the Nazi period, or had read about in works of fiction. These were the "sources" of legitimacy—not state law, not political principles, not even the Holy Bible. Because many of the original settlers had to overcome political, ethnic, and religious differences to form a community, the shared rules and tenets of kombinacja provided the basis for an expression of local culture with which everyone could identify.

Curiously, villagers' personal memories of kombinacja followed a collective pattern of remembrance and forgetting. While they recalled kombinacja as a widespread practice used to evade agricultural quota production for the Nazi Generalgouvernement, the term nearly disappeared from their recollections of the immediate postwar period from 1945 until the dawn of Stalinism in the village in 1953. Periods of silence are just as significant as periods of abundant kombinacja activity. It is unlikely that the practices themselves ended, but somehow in the discourse, *kombinacja* was unavailable as a label. Is this because these practices aligned with the postwar state's own project of self-determination?[6] Is it because the villagers had not yet formed a cohesive community? Or did it have something to do with the cosmic dimension of kombinacja existing vis-à-vis some foreign occupying power or oppressive Other? In the postwar period, the formal apparatus of the Polish state and Soviet-inspired command economy was still in the process of formation, especially in the Recovered Territories. Perhaps identity on a personal and societal scale was in flux, or perhaps people really believed that they were working together with the state to rebuild a new Polish society on the former German lands.

It was only in recalling the onslaught of Stalinism and the centralization of agriculture and industry that kombinacja reemerged in the peasants' collective imagination, positioning them antithetically to the state project and officials. They portrayed their good kombinacja as a reaction to the bad kombinacja enacted by the state and officials who found clever ways to extract labor, capital, and services from them. Some informants described kombinacja as corruption from outside that possessed and corrupted their minds. Consciousness of this "bad" kombinacja "marked" a moment of occupation, a division between "us" and "them," resurrecting dormant kombinacja techniques that they had honed during the war against Nazi occupants. It also "marked" a moment of ethnic unity between the Polish and Ukrainian peasants in particular, whose fraught relations had spilled over from the war. The nomenklatura too co-opted the kombinacja discourse to scapegoat peasants for diverting food from rural-urban state supply chains. Documents they wrote that now sit in local archives attacked kombinators, characterizing them as economic saboteurs and capitalist entrepreneurs from the presocialist era who had to be eliminated from the Soviet modernization project. The discourse of kombinacja appeared precisely at the moment when Stalinism began to take over the village. When peasant and nomenklatura class divisions crystallized in the villagers' imaginations under Stalinism, the discourse of kombinacja began to mark their struggles over village power. A "collective" imaginary formed, but not the type the state desired.

This distinction between peasant resistance and nomenklatura oppression was clearer in the memories of first-generation settlers who were born in the presocialist world than in the proletarian memories of second-generation settlers who were born under socialism and had known no other system. Whereas peasant kombinacja had been primarily oriented against Soviet collectivization, most proletarian kombinacja was not specifically oriented against the state, but was imagined as a remedy for a broken system. When workers siphoned food and grain from the state farms, they did so to feed their families, so they could have the strength to be a part of socialist modernity. They called out bad kombinacja among those who were perceived to be siphoning more than their fair share, enriching themselves and depleting limited resources in the process—in other words, displaying capitalist inclinations that by definition contributed to class inequality in the village. In one incident a state forestry official fled the village because the workers began to decry his bourgeois tendencies. While economic constraints had an enabling effect on kombinacja, workers justified it not with pro-capitalist convictions, but by framing it in terms of proletarian collectivity. State farm directors permitted, and engaged in, an economy of favors facilitated by kombinacja because doing so pacified the workers and ensured that they would not revolt. Maintaining good kombinacja relations ensured control. The more evolved the villagers became as dystopia's provocateurs, redistributing and disassembling the state along their family and friendship networks, the more they destroyed the formal economy and, therefore, their socialist selves. Systemic kombinacja in the late socialist period became the highest apex of their sense of collective utopia. In their memories, capitalist "liberation" does not provide a happy ending. Instead, they mourn the loss of their socialist selves and of socialist modernity. Today, they are invisible and isolated people living in an uncertain neoliberal world. Socialist memories of kombinacja prove to them that they were once part of a unified collective. There is a new and emerging pattern of transnational kombinacja among the second generation, and even more among the third generation, of villagers in the postsocialist period. Since the opening up of the Schengen Area in 1997 and Poland's entry in the European Union in 2004, Bursztyn has become a ghost village. The young people and families who lost state jobs and entitlements in the privatization crisis of the 1990s have moved abroad to Norway or other Western European countries in search of agricultural work. They keep their homes and land back in the village, where they return monthly, seasonally, or annually. Their dual identities as villagers and migrant workers have spawned a new kind of transnational kombinacja through which villagers pull themselves into work, forming informal guilds to negotiate prices and working conditions with Western farmers, finding creative ways to increase total annual income by shuttling cheaper food bought in Poland into their worker colonies in the West or by using kombinacja on the job, and creating their own private retirement funds because they do not believe the state will provide for them in the future. They use the border creatively to these ends.

This is not just a European phenomenon. Kombinacja has also been taking root in the Polish diaspora in the United States, where I have lived for more than twenty years. It is unlikely that American policy makers know anything about kombinacja, yet the practice is widely used in the Polish diaspora to access health-care benefits, engage in identity fraud, operate unregistered businesses, acquire fake passports, and smuggle people over the border from Canada. Kombinacja affects the implementation and success of health-care, immigration, and security policies. People in the Polish diaspora do not necessarily see these practices as negative or unethical because they reunite families, ensure the family's survival, and provide solutions not available through the formal system. They might even justify their kombinacja as retaliation against the "kombinacja" of elites in Congress who put private and party interests above the will of the people. It is important to understand and decode the underlying logic and constraints that push people to fall back on these socially sanctioned practices.

An awareness of practices like kombinacja is pertinent to today's political climate. In borderless Europe and a globalizing world, the kombinators are on the move, adapting to new economic and political systems in the global arena, creating hybridized versions of ideal types of capitalism or neoliberalism, and linking up with emerging solidarities of similar global practices that are rendering states more porous, allowing for the free flow of capital, labor, and services across state-regulated capitalism. They are finding creative and innovative solutions to the global problems created by global capitalism. With the rising tide of right-wing nationalism across Poland, Europe, and the United States jeopardizing the vision of a borderless European Union and potentially destabilizing alliances like the North Atlantic Treaty Organization (NATO) that have helped to check Russian incursions into the West, kombinacja may undergo another mutation. But there is hope, because who is more equipped to navigate the emerging world of "fake news" and "alternative facts" than the kombinator, who has historically thrived in fractured and dystopian systems? Will we all have to learn to dabble in the arts of kombinacja to survive these uncertain times? Will we all one day stand up to these forces and declare, "Je suis kombinator?"

Dystopia's Provocateurs positions kombinacja at the center of its investigation to argue that these practices are neither peripheral to the state or formal economies nor defined exclusively in relation to them; rather, these practices represent a distinct way of life, with its own histories, discourses, cultural practices, moral systems, arts, and platforms for political change. Every act of kombinacja is consequential and affects the society around it, no matter how minute or undetectable it may be. Kombinacja is a field that enables invisible people who have no access to the formal political process to alter power, capital, and labor in their locality. But it is also a field that can be co-opted by those in power to shift power further in their favor. In Bursztyn, struggles over formal power before, during, and after socialism took place in this field of kombinacja. And today, these practices are evolving across borders, identities, and economies, in Poland and beyond.

Labyrinthine World

The thing about kombinacja and elusive practices like it is that they exist whether or not one chooses to see or believe in them. Transnational kombinacja is one of many emerging practices of informality that include Brazilian *jeitinho*, Argentinian *viveza criolla*, Italian *combinazione*, Israeli *combina*, Indian *jugaad*, Angolan *esquema*, Mexican *palanca*, Russian *blat*, Hungarian *protekció*, Chinese *guanxi*, and many other practices that creatively rework state-regulated capitalism and socialism in today's global economy.[7] People who have been on the outskirts of modernity are feeling shut out of the utopian promises of capitalism and socialism, and have had limited to no access to the formal political process. But these people have a superpower: the ability to survive cataclysms like war, natural disasters, the downfall of a civilization, and major economic and political transformations that radically transform their societies—sometimes all within a single lifetime. Their socially sanctioned practices thrive on innovation and creativity to produce alternatives to the "formal rules" and "formal economies" that disenfranchise them. If we could see through their eyes, these invisible ideologies of informality, not official discourses, would be at the center of their economic lives and of global capitalism.

In the midst of these emerging global trends, informality is still a relatively new field, largely pioneered by anthropologist Keith Hart's investigation of informal-sector practices among unskilled migrants who could not secure wage labor in Accra in the late 1960s.[8] During that same period, "second economy" studies, inspired by Gregory Grossman's investigations into similar practices across the Soviet bloc, followed their own trajectory but were omitted from debate on the informal sector.[9] Scholars of informal-sector studies predominantly focused on informality as an experience particular to capitalist domination across the Global South. This academic iron curtain has led to several trends in the field since the 1970s: a tendency to portray formality as the dominant economic and political order and thus at the "center" of investigation (which second economy studies disputed with state informality); the romanticization of informal-sector practices as resistance to post-Fordist capitalism (which second economy studies disputed with socialist informality); a focus on informal sectors that are readily visible to the naked eye, such as informal vendors on the streets of Calcutta; the reliance on crisp case studies that suspend informality in relation to a formal practice in only a single and relatively stable context rather than showing its transformation over time, borders, identities, and economies in crisis; and most important to this book, a claustrophobic language of informality that describes these practices in legal or economic terms rather than exploring how the people who actually used these practices describe their history, ideology, and function in their lives. Nezar AlSayyad and Ananya Roy write that "if formality operates through the fixing of value, including the mapping of spatial value, then informality operates through the constant negotiability of value and the unmapping of space."[10] This presupposes that a stable and constant "formal" economy actually exists. As the case of kombinacja in the late socialist period shows, these engines of innovation can be co-opted by the state and also substitute for a defunct "formal" economy. Thus, I propose viewing informality not as a secondary unmapping practice that exists strictly in relation to formal systems, but as a system that cuts through and reorders capital, labor, gender, space, time, history, nationalism, discourse, and the aesthetics of power. Societies in crisis that rely on such practices can help supply a language to describe and rethink the spirit of informality and its functions.

An investigation into informality should seek to produce not necessarily a set of clear, precise answers, but insight into a mind-set that can be understood only from the inside out. Psychological concepts in works of literature, like George Orwell's doublethink in *1984*, provide a far more nuanced and perceptive understanding of the psyche of the kombinators than social science literature on informality that takes a quantitative or analytical approach. Consider Orwell's "labyrinthine world of doublethink" in which subjects can simultaneously claim multiple identities by holding, believing in, and weaving through two contradictory ideologies at the same time:

> To know and not to know, to be conscious of complete truthfulness while telling carefully constructed lies, to hold simultaneously two opinions which cancelled out, knowing them to be contradictory and believing in both of them; to use logic against logic, to repudiate morality while laying claim to it, to believe that democracy was impossible and that the Party was the guardian of democracy, to forget whatever it was necessary to forget, then to draw it back into memory again at the moment when it was needed, and then promptly to forget it again, and above all, to apply the same process to the process itself—that was the ultimate subtlety: consciously to induce unconsciousness, and then, once again, to become unconscious of the act of hypnosis you had just performed. Even to understand the word "doublethink" involved the use of doublethink.[11]

Doublethink encapsulates the idea of a volatile world where black and white blur into grayness. Survival is based on mental elasticity and the skillful navigation of a labyrinth of constraints to devise the appropriate calibration of speech, thought, and movement so that one can evade the gaze of the state or trick the Other without consequences. Those born and socialized into communities that depend on informal practices are taught to navigate this path at an early age. Doublethink, doublespeak, double consciousness—all help mark and capture the scope of survival in dystopia. This is because systems of thought that embrace liminal states of being and identity are more resilient than the fragile, temporally rigid formal systems that try to control and eradicate them. Informality is survival. But to understand these processes, one must follow the twists and turns of a labyrinthine underworld. To do this, one must enter the kombinator's mind.

Consider the aesthetics of informality. Writing about *blat*, kombinacja's Russian cousin, Alena Ledeneva notes that the entrance to this world is through a "knowing smile," a smile that breaks on the faces of those who know its open secret. It would be impossible to learn about blat by searching through archives at the Ministry of Blat. Participant observation and conventional ethnographic methods are limiting here. Blatmeister bonds are communicated through the smile. Echoing Orwell, Ledeneva writes that the smile is "partially about smiling, partially about knowing; partially about knowing, partially about not knowing yet being able to go on without questioning." The smile signals competence in doublethink as well as ambivalence about honesty and upholding values and official goals, but most of all, the knowing smile signals a belief in individuality and independence from official discourses.[12] There is a kind of utopia in perpetuating dystopia. A similar "lightness" appears in memories of kombinacja. "Ahh, kombinacja!" Villagers would brighten up and knowingly laugh when I mentioned it. Sometimes the story would be about a joke played on a state official, one that displayed the kombinator's skill in outwitting the state. Those memories too would be recalled with a smile and excitement, even though the practice itself revealed a sort of "darkness" about the economic conditions requiring and enabling such practices. Indeed, Sherry Ortner writes that even in "dark anthropology," which exposes harsh and brutal human conditions like exploitation and prejudice, there are flickers of light and hope.[13] A labyrinthine approach can helps us discover these mystical dimensions of informality, its darkness and "lightness of being," as Milan Kundera puts it.

Investigating the labyrinth of informality in any given society ought to be a counterintuitive and uncomfortable experience. Many of its practices rely on strategies that may contradict researchers' conceptions of just and equitable behavior. There is still a misalignment between what these practices signify in the eyes of the people who practice them and how they are portrayed in ethnographic literature. In his ethnography of Wisłok village in southeastern Poland during the 1980s, anthropologist Chris Hann described *kombinować* as an "ugly verb" that "refers to the whole undignified, frequently underhand and devious, maneuvers persons must make to accomplish anything."[14] To an outsider, especially a Westerner raised in a society with a strong formal economy and no major border or regime changes to destabilize it, it may have indeed looked like a sign of eastern backwardness or an indication of what was "wrong" with Polish communism. I am not convinced, however, that Wisłok villagers saw it that way; they were probably proud of their creativity and the innovative solutions they devised to fix the broken system. For them, kombinacja may have symbolized individual expression. What could be more "Western"? I remember speaking to an American several years ago who laughed when he said that when he visited Moscow in 1990: "The Russians did not even know how to use money!" He had no idea that most Russians had arranged their lives around *blat*, or the "economy of favors," in which they secured scarce goods and services in the centrally planned economy, hence the Russian proverb, "Do not have a hundred rubles, have a hundred friends."[15] To him, it was the ability to understand and use money that signified ethical behavior. Innovation around money that circumvented the money itself appeared suspect. The reality is that most people in the world do not live like "Westerners." They have to find alternate ways to access food, services, and resources because they have no money to spend. It takes more ingenuity to secure resources without money in a shortage economy than with money in a well-stocked supermarket. This is the danger of analyzing informality through formality's gaze: it is far too easy to fall into a false association of formality with justice and equality, rather than recognizing that, for example, the very construct of the "formal" is a mask for elite corruption.

Native ethnographers can play a key role in this underworld of informality and in expanding the language we use to describe it. Kombinacja feels as real in my imagination as a being that has free will and can take "possession" of an individual. Sometimes it is portrayed this way in the book. The academic in me knows that informality is just a practice or discourse that scholars study, but the psychology of kombinacja that I have personally wrestled with helps me decode and understand how being "possessed" by informality is a transformative internal feeling. It is a drug that forms a haze over one's eyes and muddles one's thoughts until one turns away from what is expected, toward that which can be destroyed or transformed for one's own needs. Kombinacja helps me keep a sense of a wilderness in my mind, a space where I can create and innovate. Using elements of memoir to translate local forms of informality is another method underused in most studies of informality that can bring these invisible practices to life on paper and in the mind. Native ethnographers can deploy their multiple identities as villagers, academics, easterners, and westerners to bridge these worlds, helping readers understand the functions of the blat smile or the history behind informal practices that could only be shared between insiders, or in specific contexts where the informants feel safe. We can help open up new avenues for exploring informality.

I did not write this book out of a compulsive need to decode the history of informality, nor is kombinacja always the dominant theme of the book. In many ways, this book reads like a typical historical ethnography of the rise and fall of the Soviet state in the Polish-German borderlands, with dates and numbers and accounts of struggles between peasants and the state. But in some ways, this book is an opportunity for informality to tell its own story, rather than the other way around. Every date could be contradicted with another date; every story could be

contradicted with another story; every attempt at continuity is jolted by disjunc-
tures and filled with fragments. There were always forces at play other than my
own intentions that dictated what made it onto paper. As I tried to plot a course
through the labyrinth of kombinacja, a new, more pluralistic historical narrative
took hold of the book. In the end, I think this is a more accurate portrayal of the
contested histories of the borderlands, layered with Polish and German architecture, with spaces representing national homelands, and populated by people who
each hold multiple ethnic, national, religious, and linguistic identities. People
used kombinacja to generate multiple identities as a safeguard against the un-
stable identity of these lands. Thus, I found informality to be a useful tool for
charting multiple histories and identities in the borderlands. This way of thinking about history deviates from conventional historical inquiry, which relies
heavily on archival evidence, historical events, media resources, treaties, and so
on, to substantiate versions of the truth. Writing history through the prism of
informality exposes the plurality and circuitousness of history. This is especially
helpful in the context of the Recovered Territories, because it allows us to think
of these contested borderlands not as "ours" or "theirs," but as a shared landscape
that has changed hands between the Slavic and Germanic people.

Taking a labyrinthine approach to the exploration of kombinacja conflicts
with the standard academic procedure of situating research in a coherent theoretical framework. For years I tried to shoehorn my research into an existing
framework. Nothing stuck. Each and every assemblage of "habitus," "métis,"
"diverse economy," and "multiple moralities" sounded good at first on paper,
but in the end did not feel right because none of these approaches provided a
holistic framework that could encapsulate the contradictory elements of kombinacja practices, nor did they provide any theoretical notion of how the practices
change over time. Choosing any one of them felt like an act of treason against the
villagers. In the end, I wrote this book by trusting my instinct for what "felt right"
to say about kombinacja. Whatever the theoretical or argumentative shortcom-
ings of the book, I am confident that the "borderless" and "exploratory" study I
have presented here captures the history of kombinacja in a way that is true to
the world portrayed to me by the villagers, as well as the boundaries and mechanisms of kombinacja that I myself know firsthand. If clear methodological and
theoretical explanations are the formality of academic literature, then this book
surely belongs to the realm of academic informality. Its framework is a labyrinth
of instinct, feelings, and detours.

What I have learned about kombinacja challenges the tendency in informality (and informal-sector) studies to portray these practices only in reference to the
post-Fordist state-regulated formal economy since the 1970s, without exploring
the logics and cultures that give life to these practices, which predate the genesis
of those formal economies—especially neoliberal global capitalism—sometimes

even helping to form them. The lack of ethnographic and historical inquiry into the history of informal practices—how they originated, transformed over time, and linked up with other economic practices—makes it difficult to expand the field's theoretical and methodological horizons. Because there are no comprehensive historical studies on informality that predate 1970, there is no effective theoretical language for understanding how informality "moves" and "changes" and how it emerges on the other end of systemic change. My exploratory research on the eighteenth and nineteenth centuries suggests that informality, born of Enlightenment ideals of freedom of association, has functioned as a competing alternative system to that of the modern state regulatory apparatus, which since the late nineteenth century has tried to control capital, labor, and movement, thereby denying those very Enlightenment ideals and freedoms under the guise of state socialism or capitalism.

Dystopia's Provocateurs attempts to find meaning in informality across many different borderlands: territorial, personal, and psychological. It traces the sites and ways in which informality intercepts our lives and is an agent of creation and destruction, lightness and darkness, exploitation and liberation. Chapter 1 explores how I found kombinacja as a research topic, both in the context of my own life and in my fieldwork in the borderlands. Chapter 2 traces the origins of kombinacja in nineteenth-century movements until the outbreak of the Second World War. Chapters 3, 4, and 5 continue following the historical trajectory of kombinacja from the making of socialism in the borderlands after the war to its unmaking in the 1980s. Chapter 6 explores the transformation of kombinacja from the socialist to the postsocialist periods, and Chapter 7 deals with the fragments of the past that continue to conjure spirits and transform us into something other than ourselves.

Notes

1. There is no consensus on the number of German expellees and Polish settlers in this population swap.

2. *Kombinatorka* is the feminine form, but I use the masculine throughout for the sake of simplicity.

3. Thank you to Russian literary scholar Alexander Zholkovsky, who used this term to describe the kombinator and who has graciously permitted me to adapt this description to the book title. Zholkovsky defines the kombinator as "dystopia's provocateur" and "the dream genre's listener-interpreter." Zholkovsky, *Text Counter Text*, 254.

4. Ledeneva, "Economies of Favors," 16.

5. I conducted interviews between one and three hours in length with sixty original settlers. Poles made up 41 percent of my interview sample—the other 59 percent were Ukrainian, Kashubian, Belarusian, German, and Lithuanian. Often interviewees' children joined the interviews to add background information; thus, the interview data include many more voices

than just those on the "official" informed consent forms. I use a pseudonym for the village and have changed all of the villagers' names, with the exception of my closest family members. I have also substituted the name of the village in the archives and the local sources in the bibliography.

6. I found the relationship between informality and the state to be symbiotic; both need the other to survive, and more often than not, narratives of informality mirrored the history of what constituted the "state" in the villagers' imaginations. It mapped their adaptations to state informality with their own informal practices against exploitation.

7. Holmes, "Peasant-Worker Model"; Jauregui, "Dirty Anthropology"; Chari, *Fraternal Capital*; Santos, "Second Economy"; Lomnitz, "Informal Exchange Networks"; Ledeneva, *Russia's Economy*; Lampland, *Object of Labor*; Szelenyi, *Socialist Entrepreneurs*; Chan and Unger, "Grey and Black."

8. Hart, "Small Scale Entrepreneurs," 101–20.

9. Grossman, "'Second Economy' of the USSR," 25–41. See also Korbonski, "The 'Second Economy' in Poland," 1–13. Seminal books in the field of informal economies like AlSayyad and Roy's book *Urban Informality* (2004) omit mention of the Soviet bloc. Books on postsocialist informality like Alison Stenning and colleagues' *Domesticating Neoliberalism* (2010) also avoid theoretical engagement with informal economy studies and informality in the Global South. A global theory of informality has yet to be developed.

10. AlSayyad and Roy, *Urban Informality*, 5.

11. Orwell, *1984*, 35.

12. Ledeneva, "Economies of Favors," 18–19.

13. Ortner, "Dark Anthropology," 49–50.

14. Hann, *Village without Solidarity*, 91.

15. Ledeneva, "Economies of Favors," 17.

1   History's Ghosts

I WAS BORN in the age of Solidarity, when our Soviet world was falling apart. My family lived on a worker-peasant (*robotnik-chłop*) farm in the village of Bursztyn, along the Baltic coast of northern Poland.[1] Just sixty miles east in Gdańsk—the epicenter of the Solidarity movement—Nobel Peace Prize winner Lech Wałęsa, the Lenin Shipyard workers, and thousands of other Poles were protesting communist rule. Pink leaflets rained down from the sky, telling us to unite and join the movement, that a better world was just beyond the horizon. Even Communist Party officials experienced epiphanies that lifted the veil of communism from their eyes and revealed the light of c apitalism. Then, boom! The Chernobyl nuclear plant exploded in Ukraine, sending gigantic, radioactive black clouds over the Baltic Sea. My parents rushed me to the hospital, where children were fed liquid iodine to protect us from the radiation, but there was not enough for the adults. For the West, the collapse of the Soviet Union was a celebration, but for us, behind the Iron Curtain, it was an explosion of nuclear confetti.

While revolution raged on in the cities, Polish villagers struggled to feed their families in the shortage economy.[2] Soviet class divisions among peasants, workers, and nomenklatura became blurred. Survival was based on the innovative ability to shift class and political identities to acquire resources. Worker-peasant farm families like ours had one foot in agriculture and one foot in industry. Everyone split their time between working in the fields, growing food to meet the agricultural quotas legally mandated by the state, and earning wages in a state job. My father was a manager and my grandfather was a tractor operator in the agricultural circle (a type of cooperative), my grandmother was a seasonal laborer in the collective farm and circle, my mother was an accountant in the state tannery, both of my uncles worked on and off in the state mechanical enterprise and state forestry, and my aunt was a biology teacher who belonged to the Communist Party in a different village. Peasants, workers, and nomenklatura alike lived as one family and, in many cases, under one roof. Throughout each village, every household—depending on where its members worked—secured different resources, rations, entitlements, wages, bonuses, and access to state knowledge through the distribution of household members across different sectors of the command economy.

In the late socialist period, a practice we called *kombinacja* was critical to finding innovative solutions to the constant instability wrought by scarcity.

Kombinacja is the practice of manipulating legal, political, or cultural rules in order to access a resource like food, commodities, labor, information, or power. Although extraordinary inflation devalued the Polish currency and chronic shortages of goods in stores rendered it worthless, it was important to keep one's day job to *wykombinować* any workplace perks. Working in state stores helped secure extra food rations, working in the factories or mechanical enterprises helped secure car parts or carpentry and building materials for the farm, being an office worker helped secure stationery, being in the nomenklatura class helped secure higher education for one's children, and so on. Peasants, workers, and nomenklatura in the family all relied on kombinacja and pooled those resources for domestic use or traded them for other necessary goods in the second economy, which had overpowered the collapsing command economy.

The privatization of state workplaces cut villagers off from these resources and flung them into poverty. When my uncle Kuba lost his job in the state mechanical enterprise, he searched the village for bottles to cash in to buy food for his four children. When the agricultural circle closed in the late 1980s, my family moved to the nearby city of Słupsk, where my father got a job as a manager in the transportation authority that was still state owned. We leased a plot of land on the city outskirts, where we harvested strawberries that we sold along the highway. In contrast, members of the nomenklatura class that had sustained state socialism became the new entrepreneurs; they privatized state workplaces, sold off assets, and pocketed profits. The capitalist transition in the 1990s did not regulate privatization, so the nomenklatura were left to their own devices and could use kombinacja to satisfy the new capitalist plan. Kombinacja did not die with socialism; rather, coupled with privatization, it compounded the class inequality that under socialism had already existed between the nomenklatura and the rest. The nomenklatura's kombinacja became critical to the formation of capitalism and the new Polish state.

The 1990s were hard times for a rural family in provincial Poland. The American dream beckoned to us with Michael Jackson videos, the *ALF* television series, colorful Coca-Cola soda cans, plastic bags at supermarkets, Mentos commercials, "refrigerators in windows" (air conditioners), sneakers, white teeth, and highways filled with cars that we could only fantasize about. In 1990 the US Department of State introduced a green card lottery. My paternal uncle, who had received asylum in America through my Jewish great-aunt during the anti-Semitic purges in Poland in the 1970s, entered my mother's name into the lottery. Her number was chosen! We packed into a large van like migrant workers for an overnight trip to Warsaw to make our case to the American embassy. In 1992 we flew into Newark International Airport, where we were met by my paternal aunt, who helped us find a home in a Polish immigrant community near Trenton, New Jersey. My father joined a Polish construction firm, my mother joined a cleaning service, and my siblings and I were sent to a new school.

In Ameryka, as we called our new country, we rediscovered the collective that we had lost through privatization. Central European and Russian families from different regions in the former Soviet bloc lived in our apartment complex. As people adjusted their languages and dialects to a less regionalized form, we were able to communicate with Czechs, Ukrainians, and Russians using a shared Slavicized language. Regardless of former lives in the military, nomenklatura, village, hospital, or university, women became cleaning maids and men became construction workers. At dawn construction vans revved their engines and groups of maids boarded minivans after dropping their children off at the apartment of an elderly woman in the complex who provided day care. We all shopped at the same stores and attended the same Catholic church in Trenton. Some tenants called the neighborhood a *państwowe gospodarstwo rolne* (state agricultural farm) because it recalled the collective way of life, and aesthetically it resembled the 1970s block buildings on the state farms. An elderly neighbor even had an ominous Nazi flag hanging on his wall that was visible through his lit window at night. Memories of the Old World were very much alive in our New World neighborhood.

Many immigrants that came in our wave quickly realized that the American dream was a mirage. It was difficult to adjust to a completely new world when one did not understand the language and lacked the financial literacy needed to navigate the capitalist system. Without inherited wealth, well-established family networks, or formal employment, many immigrant families struggled to get by. To subsidize their low pay in the unregulated and informal cleaning and construction businesses, many engaged in various kombinacja activities that they had adapted to the New World.

In Trenton, this included shuttling undocumented Polish immigrants from Canada to the United States for pay; overstaying student visas; buying fake green cards, passports, and social security numbers; going to special tax accountants who filled out taxes in a way that helped secure welfare checks and other state benefits; having babies and then filing family reunification claims; pilfering construction materials or food while on the job; selling scrap metal obtained from a workplace; "renting out" one's legal immigrant identity to undocumented immigrants so that they could acquire a driver's license, start a construction business, or buy a house; marrying a documented or undocumented immigrant for pay or other benefits; subletting rooms to undocumented immigrants to reduce rent costs; moonlighting at "no-show jobs" to earn double income; finding legal loopholes to qualify for free medical treatments before Obamacare; carving out cleaning service territories in various suburban communities and then "selling" those homes or streets to other cleaners for profit; selling car insurance to undocumented immigrants; using the gift and favor economy to get someone to translate a document, make a phone call in English, look up information on the internet, secure cheap housing in Trenton, or obtain the contact information of people in Brooklyn who sell powders with healing properties.

Because it can involve breaking the law, kombinacja can be divisive in the diaspora. It can create unhealthy competition among documented and undocumented immigrants over the limited pool of state resources available to poor families. It breeds class resentment between those who are more upwardly mobile and those who are not. It creates tensions between those who have permanently emigrated to the United States versus those who stay temporarily *za chlebem* ("for bread") with the intention of earning money and living off the welfare system before retiring to a better life in Poland.[3] It can divide families. When someone miraculously scores a two-hundred-dollar-a-month apartment or receives free cancer treatment, everyone else wants the same. Parents who speak no English pressure their children—who often serve as their de facto caseworkers—to secure those same miracles, forcing them to choose between being upright citizens and being "good" children. Its networks keep the Polish diaspora clustered together to ensure the flow of resources and people. It marries youth to the construction and cleaning services rather than encouraging them to find opportunities at university and beyond. Ultimately, it creates a climate of fear and suspicion vis-à-vis the state. While the Polish landlords participated in and benefited from various shady housing enterprises, such as providing housing for undocumented immigrants and taking bribes for repairs that they were legally required to provide for their tenants, police cars were a fixture in our complex. In the wake of September 11, 2001, there were nightly police raids and an increasing number of deportations in the neighborhood. Overall, only a handful of individuals were jailed or deported, but the fear of the state cracking down on everyone was always in the air.

Immigrants use kombinacja to manipulate legal loopholes to alleviate the everyday effects of broken systems of immigration, health care, and welfare. "Illegal" immigration reunites families and builds the diaspora even as Polish citizens remain excluded from the US Department of State's Visa Waiver Program. Housing undocumented immigrants more immediately relieves the difficulty of paying rent than does spending years on waiting lists for low-income housing. If we look closer at the problems kombinacja fixes—job security, access to housing and medical care, immigration rights, family reunification, education, access to technology—it reveals a progressive platform, one supported by those with limited representation in the American political system. Kombinacja is a way for those with little political voice to exercise agency.

In the early twentieth century, William Thomas and Florian Znaniecki wrote in *The Polish Peasant in Europe and America* (1918) that "assimilation" into American society for the Polish diaspora was an "entirely secondary and unimportant issue" relative to the "formation of a new Polish-American society out of the fragments separated from Polish society and embedded in American society."[4] *Assimilation* is a patronizing term, suggesting that immigrants do not already share American values. "Getting around" the system requires an entrepreneurial spirit, resourcefulness, and self-reliance to carve out new economic spaces, new possibilities—what could be more American? In a more recent study of the Polish diaspora in Chicago, Jason Schneider documents kombinacja (e.g., illegally marrying for green cards to become "more" American) as an "informed navigation of the state's symbols" that allows diaspora members to position themselves vis-à-vis the state.[5] Yet, according to Schneider, kombinacja is "premised on an antagonistic relationship with the state," which disqualifies it from being an effective form of political rhetoric.[6] It does not have to be, however. Kombinacja in the previously mentioned cases is a response to marginalization and an expression of agency through nontraditional political expressions. Rather than waiting for Poles or other diasporic communities to organize, studies of kombinacja can help inform legislation, target state programs, and support those falling through the cracks, those who are trying to realize an American dream in economic and political spaces between the formal economy and the political system.

While my family experienced kombinacja in an established Polish diaspora in Trenton, my uncle Kuba's family has practiced the art of transnational kombinacja between Poland and Norway. Since the Schengen Agreement opened up Europe's borders to Poland in 1997, Poles from villages like Bursztyn have sought construction and cleaning jobs in Western and Northern European countries.[7] My uncle stays in Norway for most of the year working in construction and agriculture while my aunt returns to Poland monthly to touch base with their daughter, who is finishing high school in the village when she is not working in the fields with them in Norway. When I traveled with my aunt, she fried chicken cutlets in the morning in Bursztyn, packed them, and served them that evening to my uncle in Norway. Every month, she packs suitcases with Polish meat from Bursztyn. She buys cigarettes and vodka at the airport in Norway. All of this is legal, but it is still kombinacja because it is an innovative way of cutting living costs to optimize earnings.

Migrant workers adapt kombinacja to negotiate their border identities and life in the diaspora. Many live for free in a Norwegian farmer's guesthouse or basement, cleaning his house and working his land to pay off their "rent." They also siphon construction materials during road construction to sell on the side, eat food produced on the farm (when I observed my uncle Kuba "taking" cabbage from his owner's farm, he laughed and declared, "Kombinacja!"), and employ various theatrical negotiating tactics like giving owners the silent treatment to scare them into settling on wages. It is also used as a way to keep jobs away from newly arriving migrant workers like the Sikhs and Vietnamese. Tight-knit migrant worker groups that "pull in" (*ściągają*) their own from their villages in rural

Poland act as a wage negotiation group, blocking the Norwegian farmers from creating wage competition between Poles. Sharing surplus Polish meat, vodka, and cigarettes shuttled from the village is a way to reproduce those socialist-era kombinacja networks and act as an informal guild. Migrant workers are concerned that the Polish government will not provide for the financial security of retirement, so they are creating their own private retirement funds. Rather than organizing and pressuring the state to strengthen its retirement infrastructure for future generations, they domesticate that burden to secure their own futures. They are exercising agency, but in a way that does not challenge the Polish government to reform its laws. Nonetheless, my uncle told me he is living out his socialist utopia—which Poland failed to deliver—in Norway. To him, kombinacja is like a superpower that allows him to operate in an economic dimension that Westerners—accustomed to formal systems and transactions—cannot detect. With kombinacja as his cloak of invisibility and invincibility, he inhabits multiple identities and crosses borders, associating fully with neither nation-state. And he no longer hunts for bottles on the streets of Bursztyn.

For my family and for the Polish people, the transition into the new world of capitalism remains uncertain, even a quarter century after the age of Solidarity. Nomenklatura privatization in the 1990s quickly put a damper on the notion that capitalism would clean up the corruption and patronage networks that had dominated the socialist state; instead, patronage became the building block of capitalism as the nomenklatura became the new entrepreneurs, and sons became the new commune mayors, as their fathers had been under communism. Underemployed and underrepresented Poles from rural and provincial areas have found freedom and economic stability not in capitalist institutions but in various forms of migration and creative adaptation of socialist-era kombinacja to new contexts. Some forms of kombinacja have been illegal, some have not challenged the state structure, and others, like nomenklatura privatization, have been inherent to state formation. Poles categorize and self-police this practice by making individual or group-based distinctions between what is "good" kombinacja—usually one that protects their interests—and "bad" kombinacja that does not protect their interests. Distinctions are usually made by way of contextual stories and are taught at an early age, as I have demonstrated in my own narrative.

Such kombinacja stories, however, provide a more nuanced alternative to the dominant narrative of communism's collapse conveyed by archival evidence, facts and figures, beginning and end dates, and heroic (male) figures. Over time, historical narratives that outline a single trajectory of transition do not hold up. Recently released letters from a former communist official's personal archive have exposed Lech Wałęsa—the hero of the Solidarity movement and winner of the Nobel Peace Prize—as the informant "Bolek," who worked for the state in the 1970s before he was crowned by the West as the leader of the movement that helped topple the Soviet Union. Yet, if we cast Wałęsa's predicament in the context of kombinacja—that Wałęsa became a state informant to feed his family during years of crisis or to acquire state knowledge that he later used to topple the state—it humanizes him, as the normal Pole did the same thing under communism. This is why a kombinacja perspective is critical to understanding history and transition, because it opens the floodgates for a historical narrative that blurs the communism-capitalism binary and introduces new actors, agencies, and moralities that have reworked state power, formal economies, and symbols of power.

Baltic Amber

One mid-June afternoon in 2009, I stuck my head out the window of an old train traveling north from Warsaw to the northern city of Słupsk, in the Pomeranian region along the Baltic Sea coast. As I inhaled the warm air and enjoyed the rich colors and smells of the agrarian countryside, I thought about how just in this past century, Poland's borders had shifted as often as the Baltic sand dunes. Before World War I, this same train route would have started in Russia and ended in Germany. Before World War II, it would have begun in Poland and ended again in Germany. But today, it began and ended in Poland. After World War II, Poland absorbed German lands east of the Oder and Neisse rivers. The German city Stolp became the Polish city Słupsk. I was traveling the same train route my grandmother Zofia had taken with millions of Polish "pioneers" (*pionierzy*) who settled these former German lands immediately after the war.[8]

Central and northern Poland still looked like two separate countries. The Varsovian countryside, dotted with church steeples and quaint villages surrounded by sun-kissed fields of grain, was the Poland many Westerners see and imagine. But as the train traveled northward, vast forests emerged, villages dwindled, and the fields grew larger, stretching toward the horizon. Networks of tiny tree-lined corridors—constructed by the Germans to protect horses and people from the sun—cut across the fields and forests. As we crossed the river Nogat into former East Prussian lands, the Teutonic fortress called Malbork appeared above, along with Gothic churches and redbrick farmhouses, some speckled with black-and-white timber framing. Beyond Gdańsk (formerly Danzig), the villages looked dull and gray, patchworks of red brick, black-tarred roofs, cement walls, and plastic tarps. There was no livestock in sight. Soviet-era worker apartments surrounded by stripped-down structures appeared in the middle of vast, overgrown fields. Where were the people, the animals, the agriculture?

At sundown, the train finally stopped in Słupsk near the transportation hub where my father had once worked before we moved to Ameryka. I boarded a quiet bus filled with tired passengers. As it traveled down a tree-lined road toward the villages, I caught the glimmering eyes of forest animals looking up at us from the dark forest. I was entering the wilderness. Suddenly, the bus dropped me off on the side of the road. I knew this place by the comforting smell of burning plastic, coal, and wood billowing out of the chimneys in a thick haze that coated the streets. This was the smell of my childhood. Tall streetlights spotlighted the rusty tractors parked alongside the road, but under one spot, there was a white cloud of hair peeking from above a gate—Zofia. I ran toward her and she embraced me with her thick hands as we entered her old German house. Sitting by the furnace in the kitchen, we caught up on family matters while sipping lemon tea and eating cake made from wild blueberries foraged from the forest. Her left eye was bloody; Uncle Roman, who suffered from alcoholism, was out on the streets. She made my bed in the dining room next to my brother's piano, which we had left behind. She turned on a Pope John Paul II night-light and poured hot water into a bowl so that I could wash and prepare for fieldwork the next day.

I woke up to crowing roosters and a heavy fog that blanketed the farm, the village, and the surrounding fields. I walked upstairs, where we had once lived, and looked out the back window to get a full view of the farm. The property had once spanned eleven hectares on which my family produced barley, wheat, and potatoes for the state. After privatization lifted the quota system, agricultural production collapsed across the entire village and the entire region. Since then, Zofia's farm has looked like what I had witnessed from the train: a tapestry of rusting machinery, scattered red brick, broken glass, tar roofs, makeshift tarps, agricultural wasteland (*ugory*), and imploded farm structures. Like nearly all peasants in the village, she does not receive enough money from her retirement checks to cover property taxes and keep up with the high costs of agricultural production in a capitalist economy. When I bought a half ton of coal to burn and keep the house warm, Zofia saved it for even harder times. She kept only the kitchen warm, with steam that rose from the soups she simmered on her coal stove. With most villagers subsisting on welfare and retirement checks, it has become more affordable to buy food at the supermarket than to grow food. The small-scale production that does still exist—like beekeeping, raising chickens and rabbits, and growing vegetables—supplements purchased food, is sold for alcohol money, or is exchanged for a service like a free plowing for next season. One Ukrainian farmer (*gospodarz*) who still cultivates his land with a horse and plow is supported by hard-to-secure European Union funds that villagers gossip about with envy and suspicion. Many of them do not know which funds they are eligible for or how to access the applications because that information is closely guarded by the village elites in the commune headquarters. Livestock are present only on funded farms or in isolated colonies (*kolonie*) where privatization has yet to reach, where houses still lack plumbing and electricity, and people still use former state barns and land for their production. This is how Bursztyn's villagers live today, a fate that is not much different from that of the fifty villages and colonies across the three-hundred-square-kilometer stretch of Bursztyn commune (*gmina*).[9]

It was sad to see that in the decades since my family emigrated to the United States, Bursztyn has become an empty village, with disappearing people and places. Reunification Street, which passes through the heart of the village, is filled with alcohol shops patronized by former peasants and workers like my uncle Roman, the invisible people who cannot seem to find a footing in a capitalist society during the transformation (*przemiana*). While he drinks with former coworkers, they travel into their fraternal past to escape their present poverty. Not much happens in this village, but when it does, it is tragic. Men lie by the side of the road in a drunken stupor, women walk around with bruised faces, children commit suicide by hanging, people set loved ones on fire with gasoline or push them out of windows during ritualistic bouts of drinking (*libacje alkoholowe*).[10] Zofia's neighbor was killed by a falling tree when she went into the forest with intoxicated workers. Villagers blame a weak police force, a state that no longer requires alcohol rehabilitation, dutiful women who give alcohol money to their sons, the communist army system that corrupted good Polish men, or an incurable disease. At night the police pick up drunk men from alongside the road and drive them home. One night, when the police dropped off Roman, who had blood streaming down his face from falling onto the concrete under the bus stop, they were helped by two men with bloodshot eyes waiting for a tip. The next morning, Roman sobered up and went back out to Reunification Street.

Reunification Street is also suffering from a hangover after its honeymoon with capitalism. In the 1990s it bustled with the flair of a quaint European village as young people hung out in restaurants and outdoor bars. In 1996 the state privatized the tannery and sold it to a German businessman who continued tanning pig hides for Italian shoemakers, but jobs became scarce as the wave of state agriculture and national industry (*przemysł*) receded from the region. After Europe opened its borders to Poland, working-age villagers migrated en masse in search of a better life. The restaurants, bars, theater, and discotheque boarded up after the exodus. Those who stayed behind retreated into their homes, living on state benefits and seasonal jobs. While running errands, old women wearing berets cluster together and complain about the collective alienation that has spread across the village. No one talks anymore. People suffer from this "disease of civilization" (*cywilizacyjna choroba*), as one Ukrainian woman put it. The village is dying. Its emptiness is filled by roaring transport trucks en route to Gdańsk or Germany, an occasional German family visiting their former homeland (*Heimat*, a German landscape of origin that is steeped in emotional attachment),[11] or a tour bus of Japanese tourists visiting to buy Polish sausage (*kiełbasa*). Capitalism passes by but does not set up shop. The agricultural wastelands that have surrounded the village are being erased by expanding forests, bringing the frontier and its boars and wolves to the outer edges of the village. Villagers call this encroaching fauna *Szwajcaria* (Switzerland) in reference to the nineteenth-century émigré Juliusz Słowacki's eponymous poem about searching for lost identity in a Western wilderness.

The ghettos of former agricultural workers stranded in Soviet-era apartment buildings surrounded by several hundred (even several thousand) hectares are perhaps the worst tragedy. These stretches of land were the heart of agricultural production in the region and belonged to Soviet state farms (*sovkhozy*), called state agricultural farms (PGRs) in Poland. During privatization, their directors liquidated the farm infrastructure and worker settlements into villages without stores, government offices, schools, clinics, or post offices. Today, former state farm workers live in unprivatized apartments, survive on state benefits, and produce food on their former worker gardens (*działki*). Others squat and are invisible to the state altogether. Sometimes a German or Dutch businessman (*biznesmen*) buys the land and employs them to produce potatoes for companies like McDonald's, but these ventures often fail, and the businessman leaves and waits for another buyer who has a new plan. Recently, urban professionals who want a quaint rural escape are buying this land, on which they build Varsovian red-roofed homes. They commute to the city in glossy cars while eyes from the ghettos watch from afar.

Seen from above, the steeple of the Catholic church towers over Bursztyn and the surrounding lands, but it is by no means their moral and political core. The priest has come under fire for misappropriating church and European Union renovation funds. People gossip that the priest has an alcohol problem and parties with women in other villages, where he is not easily recognized. Unlike in the rest of Poland, the Catholic Church is losing its grip over the region. One village priest—who sported a mustache and a Hawaiian shirt and smoked a cigarette while his young secretary served us coffee—told me that the Vatican considers these to be "missionary lands." Under socialism, the Catholic Church had a stronghold on these lands, but after the thaw of socialism came the thaw of ethnic homogeneity, and people who had identified themselves as Poles for decades began to show their true identities and true religions. The Ukrainian minority in Bursztyn demanded that Greek Catholic (*grekokatolicki*) mass be held on Saturdays and the only remaining church in the village is now split between two religions. To some, the church that helped topple the communist system seems to have lost its moral compass—like everyone else in the village who has been lost in transition since 1989.

The region has seen the arrival of a type of American capitalism unlike anything people fought for during the Solidarity era. In Rędzikowo, just a few kilometers north of Bursztyn, the American government is building a missile interceptor site and for security purposes has effectively frozen economic development on former state farmlands. Many feel at the mercy of American and Russian tensions. In the late 2000s Pomerania (Pomorze), the province where Bursztyn is located, became the epicenter of an American-style shale-gas revolution, when Poland's Ministry of Environment granted concession lands to American corporations and the state passed legislation allowing companies to conduct dangerous seismological testing on private land, even if the owners objected. Where was private property as a building block of capitalism? Curiously, the very people who had fought with Solidarity against the Soviet-backed Polish state found themselves having to fight again for private property against an American-backed Polish state. They blocked roads, stole cables, and petitioned the state. Government officials promised that a shale-gas revolution would make Poland a "second Norway," the youth would return from migrant labor, families could be reunited, the village could be made whole again. But as the revolution waned, companies gradually pulled out, with no government accountability for the environmental damage, and it became clear that once again the people had been lured by the promise of utopia, only to be cheated in the end.[12]

Unlike villages in central Poland that have been steeped in family farming and Catholicism for centuries, Bursztyn was a modern invention engineered by the socialist state, which might help explain why it has taken such a dramatic fall after communism. Before 1945 these lands had belonged to Germany. Bursztyn was a German village called Bernstein. It was founded in the fifteenth century on top of a Slavic Wendish settlement, under Germany's eastward expansion policy (*Ostsiedlung*), which mandated the colonization of Slavic lands. For centuries, it followed the Western narrative of the Enlightenment and the Industrial Revolution. When serfdom was abolished in the mid-nineteenth century, the city of Stolp freed the peasants from the Junker aristocracy that had enslaved them on their gigantic estates and redistributed land to the peasantry in Bernstein. In the late nineteenth century, Bernstein industrialized its paper factory, but advancements in cellulose production in mainland Western European countries weakened the economic power of these forest-rich lands. The twentieth century brought harder times to Bernstein. The East beckoned during the Bolshevik Revolution in 1919, which incited a failed uprising among the paper factory workers. When Adolf Hitler came to power, the village and the rest of the region received state subsidies that culminated in the reconstruction of the main street as Hitler Straße. During World War II, the village produced aircraft parts for the Luftwaffe and exiled its Jewish residents to Stolp, where a pogrom was taking place. The Junkers put enslaved Slavic prisoners to work in agricultural production on their estates; this was a way of domesticating the maximum prisoner capacity permitted in the Stutthof concentration camp system across the Pomeranian region. As Germany began to lose the war, the village was flooded with thousands of German refugees from East Prussia who were fleeing Red Army atrocities.[13] When Poland absorbed these lands in 1945, Polish communist authorities renamed the village Bursztyn and, with the support of the Red Army, expelled the German population.

The Soviet-backed Polish state treated this annexation as a postcolonial project. It called these lands the "Recovered Territories" (Ziemie Odzyskane) on the premise that it would "recover" the Polish identity of the lands from centuries of German colonization. Curiously, the pioneers who populated these lands were not ethnic Poles, but Ukrainians, Belarusians, Greeks, Lithuanians, Jewish Holocaust survivors, and others who arrived by choice or by force through state resettlement schemes. Polish-German groups like Kashubians and Silesians, as well as German war brides who had married Slavic officers, also remained on the lands. Although the Polish state advertised the Recovered Territories as a Polish homeland, it used the land to create a Soviet society. Until 1949 Red Army military personnel occupied the Junker estates, nationalizing them into Soviet state farms. By the 1950s these lands had become the most densely Sovietized area of Poland, with nationalized industry and collectivized agriculture, resembling Soviet Russia more than central Poland. And yet, it was on these very lands that the Solidarity movement shook and toppled the communist regime in Poland. A professor once told me it was a miracle the Solidarity movement had ever emerged, given the very atomized state of Polish society. As I looked closer at the history of the Recovered Territories, I wondered if it had ever been a Polish society in the first place. Many of the pioneers did not speak Polish. They became a highly Sovietized society composed of ethnic groups that later revolted against the very system that had organized their lives ever since the genesis of the Recovered Territories. What kind of world had these people wanted to build? I wondered. What real struggles were co-opted by Cold War narratives of the cosmic battle between communism and capitalism?

It was from that second-floor window of Zofia's house that I embarked on six months of ethnographic fieldwork in Bursztyn. At the time my objectives were hazy, but I knew I wanted to dovetail historical accounts from the state with villagers' recollections of the genesis of the state and society on the so-called Recovered Territories. How are modern states born and what kind of mythologies do they create? Did pioneers accept that mythology, or did they have their own vision for the new frontier? How did such a diverse group of pioneers transform Bernstein into Bursztyn while simultaneously undergoing their dual transformations into Polish and Soviet citizens? How did they negotiate this state-making project in the village and within themselves? I knew that some villages in the commune evaded collectivization altogether: how did they carve out spaces of resistance under extraordinary pressure to accept Stalinist reforms? I wondered if I could locate those spaces today and find out what role they played in the poverty and alienation suffered by villagers in Bursztyn and across the region. I was looking for a narrative thread of alternative history that might weave across multiple transitions while remaining invisible in history books or formal political platforms. I reasoned that ethnographic investigation would be the only way to access these memories of the state and the people, which is why I returned to my village. With my family networks there, I suspected I might be able to recover information from the original pioneers, people who were already in their eighties and nineties. Time was running short.

Why I was doing this had nothing to do with theoretical frameworks or literature gaps. I was driven by vivid memory fragments and curiosity about my origins. Until my early twenties I had been under the illusion that Bursztyn had always been part of Poland. My grandparents settling a German farm as part of a massive Polonization and Sovietization scheme had never made it into the family stories. I found out about the border shifts by happenstance, when a university professor with Ashkenazi roots in the German Silesian region just south of Pomerania asked me about them. I felt my face turn red because I knew nothing about it. During that period, my father was dying of cancer. One of the last things he talked to me about was his early life growing up in a German hay-thatched cottage in a small village near Słupsk after the war. When his parents moved to Słupsk with his three siblings, they left him behind in the village with his grandmother, a healer who spent most of her time tending to his grandfather's wounds from the Stutthof concentration camp. With few friends and missing his siblings, he spent his time reading adventure books. When my grandfather visited to take him into the city, he noticed as they rode on his father's bicycle along the German cobbled road that the fields were pockmarked with bomb craters. The sad image of a lonely boy making his way across a dystopian Stalinist landscape after the war stayed with me like a fossil encased in amber from the Baltic Sea. After he died, I felt the need to chisel away at it, to excavate that memory of those lands and meet the subjects who had lived through that time period. I left the West and took refuge in Bursztyn under Zofia's wing. As one of the original pioneers, she was the key to that past and knew those who could help recover it. We could make up for lost time. Maybe, by undertaking this project together, she could reclaim her childhood dream of becoming a geographer, a dream that was interrupted by the war. Maybe by listening to those survival stories I, too, could recover something, some source of strength and understanding that I could apply to my private postsocialist transitions in the wilderness of émigré life.

Whispers

A German woman known to everyone in the village by her catchphrase *Mein Gott* (my God) is the only villager who still lives in the same house where she was born before the war. When the victorious Red Army marched through Bernstein in 1945, "all of the documents lay in the street as if they were looking for something," she sadly recalled in her German-inflected Polish. The proof of Bernstein's existence was in the paper. Bursztyn's authorities gathered it up and sent it to Słupsk, where it was stored in a new "archival" office that coincidentally burned to the ground from an "arson attack" at the height of Stalinism in the 1950s. And so Bernstein, a village defined by centuries of industrial paper production, had been reduced to a handful of charred scraps within a matter of years. When I visited the reconstructed archives in Słupsk, I noticed that some of those scraps had been preserved in folders, not because they documented the existence of a German state, but because they appeared on the reverse side of salvaged Soviet edicts that had been printed on Third Reich administrative paper recycled by the Polish state. On one side, these pages were filled with faded, cryptic, typewritten paragraphs in Polish; on the other side was German text in black-letter script surrounded by "Heil Hitler" signatures and swastika stamps.[14] In figure 1.1, the text on the German side indicates that it was an official voucher worth 10 Reichsmarks, which could be used only for the purchase of animal fodder, seeds, fertilizer, or straw, valid until September 1, 1941, after which it would lose its value. It was issued to a farmer named Max Thrum, of Vargow, who used it on April 22, 1941, to purchase 1,500 kilograms of various types of fertilizer from a seller named Adolf Pleines, who was entitled to redeem the voucher for cash.[15] The text on the Polish side is a copy of an edict written by Władysław Gomułka, Minister of the Recovered Territories, that laid out the hospital revitalization and social care program for the Three-Year Plan of Reconstructing the Economy (1947–1949). German history was preserved by accident, not intent. Meanwhile, another German woman in the village named Krystyna, a physical embodiment of that past, clings to what she has salvaged and collected. Her bookshelf is stacked with *Heimat* literature like Karl-Heinz Pagel's *Der Landkreis Stolp in Pommern* (1989) that reconstructs German history across Pomeranian villages and towns. "I read it, and immediately, I am in Germany," she whispered, hugging the book to her heart. Just as my father read books to escape from Stalinist dystopia, Krystyna reads them to escape to the Bernstein of her youth.

German history slipped out in whispers. Lore, a German woman who lived in the Lipowa forest colony outside of Bursztyn, recalled that the Polish Catholic priest Karol had colluded with authorities to erase the symbols of German Protestant identity: "They destroyed everything of [Bernstein's] cemetery and they made a road [out of it] by the bakery," she whispered. I found Strażacka (Guard) Street covered by a thick layer of asphalt, but bits of marble engraved with words like *Die Liebe* (love) in black-letter script still protruded along the sides, revealing a subterranean path paved with tombstones—a marble brick road to socialist utopia (see figure 1.2). I dusted the dirt off with my hands and snapped several photographs, but the next day, someone poured cement over the fragments and wrote *Seba* on top of it, violently erasing these remnants of history.[16] The

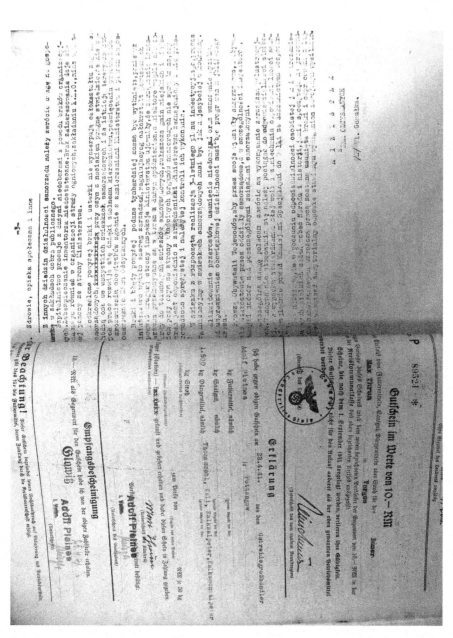

Figure 1.1. Third Reich administrative paper recycled by the Polish state. Courtesy Wojewódzkie Archiwum Państwowe, Koszalin.

Figure 1.2. German tombstone road. Photo by author.

cemetery where the tombstones originated was right behind Zofia's farm, and indeed, the oldest tombstones dated to 1945, but I also noticed a shard of black marble with black-letter script reading *Hier ruhen* (here lie) that looked as if it had been salvaged by some sympathetic witness and intentionally pasted onto one of the cement pillars that surrounded the cemetery. When I later interviewed the retired priest Frederyk—a Silesian—in a presbytery lavishly furnished with German antiques, he said knowingly in a thick Germanic accent that the first priest, Karol, had worked with the state to "make room" for new Polish corpses. Konrad, Zofia's husband and my maternal grandfather, took part in that operation, but Zofia always insisted that it was obligatory labor he had to perform for the state.[17] Still, whenever I asked her, she ended the discussion with a long silence. There was something more to the story that she was not telling me; I always sensed it. At times I found her hunched over the fence, looking out onto the cemetery, contemplating.

This "resourceful" recycling of German tombstones as construction material was a pattern across the commune as the church and state worked together to extend the reach of their power over the German lands. In Bursztyn newly formed state construction crews built roads and walls out of the tombstones. After the state nationalized forests and formed the state forestry divisions on the outer perimeters of the village, newly minted state forestry workers planted trees on top of German cemeteries, both to hide them and to demarcate the forestry division's new property lines. In a neighboring village called Podwoda, which the state had mostly settled with Belarusian repatriates, a group of peasant men approached me on the street and pointed to a state kiosk they said had been constructed on the foundations of synagogue. Evidently, this de-Germanization took place throughout the Recovered Territories, and media sometimes report on skeletons sticking out of fields and tombstones protruding from walls that surround schools or parks, or embedded in cobblestone roads.[18] In one television interview, a Polish historian in Wrocław (formerly Breslau) stated with an upbeat tone and a tinge of pride that during material shortages in the postwar period, clearing the German cemeteries was a totally "natural process" of recycling materials toward state construction projects.[19] I was disturbed by the way such expressions of pride failed to acknowledge the erasure of history and memory that this innovative resourcefulness entailed.

Curiously the de-Germanization campaign was absent from Bursztyn's archives. How did the state systematically carry out ethnic cleansing without a legal architecture? Historians have tried to find evidence of this ghost statecraft across these territories. Gregor Thum writes in *Uprooted: How Breslau Became Wroclaw* (2011) that a secret directive sent by the minister of the Recovered Territories in April 1948 is one of the "few extant documents confirming the rigid and methodical nature of the de-Germanization campaign in the western territories."

The de-Germanization of the territories included eliminating use of the German language, removing all German inscriptions, Polonizing first and last names, and cleansing the lands of Nazi and German ideologies. Removing all German inscriptions encompassed, according to the directive Thum quotes, "'churches, chapels, cemeteries, wayside crosses, and other religious objects, except those of outstanding historical value, which in case of doubt should be determined by the competent authority.'"[20] Officials were given an extraordinary amount of improvisational power to purify the lands without strict adherence to a legal architecture or parameters on the socialist spirit of this revolution. Jan T. Gross and Irena Grudzińska-Gross's *Golden Harvest: Events at the Periphery of the Holocaust* (2012) emphasizes the sinister undertones of officials' "improvisation" techniques, which the authors assert was also key to creating the Holocaust: "No matter how large or small the domain over which they presided—a work detail, a barrack, a ghetto, or a camp—the men in charge of solving 'The Jewish question' were improvisers." Since there were no well-defined procedures for getting rid of the Jewish people in villages and cities, faceless German bureaucrats and local officials had to "work toward" the Final Solution by improvising and finding ways to catch, expropriate, and transport Jews to the concentration camps.[21] This fetishization of resourcefulness was not only state orchestrated. In *Fear: Anti-Semitism in Poland after Auschwitz* (2007), Jan T. Gross writes that "communal Jewish property, such as cemeteries and synagogues, was in large part devastated after the war as the local people carted away tombstones, bricks, roofs, anything useful for their own construction projects."[22] Common interests in disassembling and recycling the German and Jewish features of the former landscape likely forged a foundational political bond between the pioneers and the new postwar regime.

Improvisational statecraft was key to the genesis of Bursztyn. Although a key pillar of Marxist-Leninist proletarian revolution has been the liberation of peasants and workers from feudal bondage in the form of labor and tithes, Bursztyn's archives reveal that state officials liberally imposed feudal systems such as unpaid labor obligations called corvées (*szarwark*) and monetary tithes (*daniny*) on the German denizens and the incoming Slavic pioneers to patch up systemic labor shortages faced by the nascent command economy. This is ironic because corvées were often used by Western European powers as a form of slave labor across their colonies, yet here, officials were using corvées as a means of "colonizing" the Germans as well as the peasant pioneers who had been drawn to the region by socialist propaganda. When the new state forestry divisions needed to fill their logging quotas, the officials sent the peasants and Germans; when the Soviet state farms were ready for plowing and harvesting, they sent the peasants and Germans; when the newly formed state schools needed additional budgets, they squeezed tithes out of the Germans. Officials creatively co-opted feudal institutions—what they knew "worked"—in creating a protosocialist state on the backs of the Germans and the peasants. I can only imagine the peasants' confusion when they arrived in the lands as "pioneers" and instead found themselves working alongside their German enemies in corvées for the good of the socialist revolution. This improvisational state making, supported by an on-the-ground Soviet military architecture, proved an effective tool for usurping economic and political power, because the officials could do whatever they wanted to "work toward" the secret edict, while those whom they controlled had no way of lodging protest. By the 1950s, however, minutes from commune meetings record peasants publicly questioning the "rationality" of an economic system that forced them to labor without compensation.

While conducting fieldwork, I sensed tension in the ways Bursztyn's villagers remembered this period of postwar improvisational state making. Not everyone liked me asking questions, hence the cement-covered tombstone. The national archives director in Słupsk commented that I was treating my own people as "monkeys" before he delivered scraps of the salvaged archives. Then, he charged me a hidden fee for taking photographs of the archive documents, and when I refused to pay it, he erased my name from the log and threatened that the state would sue me if I ever used the data. The very function of an archive director is to preserve history, yet he erased me from it in Stalinist fashion; there was no indication in the log that I had even asked the questions. I only pretended to erase the photographs on my thumb drive, and when I returned to Zofia's farm, I plunged into them on my computer. The archives were divided into thirty-two booklets, each marked with the type of government correspondence and the date on the front cover, but inside, there was no clear page-numbering system. Documents from 1947 were in folders from 1946, and each booklet was stuffed with loose notes that tackled local problems. Years later, I received official permission to publish the information in the national archives, but when I asked another archive director in the Wrocław branch if I had to pay for the photographs, she was completely perplexed by the strange question. "Of course they are free," she replied.[23] This was not the case, however, in the provinces and in the village, where nothing was offered free of charge. For example, a source told me she would introduce me to the former school director under communism if I brought cake and hosted him with her. The village teacher wanted to sell me old photographs that she had gathered from villagers for a school project. A librarian did not believe that my student identification card belonged to a real university. A secretary would not share Bursztyn information with me because she was supposedly working on the same exact research project. Other government office secretaries claimed they did not understand my Americanized Polish accent. The director of a department where I was a visiting scholar in Warsaw before my fieldwork also stopped me in the hallway and told me to pay up several hundred dollars as a charge for affiliation—I had not been informed of any such charge when I accepted the position. When my mother attempted to secure her pension from the Polish government, she learned that during privatization, someone in Słupsk had bought the work records from the state factory that she needed to prove to the state that she qualified for retirement. When we went to Słupsk, we had to pay the woman for the archives while she looked for them in a filing cabinet by her dining room table. To access history, one had to pay the price of entry.

Villagers were very protective of this improvisational statecraft. My aunt, the retired biology teacher who had been part of the Communist Party in another village, confronted me one day on Zofia's farm. She had heard years ago, she said, along with a "witness," that I had once said that I "hated all Poles." I could only feel that way, as she put it, because in America, "they do not know what war is." I have heard this myth before. It went like this: because Poles had suffered so greatly at the hands of the Germans during the war (which is not in dispute here), any injustices committed against Germans during the postwar period were legitimate and understandable, and as a young person who never went through it, I have no right to question it. This was not the Piast myth of the Recovered Territories, the one that says that the lands had always been Polish because the Piast dynasty ruled them a millennium ago. This was the myth that washed state officials' hands of all wrongdoing in the postwar period. I was perplexed that my aunt, the daughter of Zofia, who had been put into corvées by the Soviet authorities, was defending this myth and putting me "on trial" rather than taking a personal interest in the project as an educator and scientist. In the village, the nomenklatura liked to dictate, not explore, the past.

I observed something during my fieldwork that might help explain this protectionism. It happened when I was following a lead on what the state did with the German bones. No one knew. No one saw. Zofia at some point hinted that they were ground up with the tombstones into the same mass of construction material that made up the streets and "cement" walls. One day my driver Marek took me and Zofia to visit the widow of a former state forestry director in Lipowa, where Marek had been raised, and where as a child he fondly recalled plundering nearby German graves to look for gold and other treasures. Another resident of Lipowa told Marek that after the war, the widow had found piles of "animal" skeletons in her attic. At first we drove right past her house because it looked like nothing more than an uninhabited ruin surrounded by scattered German-era bricks. But when Marek later walked around the ruins, he found a single door. We stepped through into a dark kitchen. A dim light emanated from an adjacent room, and in that room we found the tiny, frail, old widow, propped up on her bed, next to an old German ceramic furnace on full blast at the height of summer. She whispered that she was "waiting for death" (*czekam na śmierć*) and did not have the strength to answer even a single question about her life. We begged her, knowing it was our only chance to extract that memory about the bones, but then her son arrived and ushered us out. When we walked out, a strange scene unfolded in front of us. We noticed that a group of men had arrived along with her son to pick up the red German bricks scattered around her home. This woman was not yet in the afterlife and already these vultures were circling around the carcass of her German house. Fragments of the German past were not only being erased; they were being efficiently and resourcefully disassembled at every turn, naturally, without question. Surely, it was a "natural process," but I was bothered by what seemed a fetishization of resourcefulness that was erasing from the landscape physical markers of a past few wanted to remember. They were continuing a domestic form of improvisational statecraft by socially reproducing a Soviet development plan years after the fall of communism.

Postwar myths that positioned all Poles as victims of the past protected not just the state officials' improvisational techniques but also the resourcefulness that binds villagers to these lands through the recycling of German materials even today. Just as the state officials used this sort of creative resourcefulness to build the state, the people must have used it to build their lives, but in doing so, they became addicted to erasing the German presence and history from the land. Meanwhile, the Soviet-backed Polish state fed off that effort to build its socialist revolution by initiating people into socialism through denazification projects wrapped up in state development projects. The postwar state began through a collaborative effort by the pioneers and the state to rid the lands of the Nazi plague that had oppressed them. This could help explain why even after the communist period, people still believe in and protect the idea that the Polish state was constructed under the heroic circumstances of "recovering" the Polish lands Germans had colonized. Polonization and Sovietization were so intertwined that they were nearly inseparable, and even after the fall of communism, some people continued to cleanse their landscapes and memories of the German past.

In *Native Realm* (1968) Czesław Miłosz writes about the "injustice" of having to resurrect the history of his home city of Wilno with only fragmented memories and photographs from before it was ravaged by war, annexed by the Soviet Union, and transformed into Lithuanian "Vilnius" in 1945: "A Parisian does not have to bring his city out of nothingness every time he wants to describe it. A wealth of allusions lies at his disposal, for this city exists in works of word, brush, and chisel; even if it were to vanish from the face of the earth, one would still be able to recreate it in the imagination."[24] I felt a similar sense of injustice while attempting to recover the fragile past, and an even greater sense of injustice when it was being actively erased in front of me.

But I was equally surprised at history's resilience and the way villagers preserved fragments of the "German-era" (*poniemieckie*) past. The fragments could be anything: redbrick buildings, coats-of-arms adorning the entrances of homes, trees lining country roads, cobblestone roads, personal belongings, decorations, or garden plants. They all had stories, memories attached to them by those willing to share. Marek showed me many ghosts of the past that were invisible to the naked eye—plundered German cemeteries, former German train tracks that the Red Army dismantled as war reparations, and empty fields where a Junker estate had burned to the ground. Domestic spaces in particular retained an eerie German presence. One day Marek drove me to a Junker estate managed by a warden, the former state farm director's son. When the man realized I was not a *Heimat*-seeking German, he ushered me into the eighteenth-century neoclassical Junker filled with gigantic staircases, dusty German furniture, old ceramic furnaces, Persian carpets covering skylights of shattered stained glass, a majestic ballroom with a crumbling fresco of angels on the ceiling. Its interior was frozen in time, and I later began to notice the same kind of aesthetic inside villagers' homes. Villagers call these German-era relics in the form of furniture, wallpaper, orchards, rooms, or wall decorations *gotyks* (gothics), or "memory gifts." Some gotyks included German black-letter script, like the cobwebbed decorative plates declaring *Gott schütze unser Heim* (God bless our home) that still hung on the villagers' walls. Each gotyk had a vivid story behind it about pioneers' relations with the German owners before they were resettled over the new border. When I listened to the stories behind them, I realized they filled in a history that the archives could not, a nuanced history that deviated from the official narrative of "recovering," revealing instead a reconciliatory narrative of joint oppression by Soviet authorities in Bursztyn. I would like to think villagers preserved gotyks instead of sacrificing them to the de-Germanization purges as a way of resisting both ethnic cleansing and the state's takeover of the German landscape and elimination of property that was private and personal. I would like to think it was a way to link with and preserve Western modernity.[25] But they could also be trophies of Poles' postwar "recovery" of these lands.

Accessing history in Bursztyn meant figuring out the secret safe combinations to open it. When Zofia and I began to interview original pioneers, she said that I needed to "know how to talk" to them. Zofia was my gatekeeper in Bursztyn. I had to help her around the farm in the morning—foraging, cooking, cleaning, killing chickens, picking vegetables, trading farm goods with neighbors—to make time during her workday. Then, we would walk down her street to talk to peasants, south to interview former factory workers near the tannery, toward Reunification Street to talk to former officials, or toward the village outskirts to speak to former forestry workers. There was no public space like a coffee shop where we could meet and talk with interviewees, nor could we canvas their homes. Most villagers keep guard dogs like Rottweilers or German shepherds chained in front of their houses, and some even released them into the streets. Most interviews had to be arranged ahead of time through a phone call or a drive up to the house, which formalized the entire encounter between host and guest.

Interview subjects had to be approached with the correct gatekeeper, and that too came at a price. My mother, Bogusława, helped me secure gatekeepers through her socialist-era network of friends and acquaintances (*znajomi*) from the factory and circle who aided me with my project in exchange for gifts like alcohol, money, chocolates, and continuing good relations with the Materka family living in Ameryka. Taking me places also helped my gatekeepers establish new relations with other villagers, which facilitated such activities as buying cheese from a European Union funded farm, exchanging information about prices of potatoes and eggs to buy, foraging mushrooms, and acquiring high-quality apples from former state farm workers who lived off the apple orchards. They might be gifted with jars of raspberry jam, cake, or coffee. There was always some form of economic activity going on during the interview. Former factory workers took me to a small village occupied by a single Polish family; there, the Polish farmer gave me a cut of pork, still warm from the kill that day. These villagers helped me taste the last flavors of a disappearing agrarian past that few outsiders would likely have access to without a gatekeeper.

There was also a unique way that villagers who were not part of the ruling class spoke about early postwar history by "unmapping" or dislocating themselves from official language, divisions of space, and ways of telling historical time. When we spoke about "origins" (*pochodzenie "ze starych stron"*), villagers "placed" themselves not inside pre-1945 state borders but in fluid and ethnically diverse historical regions that crossed state borders. A Belarusian repatriate would say that he was "from beyond the Bug River" or Kresy (eastern borderlands); a Ukrainian who had been forcibly resettled to the lands would say he was from Wołyń (Volhynia) or Podkarpacie (Subcarpathia). It was impossible to tell whether either of them had been "Polish" before the war, but these forms of dislocation were ways in which villagers "distanced" themselves from authorities. I understood this because of the ways that Zofia dislocated me from my official identity as a researcher during interviews. She created a special lineage for me that connected me to each interviewee (e.g., "Edyta, the daughter of Czesław, who worked in the circle with your husband") and said I wanted to learn from the elderly about village history. She branded me as a subject myself, explaining that my questionnaires and consent forms were something that I had to do for my "London professors." Consequently, villagers gave me one answer to "tell London" and another "real" answer. To defuse ethnically charged topics, Zofia often said, "We were all like one family" and "There were no problems" to convey unity, or "There are [good] people and there are [bad] people" (*Są ludzie i ludziska*). This dislocated discourse also affected the way that villagers spoke of time. Their narration of the transition from socialism to capitalism did not begin after the fall of the Berlin Wall in 1989 but followed the asynchronous liquidation and privatization of the arms of the state that pertained to them. Peasants who had endured decades of agricultural quotas said that the state had collapsed in 1983, when the quota system was lifted. Shop workers who owned the first private restaurants said that the "ghost of communism" (*duch komunizmu*) already existed in 1987. Workers who lost their jobs when the tannery was privatized said that Communism ended in 1995. Such discourses played an important role in shaping identity and solidarity that bridged ethnic and class divides between the original pioneers, but in a way that distanced them from the official state discourses.[26]

Villagers entered history through their bodies, their own irrefutable documentation of historical events. Their "archives" were wartime gunshot wounds from messy escapes from state violence, back pain from feudal labor obligations, abnormally swollen hands and feet from working with hazardous chemicals in the state tannery, overworked hands and backs from decades of producing state quotas in the fields, mutilated fingers from freak accidents in the mechanical enterprise, thyroid cancers after Chernobyl, and psychological anxieties (*nerwica*) caused by economic abandonment under market capitalism. Just as their homes were collections of gotyks that told stories of the German past, their bodies were collections of pain (*ból*) that documented their encounters with the state. They shed light on events that were camouflaged in the archives. After a Ukrainian couple complained about back pain from years of hard work in the fields and feudal forced labor on the roads and in the forests, I discovered that the archives had in fact camouflaged the practice under an official term: *świadczenie w naturze*, or "obligatory voluntary labor." I found it fascinating how bodily pain provided a platform for political grievances. For some, the thaw of their bodies coincided with the thaw of the communist state: "The human worked and worked, but now, everything is coming out [*wychodzi*]," one Ukrainian forestry worker said, showing me her hands. Under communism, pain was suppressed, but in the atmosphere of alienation and abandonment that capitalism ushered in, the pain accumulated under previous governments surfaced and rippled through the body like an aftershock. Others felt that "not much has changed" and their bodies still worked "like a machine" (*jak maszyna*); they used their bodies as a political medium to question the "success" of the transition. The villagers' stories about pain reflected not pride in hard work but a perception that they had been, and still continue to be, cogs in the wheels of states and the officials who run them.

There might be something to these narratives. Some of the original officials whom Mein Gott and Lore whispered about were still alive, and Zofia was an important advocate for the truth during my interviews with these men. When we went to interview Kacper, a former state official and son of a military official called Houdini, his partner, a former factory worker, told me, "He does not remember history" (*on nie pamięta historii*). Zofia, shocked that he had "forgotten" how his family had enslaved the peasantry, gossiped about the encounter to other villagers. This was evidently effective, because when I returned later, they were happy to sit down for an interview in which Kacper admitted that the officials had used corvées—the "obligatory voluntary labor" mentioned in the archives. When another official, Orzeł, recalled that he had been one of the founding state officials and also lived on forty hectares of farmland in the village, Zofia called him a *kułak*—a term borrowed from Russian that was applied disparagingly to wealthy peasant farmers—a term that state officials like him used to pressure peasants like Zofia to collectivize their land into Soviet collective farms (*kolkhozy*). When we interviewed Motylek, the Stalin-era official who implemented collectivization, he initially said he had arrived only after Stalinism and denied that collectivization existed altogether. When Zofia mentioned her work in the *kołchoz* (*kolkhoz*), he "corrected" her, explaining that it was a *rolnicza spółdzielnia produkcyjna* (agricultural production cooperative), even though structurally they were identical. Renaming Soviet institutions was a common form of state propaganda, meant to give the impression that the Poles had not been colonized from the top down but had adopted Soviet institutions on their own initiative, to better themselves. Before we left, Motylek let me take photographs of him with about a dozen Party awards he had once received, which he propped up on his body like badges of honor. These discussions between Zofia and the officials exposed the cold war that still raged between peasants and officials over words and definitions, what existed and what did not exist, what was forced by the socialist revolution, and who were the actual architects of socialism on the ground.

History was accessed through corridors and labyrinths, real and imagined. One day, the retired treasurer who had once worked with my father in the agricultural circle said that she could introduce me to the mayor—the son of a former mayor under communism—at commune headquarters on Reunification Street. When we entered the building, she walked freely past the line of nervous whispering peasants queuing behind a single door, opened office doors without knocking, chatted with the secretaries, walked up the stairs, and got me face-to-face with the mayor in minutes. He asked me about my project, but then refused multiple times to be interviewed, even after the treasurer insisted he do so as a favor to her. He deflected and said to "find history among the elderly." On our way out, the treasurer opened up the main conference room for us to see: it was lavishly furnished with antique German furniture, beautiful carpets, wooden beams, and dusty, socialist-era patriotic banners. There, sitting at the mahogany table, was a former state farm director dressed in a full suit and thick glasses as if he were reflecting on a meeting from the distant past. He gladly agreed to an interview, speaking with pride, clarity, and moral authority, as if he were still in power, sitting at Bursztyn's political heart.

History in Bursztyn was like the fog that covered the countryside in the mornings, evaporated during the day, and every so often returned unexpectedly. It had nothing to do with dates, facts, laws, or structure, and everything to do with everything else—improvisation, resourcefulness, genesis myths, fragmented memories, tombstones, bodily pain, forgetting, silence, gotyks. Of his own attempts to recover history and memory from Pomeranian lands in his memoir *Peeling the Onion* (2006), Nobel Prize–winning German novelist Günter Grass writes:

> Memory likes to play hide-and-seek, to crawl away. It tends to hold forth, to dress up, often needlessly. Memory contradicts itself; pedant that it is, it will have its way. When pestered with questions, memory is like an onion that wishes to be peeled so we can read what is laid bare letter by letter. It is seldom unambiguous and often in mirror-writing or otherwise disguised.[27]

Likewise, I got the sense that I was spiraling into a different dimension, one dislocated from space and time. What counted as history was also in dispute. Villagers said that they did not know "history," as if it were a separate entity that belonged only to the state. If I wanted to learn about "historical structures" (*struktury historii*), villagers whispered, I would have to see Fidelis.

Dystopia's Provocateurs

Fidelis was a ninety-year-old Kashubian who lived in a former state forestry settlement up the street from Zofia's farm. The Kashubians are a Slavic ethnic group in present-day northern Poland who were Germanized during *Ostsiedlung* settlements of Eastern Europe. Before 1945 their ethnic region was split into German and Polish Kashubia. German Kashubia was located closer to the city of Danzig, while the adjacent corridor of Polish Kashubia stretched up to the Baltic Sea. The border changes in 1945 unified Kashubia, and its people were deemed "Polish" enough to be "repatriated" back to Poland. Fidelis was from German Kashubia. He sported a platinum crew cut and spoke at least five languages, including Esperanto. After the border change, he said, the Soviet-backed Polish authorities viewed him as an "uncertain person" (*nie pewny człowiek*). In 1947 they seized "his documents from the Gestapo" (*moje dokumenty z Gestapo*)—"you know," he added in a higher octave, "the German security service." The octave jump caught my attention because Poles often use it to downplay the gravity of any situation. When they found him in his forest hideout, they stripped him of his rifle and threw him in jail. I asked why, but he replied that it was irrelevant. Fidelis did not want to talk about the war. His wife, Jadwiga, drifted in and out of our interview like a ghost, dutifully serving us coffee and cake. But when she recalled how Fidelis's house in the forest had been adorned with beautiful furniture after the war, he abruptly changed the subject. My eyes searched his face for any indication of breaking character, but in the end, there was little I knew for certain about him. Was Fidelis a Gestapo prisoner or imprisoner? A freedom fighter or war criminal? He was a step ahead of me and in full command of the answers before I even asked the questions.

One thing was clear: Fidelis was a shape-shifter. After his release from jail, he climbed the ranks from state forestry worker to Communist Party activist and then to state forestry director; eventually he became a state official at the Bursztyn commune headquarters located in the heart of Bursztyn. His transformations reminded me of the Czech literary character Josef Švejk, a dealer of stolen dogs who gets swept up in the upheavals of World War I in Jaroslav Hašek's novel *The Good Soldier Švejk* (1923). Although an antimonarchist himself, Švejk presents himself as a model Czech soldier of the Austro-Hungarian Empire who always agrees with his superiors through "double-talk" ("Humbly report, sir, I don't drink spirits, only rum"[28]) that deflects their attention, triggering a series of events that ultimately keep him from ever reaching the front lines to fight the Russian Empire for the monarchy.[29] Hašek portrayed this kind of liminality as the everyman's form of agency in the chaos of war that wrought havoc on Central Europe: "Every man in the course of his eternal life undergoes countless changes and has to appear once in this world as a thief in certain periods of his activity," because, as Hašek put it, "it's the self-determination of man."[30] Likewise, Fidelis shape-shifted to survive the transfer of his Kashubian lands from Nazi Germany to Soviet Poland. He seemed to have a different face for every scenario. His identity was as fluid as the Polish-German border had been over the course of his life. At one point in the interview he vehemently critiqued what he called the spread of the Soviet "plunder economy" (*rabunkowa gospodarka*) in the late 1940s—"We were producing shoes for the revolution in China but we ourselves had no shoes on our feet!"—but he later revealed that he had been a party activist during that same period. He had traveled the Bursztyn commune spreading the socialist revolution and persuading peasants to collectivize their land into Stalinist collective farms. I wasn't sure if the villagers had sent me to Fidelis because he could tell me official history or because they saw him as the physical embodiment of the state. Nevertheless, it was this shape-shifting capability that gave Fidelis the power of mobility and a particular insight into the unraveling of Stalinism across the commune.

As an "anti–Communist Party activist," Fidelis witnessed the growing contradiction between the socialist utopia he advocated and the emerging shortage economy spreading across the commune. As the Stalinist command economy took shape, a curtain of aesthetic dullness (*szarzyzna*) fell upon the region and crept into people's minds, transforming them into "dull people" (*szarzy ludzie*), the shadowy collective suspicious of otherness: "Słupsk or Bursztyn itself, it was dull! It is not the case that a house would be painted somewhere because immediately [people suspiciously asked], 'How does he have money? From what has he made money?'" Then Fidelis seamlessly switched voices, as if speaking from the perspective of the villager held under suspicion: "And as a matter of fact, one did not buy paint, because there was no paint. One might have had that type of money, but he could not do it because he did not receive it [through the state plan], so he stole it from somewhere. Because, simply put, back then, it was not called 'stealing.' It was called 'kombinacja!'" Resource-strapped workers devised creative strategies to extract resources like paint from sites like mechanical and construction enterprises where they worked or had personal connections. And of course, stealing could not exist in a society where the proletarians owned the means of production. This manipulation of socialist propaganda to extract state resources put state directors and officials in a bind, because cracking down on this practice would have exposed the state as the exclusive proprietor of its property and could have incited unrest. By exercising creative thinking to carry out their kombinacjas, workers created ideological loopholes, and in doing so, to use Fidelis's metaphor, they reclaimed the lightness of self-awareness from the dullness of collective assimilation.

Long before speaking with Fidelis, I knew the term *kombinacja*. Growing up in the Polish diaspora in Trenton, I had heard Poles use it to describe duping the state or beating the odds to acquire a government-subsidized apartment, free health coverage, or welfare. My mother once told me that kombinacja was a way of "thinking"—as Fidelis claimed—but also "corruption of the mind," a dystopian form of agency. The way she described it, kombinacja was a mental virus that the Polish people had contracted from a perpetually corrupt economic and political system under communism, and it had spread to the point that they could no longer control it. Kombinacja went straight to the brain, unleashing a sense of anarchy that felt so human. To write a book about kombinacja, she added with a mischievous smile, I too would have to use kombinacja to give it form and capture it on paper. Her words brought to mind émigré novelist Witold Gombrowicz's observation, "Oh, the power of Form! Nations die because of it. It is the cause of wars. It creates something in us that is not of us."[31] In his anarchist novel *Ferdydurke* (1937), banned under communism, schoolchildren held chaotic duels in the school yard, where they magically morphed their faces to determine who could contrive the most grotesque face. Likewise, in my mother's tale, kombinacja became a race among Poles to see who could contrive the most ingenious way to shape-shift around "form," duping the system that had corrupted them. The very existence of kombinacja means that we live in a dystopian present where we are perpetually excluded from our fair share, where we must shape-shift to restore some semblance of justice. But by tipping the balance in our favor, we strip others of their share. This process spirals us deeper into the bowels of dystopia, where we feel more oppressed, driving us to further dismantle the system and then concoct new kombinacjas to survive. We all become dystopia's provocateurs. "The whole world is one big kombinacja"—a cycle of corrupt states and corrupt states of mind—my mother said, while making a circle with her finger in the air.

Kombinacja must have been a concept I was in the habit of taking for granted. When I later reviewed interview transcripts, I was surprised to find that before interviewing Fidelis, I had never noticed when villagers used it to talk about their history. After Fidelis, statements like these suddenly stood out:

The mind had to work! Kombinować! Without kombinacja, no one would have made any money.

Before, there was a lot of poverty, and people had to kombinować—everywhere.

If I could not purchase it, I had to kombinować.

There were prices imposed from the authorities for the products which the [state farms] purchased and sold. It was calculated in a way that nothing was left. One had to kombinować so that he could at least get [a bonus].

When [state workers] dug out the potatoes, one took some potatoes in one's pocket or in a bag for dinner. I did not consider that stealing.

Their kombinacja stories were rich data points that revolved around identifying a limited resource, determining where that resource could be found, devising a plan to extract the resource, identifying who was competing for the resource, and devising a way to use that resource or hide it from state surveillance. Many of these stories were funny anecdotes in which ordinary people outwitted state officials, escapades that sounded a lot like the kombinacja used by Poles in Trenton. Whereas I had always thought of kombinacja as a recent practice, here I was hearing interviewees using the term to describe the distant past. It took someone like Fidelis, who had learned Polish as a second language, to not only isolate the concept but also allow me to understand its significance. This art of shape-shifting unlocked the history of these borderlands.

Usually, kombinacja was practiced by individuals and small networks of people, but Fidelis described to me a period of postwar history when villagers scaled up the practice to check the spread of Sovietization. As a party activist Fidelis was amused to see how some villages evaded the collectivization drive altogether: "Simply, they promised that, 'We will collectivize at such-and-such time.' Those who were establishing the *kołchozy* could then overlook it. They had to." By comparing his recollection and the archives, I began to understand that in the postwar transition to socialism, during bouts of poverty, peasants did not accept the economic rationale behind the plunder economy by which the state systematically extracted resources from them to feed the cities. Dislocating from the Soviet economy was a way of keeping food in the village. Thus, just like the fictional Czech soldier Švejk, peasants practiced kombinacja by giving the impression that they agreed with state collectivization goals. Meanwhile, activists like Fidelis, who spread a revolution they did not believe in, turned a blind eye to the peasants' evasiveness. Collectivization was outdoor theater: activists and peasants all performed when they needed to, but when everyone went home, they returned to their original selves, and the land remained uncollectivized. These carefully planned moments when people shifted identities between good citizen and economic saboteur became a means of resisting collectivization. If Fidelis's version of events was true, then peasants' applications of kombinacja under Stalinism were likely the key process that resulted in the checkerboard pattern of collectivization that I had wondered about when I first arrived to start my research. And since villagers today claim that some villages are wealthier than others because they evaded collectivization during the Stalinist drives, I began to consider kombinacja as not just a colorful folktale about outwitting the state but a real process that checked state development and had longer-term effects on future development projects that provincialized the borderlands away from Warsaw. I also must admit that a story of villagers without the power to vote or unionize who were crafting strategies to check Stalin's vision was just the kind of rebellious history I was looking for when I started my fieldwork. There was something comforting about imagining my village as having always been on the "right" side of history and outsmarting a big, brutal state.

I began to understand why my mother spoke about kombinacja as corruption of the mind when Fidelis told me something in the same diminutive tone he had used to describe the Gestapo as the "German security service." Former officials like himself—the very face of the state—were also victims of the shortage economy, he said, and they had no choice but to use kombinacja to get by: "Party officials who sat at a certain pig sty, also lived in poverty. They also stole, they *kombinowali*, but they just had a better chance to *wykombinować*." I liked Fidelis because he seemed so much more "Western" than the other villagers and I felt like he understood me. It was tempting to just accept everything he told me and imagine officials working alongside workers and peasants trying to carry out a local effort against the encroachment of state control in the village. But, when he revealed to me his own use of kombinacja as an official in the state forestry, I sensed kombinacja's more sinister undertones:

> I used kombinacja because this home required renovation. Completely. I did not receive any [state] ration of wood or anything. But I thought to myself, "I will continue working in the forest; there, I can manage to acquire the wood." I got the wood, some of it I stole—well no, I did not steal it, I used kombinacja. Because the forestry director was a buddy. We were forestry directors together. He allotted some wood which I measured myself. I brought it home. The second batch, I measured, cut it so that the guard would not catch me, but the guard would not go to my house to see if I had the first batch or not. That is how it was done!

Indeed, just as workers and peasants alternated between good and bad citizen personas, he shifted along the "villager who broke the state rules" and "official who enforced the state rules" spectrum of identities. But it was far from a level playing field, because when officials like Fidelis were the "state," they, or their friends in power, loosened the laws when it suited them. While he needed to fix his house, other villagers were cheated out of wood rations that would have warmed their houses or boiled the water to cook food. Fidelis's story reveals that he was only trying to benefit himself by outsmarting the ration system. And when recalling the past after communism collapsed, he could spin his story so that he was either the activist who stayed silent when the peasants used kombinacja or the forward-looking entrepreneur who circumvented the laws using his patronage networks. He was always part of the struggle to fight the system. It was then that I began to think about kombinacja not just as a practice that everyone claimed to have used but as a kind of discourse for talking about the past. The thing about kombinacja is that in the Polish language, the term is so vague that it is impossible to tell what the kombinacja really involved unless the storyteller volunteers the information. Having full control of the story is a kind of power in itself.

When I returned to my interview with Motylek where he argued with Zofia—a former collective farm worker—about whether or not a Soviet "collective farm" actually existed in Bursztyn, I noticed that he used the discourse of kombinacja in a similar way. When he spoke about the early days of state making in the commune, he said that he had been allocated "a very small budget and one had to kombinować so much, so that everything played right, so that everything would work out fine, for there to be help at school." He bought a German carpet on the black market with state money to ensure that the new state school director had a carpet in her new office, to emphasize her new role of state authority. But to Motylek, not all kombinacjas were equal. Later in the interview, when he spoke about workers' kombinacja, his voice boomed with aggression: "Do you think they did not pilfer in the enterprises? They kombinowali! Everyone scratched something here and there. Sometimes a small screw or something or other. Yes! He scratched! But not en masse! Normally! Because if someone fell in, he immediately went to prison. There was no choice. There was rigor." When Motylek used kombinacja, it was for the good of the state; if anyone else did it, they were state saboteurs. I located a state order in the archives that Motylek had written at the height of Stalinism in 1953—at the same time he said he had used kombinacja—advocating for the "abridgement of speculation and forcing [the submission] of kułaks, *kombinators*, and those peasants who are in this era, for the national economy, not meeting their citizen duties, and sometimes even their own economy, in the meeting of their duties within the State."[32] I not only had textual proof of kombinacja subverting state supply chains, but evidence that Motylek had waged a Stalinist witch hunt against the "kombinators" who were diverting resources from the command economy's supply channels linking villages and the industrializing cities. Kombinacja was not just folklore; it was a practice the state sought to eliminate during its Sovietization campaigns, and Motylek was "the state" in Bursztyn.

Former workers and peasants had no sympathy for former officials who used kombinacja. They saw it as simple corruption:

> I am telling you, when there was that corvée, there was Houdini (Kacper's father), let him rest with God in peace—he is long dead—but he was such a kombinator! And a liar!

> Kombinacja was everywhere. On the state supplies there was kombinacja, in the local governments where one tricked the other.

> Everyone kombinowali—even the higher officials, they also kombinowali. But they kombinowali in such a way that we did not know. People knew less about the government officials.

> They even took [resources] out of bureaus, they took out everything.

> They [officials] were looking through their fingers [bribery for silence]!

> Whoever woke up first that day, ruled.

Tracing the ways in which the villagers related to one another through the discourse of kombinacja exposed class tensions between officials and villagers over who got to pilfer state resources. When I cross-referenced their kombinacja stories, I learned that villagers' claims during interviews that "there were no problems" and "we were like all one family" were a protective measure. Rather, those who were and were not in state power were out for themselves and sought control over labor, property, access, redistribution, legitimacy, and power in the postwar period and beyond. By the late socialist period, around the 1970s, this class division became increasingly blurred because second-generation villagers diversified every family's reach across sectors of the command economy and kombinacja networks included party members and nonmembers alike. I was intrigued by this kombinacja narrative and decided to follow its migrations, in the way people told history, from socialism to postsocialism.

Taking a step back from the interviews with Fidelis, I began to scaffold kombinacja in my mind as a practice and as a discourse, each serving slightly different functions. As a practice, kombinacja was the very general process of bending the rules, a practice anyone could use for any purpose. In the context of a shortage economy, villagers used kombinacja to secure limited state resources. This created a tragedy of the commons scenario where too many people wanted a limited amount of state resources. They developed the discourse of kombinacja as a policing mechanism told through kombinacja stories shared in real time. In general, kombinacja used by "us" was cast in a positive light; kombinacja used by "them," the perceived competitors, was cast in a negative light. Explaining why one person's kombinacja was good and another's was bad became a way of expressing how the storytellers perceived themselves in relation to the world around them. Villagers sometimes used good kombinacja stories to set the record straight about a controversial moment in their pasts or to convey the idea that they had been on the right side of history all along. When they called out "bad" kombinacja in interviews, I also wondered whether this had anything to do with the truth, or with ending the practice of kombinacja itself (because no one in their right mind would want any resource pool closed off), or whether it had more to do with using the tools they had at their disposal (gossip, humor, shaming) to shed light on historical patterns of corruption that the same families practice to this day. Good and bad kombinacja stories are just as important in exposing class, political, and ethnic tensions among villagers today as they are in the historical context. They expose the persistence of those tensions. And sometimes it was really difficult to tell whether the storytellers were talking about the past or present.

There was a bodily dimension to kombinacja stories. When I asked some villagers to tell me about kombinacja in person, it was as if a light bulb appeared above their heads. Their eyes brightened and their lips widened into a smile. "Ahhh! Kombinacja!" they would say knowingly, and then they would chattily dive into the narrative of how everyone practiced it under communism, how it was a necessity, before sharing their personal stories. An award-winning milkmaid became a *kombinatorka* whenever the state director diverted his gaze to some other part of the farm and lived to tell the tale. The thrill! In contrast, "bad" kombinacja stories that harmed "us" were nestled in feelings of anxiety and oppression enacted by another person or group who bent the rules in their favor. The speaker's face would wrinkle with nervousness, voices grew louder and more panicked as if the apocalypse was nigh: "In Poland, they do not know how to value the worker. But with a dodger or a kombinator, oh! Those, yes!" or "Oh! What a kombinatorka! She is doing everything for herself!" The dark and sinister tone sounded like it belonged to a witch-hunt, as a kind of "unmasking" of the evil kombinator gaming the system. At times a villager who described her own good kombinacja would later speak about the bad kombinacja of others in the same interview. I could see how the dual narratives could be an effective storytelling device that logged who was in one's network, what was taken, and what sorts of activities a person supported or not, but the level of accusatory rhetoric about "bad" kombinacja sometimes reminded me of the language in Motylek's archive. Had villagers helped the local militia or the state officials identify the "bad" kombinators on the prowl in the village at some point? In hindsight, we know that communism collapsed; but back then, during such uncertain times, villagers had to walk a tightrope daily: one minute they could be kombinators and the next they could be helping the state catch them.

There was another peculiar pattern: villagers collectively remembered and forgot kombinacja. Their memories of kombinacja were present in recollections about some eras and not others. For example, kombinacja was absent from their childhood memories of the interwar period from 1919 to 1939. It surfaced in stories of surviving the Nazi occupation between 1939 and 1945 before dipping into obscurity again during the postwar period from about 1945 to 1949. I wondered if that postwar invisibility had anything to do with the origin myth in which the state was on the villagers' side, and vice versa. Villagers began to use the term frequently only when talking about the Stalinist period (when it also appeared in the archive) until the end of communism in 1989. In discussions of the period after that, its use is less consistent. Some still use it to describe today's struggles ("Where in this world is there no kombinacja?"), while others have stopped ("No, there is no need today for kombinacja"). This fragmented historical narrative of kombinacja appeared curiously symmetrical. Did memories of kombinacja represent the "memories of the state or memories of the people"?[33] What could explain this collective amnesia? Did the state co-opt kombinacja practices in the early state-making period, or did people co-opt the state's campaign against the kombinators and make it their own? To answer this, I first had to investigate the history of this invisible practice in the Polish imagination before I could explore its role in shaping the history of Bursztyn.

When I began to map kombinacja's evolution across communism and capitalism, from Bursztyn to Trenton, I realized there were many paradoxes. As a historical discourse, it appeared and reappeared in villagers' narratives of certain historical events but not others. Villagers used it as a discursive device to retell the history of both state making and state breaking. As a practice, kombinacja was a means of resisting and accommodating the state, but it could be used just as readily by the state and its elites against the people. Some associated it with the state's corruption of the mind, while others considered it a kind of Enlightenment and liberation from Soviet structures. Then there was the ethnographic conundrum: while kombinacja felt like a real phenomenon in the villagers' imaginations and in their personal histories, it was nearly invisible in any textual form on the local level that could help anchor it to any historical event. The polysemic evolutions of kombinacja were interesting to map across history and reconstruct into a narrative, but they rendered it very difficult to put kombinacja in conversation with ethnographic and theoretical literature. There are many ethnographic records of similar practices—*blat, guanxi, combina*, to name a few—but most of these concepts are static and situated within particular time frames. There is no history of these concepts, especially not predating the 1970s. Likewise, theoretical concepts like Scott's *mētis* (practical experience), Bourdieu's habitus, or J. K. Gibson-Graham's diverse economies are limited because scholars have tended to politicize and romanticize them as working against state hegemony and formal economies.[34] That people who represent the state or regulate formal economies also use these practices in clever ways to consolidate or preserve state and formal power is an important aspect of kombinacja. Overall, I found a lack of theoretical language for explaining the inner workings of these concepts, how they evolve over time and across space and economies. To talk about kombinacja, we need flexible language that allows for its polysemic and antithetical expressions as a practice and discourse across history. Since the very objective of kombinacja is to evade form, to neatly package it into a theoretical model or unified argument would be to miss the point entirely. Fidelis gave me the key to unlock the village past and the way that villagers spoke about it, but unfortunately, by the time I began to grasp the complexity of kombinacja as a practice and discourse, its transformations over time, and its significance in uncovering unknown pasts, he had passed away. He had completed his final transformation. I visited his grave in the cemetery behind Zofia's farm, right by several shards of black German marble engraved with black-letter script. I never got the chance to inquire more about his Gestapo comment, to find out how he learned about kombinacja in the Recovered Territories. But Fidelis gave me a gift of awareness about kombinacja which taught me "how to talk" to villagers and feel a sense of belonging among them. These stories revealed a cosmic struggle between the villagers and the world around them. The resistance strategies they devised did not win them a Nobel Prize or even make it into history books, but these strategies were their own way of surviving desperate times. The kombinacja stories that were passed down over generations were codes for survival, should anyone need them in the future. In kombinacja stories, villagers identified oppression and exploitation that did not catch the attention of the international media or cause an investigation by human rights groups. They used kombinacja to seek justice for themselves as their oppressors walked among them. Fidelis had shown me the fossil in the amber, but I would have to extract it myself.

Notes

1. In Polish *Bursztyn* means "amber," fossilized tree resin resembling a stone, found in copious amounts along the Baltic Coast.
2. Kornai, "Reproduction of Shortage."
3. Also see Erdmans, *Opposite Poles*, 21; Zaretsky, "Epilogue," 123.
4. Thomas and Znaniecki, *Polish Peasant*, 107.
5. Schneider, "Inventing Home," 183–84, 200.
6. Ibid., 218.

7. See Napierała and Trevena, "Patterns."

8. I use *pioneers* and *settlers* interchangeably.

9. Bursztyn is the largest village in Bursztyn commune. The political headquarters of the commune are located in the heart of Bursztyn village.

10. See Zbierski-Salameh, *Bitter Harvest*, and Schneider, *Being Góral*, on alcoholism in rural Poland.

11. Lekan, "German Landscape," 141.

12. Materka, "Hybridizing Postsocialist Trajectories" and "Poland's Quiet Revolution."

13. Pagel, "Rathsdamnitz," 800–812.

14. This black-letter script (also called Fraktur), was used in German texts through the mid-twentieth century, long after it was abandoned by typesetters elsewhere. It therefore has a distinctly "German" appearance. Many thanks to Aliza Krefetz for this clarification.

15. Many thanks to Aliza Krefetz for this translation.

16. *Seba* is slang for "Sebastians," a right-wing subculture of young, working-class men who shave their heads, wear tracksuits, breed aggressive dogs, and are often associated with hooliganism, trickery, and gang violence. In 2017, my mother reported that "all of Bursztyn" knew about this incident.

17. I always thought that the tombstone road had been built immediately after the war, but in 2017, my mother recalled to me that it happened sometime between the late 1950s and early 1960s. She remembered being afraid of German ghosts in the cemetery as a little girl. When I asked what happened to the bones, she said, "The bones were brittle. They disintegrated." The priest in charge of the operation, she recalled, left and moved to Słupsk with his mistress.

18. See "Zniszczony niemiecki cmentarz" (Destroyed German cemetery), *Gazeta Wyborcza*, July 31, 2002, http://wyborcza.pl/1,75248,956159.html; "Trzeba przenieść grób niemieckich lotników" (The graves of German pilots must be moved); *Gazeta Kaszubska*, May 25, 2011, http://www.gazetakaszubska.pl/12837/trzeba-przeniesc-grobniemieckich-lotnikow; "Ludzkie szczątki na wysypisku—do prokuratury" (Human remains in the landfill—To the prosecutor's office), *Gazeta Wyborcza*, July 16, 2010, http://wyborcza.pl/1,75398,8143700,Ludzkie_szczatki _na_wysypisku_do_prokuratury.html; Agata Grzegorczyk, "Gdynia: Fragmenty żydowskich nagrobków będą pełnić funkcję edukacyjną" (Gdynia: Fragments of Jewish tombstones will play an educational function), *Dziennik Bałtycki*, November 7, 2011, http://www.dziennikbaltycki.pl /artykul/469587,gdynia-fragmenty-zydowskich-nagrobkow-beda-pelnic-funkcje,id,t.html.

19. Tamara Barriga, "Miasto z nagrobków. 'Próbujemy sobie radzić z tą sprawą'" (City of tombstones: 'We are trying to deal with this issue'), *TVN24 Wrocław*, March 29, 2015, http:// www.tvn24.pl/wroclaw,44/poniemieckie-nagrobki-we-wroclawiu,528193.html.

20. Thum, *Uprooted*, 271–72.

21. Gross and Grudzińska-Gross, *Golden Harvest*, 66.

22. Gross, *Fear*, 45.

23. My mother later told me that she gave the archive director a bottle of liquor to ease tensions so that he would sign the archive permission form. She recalled that he "remembered you and did not remember you."

24. Miłosz, *Native Realm*, 54.

25. Many thanks to Molly Mullin, whose comments helped me reach this conclusion.

26. At times, interviewees answered questions nervously, as if taking a test. They would give me their "formal" answers and then tell me something completely different "behind the scenes." Some villagers refused to be interviewed, and others were hostile toward the questionnaire. I realized pretty quickly that if I admitted to having written the questionnaire and interview questions, I would get a negative backlash from the interviewees. In one interview

a former party official verbally attacked me for the "stupidity" of the questions. However, if it was inferred that "London" had sent me to fill out this predesigned questionnaire, I would be put into the "local subject" position and would not be considered at fault. Each informant received a box of chocolates at the end of the interview. The decision to give chocolates came from Zofia. She said that one box should be enough and that it should be given after, not before, the interview. I must admit that in some interviews, especially with ex-officials or other members of the nomenklatura, I gave the chocolates first so that the interviewees would feel indebted enough to open up. If I detected in the "network" introductions that the person seemed reticent or reluctant, I took out the chocolates. I was drawing on their old socialist-era practices.

27. Grass, *Peeling the Onion*, 3.

28. Hašek, *Good Soldier Švejk*, 106.

29. Parrott, Introduction, xv.

30. Hašek, *Good Soldier Švejk*, 613.

31. Gombrowicz, *Ferdydurke*, 80.

32. Numer 13, 1953–1954, VIII/53 Sesja nadzwyczajnej G.R.N. [Bursztyn], Prezydium Gminnej Narodowej w [Bursztyn], (Referat Ogólno-Administracyjny), Protokoły z sesji Gminnej Rady Narodowej 1953–1954r. (Zespół: Gminy wiejskie powiatu słupskiego), 51–52.

33. Davis, *Memories of State*, 227.

34. See Scott, *Domination and the Arts of Resistance*; Bourdieu, *The Field of Cultural Production*; Gibson-Graham, *A Postcapitalist Politics*.

2 Kombinacja's Histories

KOMBINACJA MIGHT APPEAR to be a specifically Polish concept with no precise English equivalent, but to understand its origins we need to begin in eighteenth-century Great Britain. At the start of the Industrial Revolution, a "combination" was a type of association used by skilled workers, called journeymen, and their employers, called masters, to negotiate workplace conditions.[1] Before the advent of trade and labor unions, the minimum wage, and individual employment contracts, workers and employers negotiated the terms of employment in each workplace and for each trade—for example, in the textile, shipbuilding, or printing industries.[2] Employers for a given trade "combined" in private to discuss wage limits, working hours, and the number of apprentices on the workshop floor. Likewise, workers of the same trade "combined" in private to agree on their own requirements regarding wages, hours, and numbers of apprentices. In this way employers avoided hiking wages in competition for skilled workers and workers avoided accepting lower wages in competition for jobs. Master and worker "combinators" met seasonally in their respective workplaces to negotiate the terms of employment.[3] In *The Wealth of Nations* (1776), Adam Smith argued that this combination system benefited the employers because they were fewer in number and could combine more easily, because financially they could hold out longer during gridlock with workers, and because only negotiating for higher wages— not lowering wages—was illegal under British law. Nonetheless, combinations served an important self-regulatory function in the gray zones of Britain's transition to industrial capitalism when control over labor and capital was in flux, there was no general consensus on the value of labor, and the modern British state was in the making.

Following the outbreak of the French Revolution in 1798 and rapid collapse of the ancien régime by 1799, fear of an insurrection rippled across the English Channel. To repress the brewing Jacobin "conspiracies" of the working class against the bourgeoisie, Parliament passed the Act to Prevent the Unlawful Combinations of Workmen in 1800, which banned worker combinations, picketing, strikes, and trade unions under British conspiracy law, and mandated such punishments as two months of hard labor.[4] Only one clause imposed a fine on master combinations (of £20), but there is no existing record of any master having to pay it. With industrialization intensifying and expanding, the aristocracy wanted a monopoly on labor and capital. Mechanization was already derailing the journeymen's monopoly on industrial labor across Britain, including labor in the textile, shipbuilding, cotton spinning, and printing industries, and in every other industry across Britain.[5] Cities swelled as unskilled workers migrated from the countryside in search of manufacturing jobs in the emerging factory system. With worker combinations kept at bay, masters could employ the uncombined surplus labor on new machines with little training, lower wages, and longer working hours.[6] E. P. Thompson wrote in *The Making of the English Working Class* (1963) that political repression and economic reality "forced the trade unions into an illegal world in which secrecy and hostility to the authorities were intrinsic to their very existence."[7] Fearing for their livelihoods, skilled workers retaliated by staging arson attacks on industrializing factories, breaking new machines (e.g., in the case of the Luddites), bribing and threatening uncombined workers to leave, and terrorizing their employers to keep them from introducing machinery and employing unskilled, uncombined workers.[8] Britain became a hotbed of class warfare as skilled workers and their employers struggled for control over the direction of the Industrial Revolution.

After a quarter century of violence and gridlock, Radical members of Parliament Francis Place and Joseph Hume helped repeal the Combination Act in 1824.[9] But the subsequent eruption of violence against employers swiftly led to the passage of the Combinations of Workmen Act of 1825, which revived conspiracy law to apply to combinations that used or benefited from violence as a negotiation tactic.[10] This caused a public split in the combination movement. Part of the problem was that the flow of unskilled labor was unstoppable, so to reclaim control over it, skilled workers had to convince unskilled workers to enter the workforce through their apprentice systems. Peaceful combinations established a more public presence by printing advertisements, staging theater performances, and opening clubhouses like Friends of Humanity, Blood Red Knights, and Board of Green Cloth with room and board.[11] In *Lloyd's Weekly London Newspaper,* a combined tin-plate worker explained that "when a poor, way worn countryman of his comes amongst us Saxon combinators; he would see the supper provided for him, the cheering but temperate glass, and then the bed, with instructions where to go to look for work in the morning."[12] By 1844 there were more than one hundred thousand combined workers in London alone.[13] As they grew financially and in numbers, trade combinations created constitutions, paraphernalia, and pamphlets. They sent letters to parliament calling for minimum wage laws and the decriminalization of strikes and picketing. They influenced public discourse by making public announcements. They fought for better working conditions and higher wages in an attempt to keep laborers from leaving the country in search of jobs in North America.[14] They traveled to isolated communities, where they stood up for workers overpowered by their employers.[15] This inclusion of unskilled labor in the combinations gave rise to a new working-class consciousness on a national scale.

Conversely, violent combinations were diffuse, had no constitutions, and lacked any center of organization, but it was their very unpredictability that created an ominous atmosphere of uncertainty for those in power.[16] The boundary between worker combination violence and violence disguised as combination was blurry. In 1833 the *Poor Man's Guardian* reported that several "combined" workers from Cork randomly broke into "uncombined" rope-makers' homes and beat them up: "These wanton outrages it is supposed originated from the injurious system of combination which prevails to a great extent in this city."[17] But since the printing industry was strongly biased against combinations, it was unclear if these were indeed "combined" workers. Where the peaceful combination ended and the violent one began was equally blurry. In an 1834 address to the West Riding of Yorkshire Operatives, a known combination and strike leader, John Tester, called for an end to violence because "the vain pursuit of an imaginary good is met by the infliction of a real and lasting evil."[18] In contrast, in 1838, a worker from the Cotton-Spinners' Association in Glasgow said at the House of Commons "Select Committee on the Combinations of Workmen" that the objective of the combined trades was to limit competition over labor "and if those objects cannot be obtained by other means, to employ intimidation and violence without any reserve."[19] During a gathering of one thousand combined workmen in Glasgow that year, the police themselves did not make arrests because they were afraid of intimidation and the "mob."[20] The "invisible hands" of violent combinations kept authorities at bay and allowed the movement to grow.

Control over the discourse regarding combinations was just as important as the combinations themselves. Employers co-opted the notion of the invisible hand of supply and demand, branding their combinations as pro-market and worker combinations as anti-market. In an 1832 article one master explained to workers, "The evils which afflict your class are not the result of unjust combination of the rich against the poor—a combination which, if attempted, would be impracticable. They are not the result of any unfair division of the price of the commodity produced."[21] Employers did not lower wages out of "selfishness," he wrote, but in response to the "fluctuations of the markets, in changes of habits and tastes, in the disturbance of commerce by unforeseen accidents, which no wisdom can anticipate or prevent."[22] At the 1838 House of Commons inquiry, employers complained that workers negotiated on the basis of the perceived—not actual—value of their labor. Such "evils of combinations," a master from Dublin's shipbuilding industry claimed, redirected investment to Liverpool, which had a weaker worker combination movement.[23] A timber merchant complained about cross-border combinations; when he sent his sawyers to sell timber in North America, they refused to cut it for the clients because that had not been negotiated.[24] Another claimed that workers had "but one political creed—the accumulation of wealth—and but one system of morality—the attainment of it for themselves," which in turn "prevent[ed] capitalists from competing with other nations."[25] So, in 1838 when a master lowered wages by 60 percent to keep a Glasgow cotton-spinning factory "competitive," his action was legal and patriotic, whereas workers' strikes that erupted in response were not.[26] By fixing the state's gaze on workers' anti-market combinations, employers erased their fingerprints from the crime scene of poverty that their combinations inflicted on the population.

Unmasking employers' combinations and delinking their natural, God-given right to power had been a key project of the Enlightenment. Thomas Paine wrote in *Rights of Man* (1791) that the legislative house was a "wretched scheme of an house of peers" and that "as a combination, it can always throw a considerable portion of taxes from itself; and as a hereditary house accountable to nobody, it resembles a rotten borough, whose consent is to be courted by interest."[27] Those who question the existence of master combinations, Adam Smith wrote, were "as ignorant of the world as of the subject." He emphasized that master combinations were in fact a real phenomenon:

> Masters are always and every where in a sort of tacit, but constant and uniform combination, not to raise the wages of labour above their actual rate. To violate this combination is every where a most unpopular action, and a sort of reproach to a master among his neighbours and equals. We seldom, indeed, hear of this combination, because it is the usual, and one may say, the natural state of things which nobody ever hears of.[28]

Enlightenment thinkers wanted people to see employers' power not as a mystical or impenetrable force that organized their lives but as a product of employers' co-optation of economic and political power to protect their class interests at workers' expense. Capitalism too was a human construct, not a natural evolution. Unmasking employers as the human face behind exploitation and oppression reoriented the common folk's worldview away from a sense of powerlessness and instilled in them a sense of consciousness with which they could negotiate the conditions of their oppression by outmaneuvering their employers. Combination at this time acquired a secondary meaning—"thinking" and "scheming"—because it represented a certain consciousness of independent thought as a powerful force of change. But as the Industrial Revolution continued, it became clear that consciousness was not enough; employers would adopt new discursive strategies to reverse workers' progress and naturalize their claim to power in novel ways; and in turn, workers had to find novel ways of unmasking and countering employers' combinations because it was the only way of creating space for change and reform.

In London and Paris, Karl Marx witnessed the drama of worker combinations unfolding across the industrializing landscapes of Western Europe. In *The Poverty of Philosophy* (1847), Marx defined combinations as a "common thought of resistance" that did not belong to any particular class or cause; rather, throughout history, people entered into combinations in different ways toward various ends.[29] For example, the bourgeoisie emerged from the "partial combinations" that formed against feudal lords: "We must not forget that strikes and combinations among the serfs were the hotbeds of the mediaeval communes, and that those communes have been in their turn, the source of life of the now ruling bourgeoisie."[30] Combinations were everyday forms of plebeian resistance that broke down ideal types and utopian promises, which in turn provoked those in power to make incremental adaptations to the system to survive, and therefore incrementally changed the system over time.[31] "If combinations and strikes had no other effect than that of making the efforts of mechanical genius react against them, they would still exercise an immense influence on the development of industry," Marx wrote.[32] Other combinations fizzle but still hold moral and political significance in that they prevent common people from becoming "apathetic, thoughtless, more or less well-fed instruments."[33] As economies grew, he argued, an increasing number of people would be affected by the same burdens. Over time, such combinations would evolve into a peripheral "economic system" that would grow and encroach on the center: "As soon as combination becomes an economic fact, daily gaining in solidity, it is bound before long to become a legal fact."[34] As systems turn over, a new elite class emerges, but its fate is finite, for it is broken up by new class combinations against it, and so on. Similar to the way Darwin's theory of evolution explained the development of species, the theory of combinations helped explain how people change and create new kinds of political and economic conditions.

Marx believed that the combinations movement in nineteenth-century Europe represented the nascent stages of a proletarian revolution against the bourgeoisie. In "Chartism" (1853), he wrote that "the first attempts of workers to associate among themselves always takes the form of combinations" because it is their collective response to "the combination of capital [that] has created for this mass a common situation, common interests." In the emerging world of supply and demand, workers' combinations had a "double aim, that of stopping competition among the workers, so that they can carry on general competition with the capitalist."[35] In doing so, they staked "their right to share in the prosperity of the country, and especially in the prosperity of their employers."[36] This put them in conflict not only with "economists" like the employers who sided with the language of supply and demand but also with "socialists" like the French Fourierists and English Owenites who believed in systemic revolution, not incremental reform:

The economists say to workers: Do not combine. By combination you hinder the regular progress of industry, you prevent manufacturers from carrying out their orders, you disturb trade and you precipitate the invasion of machines which, by rendering your labour in part useless, force you to accept a still lower wage. . . . The socialists say to the workers: Do not combine, because what will you gain by it anyway? A rise in wages? . . . Skilled calculators will prove to you that it would take you years merely to recover, through the increase in your wages, the expenses incurred for the organization and upkeep of the combinations. And we, as socialists, tell you that, apart from the money question, you will continue nonetheless to be workers, and the masters will still continue to be the masters, just as before. So no combination! No politics! For is not entering into combination engaging in politics?[37]

The political elite did not really know what to make of workers' combinations, because they did not fit into the ideal types of socialism and capitalism. "Does this mean that after the fall of the old society there will be a new class domination culminating in a new political power?" Marx asked.[38] Unlike the bourgeoisie, which created a class-based society out of the feudal order, this particular spirit of worker combinations, Marx theorized, would eliminate class altogether, for "the condition for the emancipation of the working class is the abolition of every class, just as the condition for the liberation of the third estate, of the bourgeois order, was the abolition of all estates and all orders."[39] What was the end goal of worker combinations—reform or revolution?

There is no suggestion from the primary or secondary material that workers used combinations to bring down the old society altogether and build a proletarian revolution. In fact, it was not always clear who was trying to preserve the old system and who was trying to create a new one. Both employers and workers adopted the strategy of combination to organize around ideas of changing and preserving the existing order in ways that most suited their interests. Employers adopted combinations to extract cheaper labor so that they could remain competitive in the emerging industrial order and preserve their old positions of economic and political power; meanwhile, workers adapted combinations to maintain their wages so that they could preserve their control over the workplace. Workers' agile economic adaptations to the oscillations of labor and capital in real time consequently exposed the rigidity of the class and legal systems still heavily saturated with employers' economic and political interests. Furthermore, one could argue that the formalization of the trade and labor unions was the upper classes' act of self-preservation because they could no longer contain the combination movement. Marx overestimated the political trajectory of the workers' combinations and underestimated employers' combinations, namely their ability to adapt to and reverse workers' progress. In hindsight, it was exactly that gridlock between employers' and workers' combinations that thwarted Marx's utopian vision. Even if a proletarian revolution was successful, Marx provided no guarantee that the workers (or a new kind of economic actor) would not evolve into a new oppressive class. Exploring those questions would have tarnished the utopian promise of a proletarian revolution.

Instead of a proletarian revolution in the latter half of the nineteenth century, reformers called for a solution to the combinations and a redefinition of the modern state.[40] John Stuart Mill's *On Liberty* (1859) made the case that the right to combine was the foundation of a free society. Individual liberty included the freedom of consciousness, the liberty of tastes and pursuits, and the liberty "of combination among individuals; freedom to unite, for any purpose not involving harm."[41] However, there were limits insofar as the state ought not to be aligned economically against a particular group, but should be a medium through which that group could enact its agency. "No class," he added, "likely to combine, should be able to exercise a preponderant influence in the government."[42] A modern state ought to help, not restrain individuals: "It is asked whether the government should do, or cause to be done, something for their benefit."[43] Finally, two acts—the Trade Union Act of 1871 and the Conspiracy and Protection of Property Act of 1875—legalized trade unions, picketing, and boycotting, and charged violent combinations under common law, not conspiracy law. These reforms opened the floodgates for improved working conditions, the eight-hour day, and minimum wages.[44] Eventually, in Britain the term *combination* was replaced by *collective bargaining*, *right of association*, *trade union*, and *monopoly*, but the spirit of combination traveled on the wave of revolutionary fervor and industrialization that swept across the European continent.[45]

The Republic of Imagination

The revolutions of Western Europe captivated an underground Polish nation that had been struggling to survive since 1795 under Russian, Prussian, and Austrian partitions. Congress Poland, a client state of the Russian Empire, was but a mangled carcass of the former Polish-Lithuanian Commonwealth that had once stretched to Moscow's doorstep. As colonial power became more entrenched, revolts became futile. In 1864, after tsarist forces crushed the January Uprising along the banks of the Vistula, Russia intensified its Russification campaign across Congress Poland, banning the Polish language from public spaces and institutions. It also heavily taxed, deported, and executed the Polish elites—nobles, clergy, intelligentsia, bourgeoisie—who led the insurrection and kept the ideas of revolution alive across the partitions.[46] Times were changing rapidly in many ways. The abolition of serfdom in 1864 created a free Polish peasantry in search of work and land, and the rapid industrialization of Polish cities created an unprecedented demand for cheap, unskilled labor to bolster competition with the textile industries in Western Europe. Peasant and working classes needed to be integrated into the underground Polish society if they were to be protected against state-run de-Polonization campaigns as well as the new church of industrial capitalism, which preached supply and demand.[47] A new, more democratized ideology was appealing to many who wanted to hold the nation together amid all the forces tearing it apart. It was in the trenches of these battles over the Polish mind that I discovered kombinacja.

Licking their wounds from their failed insurrection, Polish elites in Congress Poland reoriented their nationalist liberation strategy away from costly insurrections and toward a new Western ideology called "organic work" (*praca organiczna*), also known as Polish positivism, in a movement that lasted from 1864 to 1900. Influenced by Herbert Spencer's idea of society as a social organism, this sociocultural movement prioritized grassroots nation building through quotidian labor, education, and ethnic economic networks.[48] In the countryside, Catholic-run cooperatives called agricultural circles (*kółka rolnicze*) linked Polish peasants to creditors, distributors, and consumers. Circle headquarters that sold Polish produce in villages often doubled as school rooms, community centers, and courts.[49] As they spread across the partitions, they created constellations that operated more like a surrogate nation-state. In the cities, "flying universities" (*uniwersytety latające*) secretly taught Polish university courses in private homes to students like future Nobel laureate Maria Skłodowska-Curie, moving from place to place to evade the Russian military. Meanwhile, publishing houses in Warsaw printed underground journals like *World* (*Świat*) and *Ivy* (*Bluszcz*) that distributed excerpts of realist nationalist fiction by Nobel laureates Władysław Reymont and Henryk Sienkiewicz. Such publications helped to keep the Polish language and national discourse alive for a new mass readership and evaded the censors.[50] The birth of Poland as a modern nation in the latter half of the nineteenth century was premised on Poles' participation in this "common thought of resistance," finding creative ways around the foreigners to preserve their identity whether by joining a circle, reading a journal, or buying cereals produced by Polish peasants. Politics and resistance was no longer the realm of military men or elites (although they remained in charge) but had become the work of the "invisible hands" of all Poles. To reproduce the quotidian was to resist.

The Polish nation renewed itself as an underground "republic of imagination."[51] Polish artists emerged as the bards of nationalism. A new school of realist Polish painters like Józef Chełmoński, Jan Matejko, and Aleksander Gierymski focused on capturing everyday life in the midst of broader historical events, often set in the past to evade the censors, but with subversive undertones. Jan Matejko's painting *Stańczyk* (1862) depicts a contemplative Polish court jester sitting (or scheming) behind a curtain after hearing that Poland has been partitioned, while a Russian aristocratic party continues on as if nothing important had happened

Figure 2.1. *Stańczyk*, by Jan Matejko, 1863. National Museum in Warsaw.

(see figure 2.1). The jester, an object of entertainment, transforms into a political subject. Chełmoński's utopian paintings of the countryside depicted the peasants' encounters with the emancipatory ideas of the Enlightenment. In his painting *Bociany* (1900), a peasant and his son sit in the fields, engaging in a new kind of mental work as they look up at the sky to contemplate a flock of migrating storks (see figure 2.2). Chełmoński captures the moment in which the freedom of the migrating birds mirrors the newfound independence of the Polish mind in the fields. Artists nurtured exclusive spaces of nationalism by honing the ability of Polish minds to detect nuances that evaded an outsider's gaze. Likewise, veering away from romantic literature that glamorized the decadent life of the nobility, Polish writers, often writing in exile, translated the lessons of the worker revolutions in France and Great Britain for the Polish masses. This new modernist Young Poland (Młoda Polska) literary movement focused on the bewildering upheavals brought on by the arrival of industrial capitalism from foreign shores, creating ambiguous spaces, liminal states, and "newcomers to capitalist society" like the entrepreneurial tricksters. These tricksters assumed new polysemous identities to bridge the gap between the nationalist organic work movement where the flow of capital was stratified along ethnic lines versus industrial capitalism where success

Figure 2.2. *Bociany*, by Józef Chełmoński, 1900. National Museum in Warsaw.

was dependent on the free flow of capital across boundaries.[52] While British combinations were documented in newspapers and archives, Polish kombinacja emerged in this fictional literature where the boundary between fantasy and reality was blurred, and liminal characters became the new norm.

The Promised Land (1899), a novel written in France by Nobel laureate Władysław Stanisław Reymont, warns against the dark and mystical force of *kombinacya* overturning the agrarian moral order, possessing people's minds, and transforming them into amphibian creatures in the rapidly industrializing textile industry of nineteenth-century Łódź in Congress Poland. Reymont's Łódź is a dystopian place where Polish nobles, stripped of their God-given feudal privilege after the end of serfdom, attempt to become the new class of industrialists but find themselves in competition with German and Jewish *Lodzermenschen*—the city's capitalist, entrepreneurial class that had received land concessions from the Russian tsar to expand the city's factory system.[53] In a scene between two Polish noblemen who became new textile industrialists, Kurkowski says to Borowiecki in a tone of awe and bewilderment:

> Think, what is this strange *kombinacya* that is unfolding today in the world: the human enslaved nature's forces, discovered masses of strength—and went

on to be shackled by these very forces. The human created the machine, and the machine made him its own slave; the machine will expand itself and grow until infinity and so will the human's enslavement expand and grow. Voilà! Winning always costs more than losing. Beware.[54]

Echoing Marx's idea of combination as a "common thought of resistance," Reymont captures the hazy moment of enlightenment when the Poles become conscious of a higher-level power at play—presumably the invisible hand of industrial capitalism—fettering the people and the landscape to the machines, and creating a dystopian order that benefits only a foreign entrepreneurial class. As Reymont's Poles find themselves at the bottom of the foreign caste system created by this mystical force, they gradually become enchanted by it, wanting riches and upward mobility, but eventually at the cost of their Catholic Polishness.

Reymont's characters become possessed by the capitalist demons of kombinacya. Karol Borowiecki slips into a dreamlike state as he transforms into a manufacturer: "Doubts ate at him, thousands of thoughts, numbers, conjectures and kombinacyas circulated beneath his skull, (to the point that) he forgot where he was and where he was going."[55] He "wandered around and walked on the sidewalk exposed to the sunlight, drowned in some financial kombinacya, because he did not see his friends who bowed to him. He looked at people and the city with a blank stare, lost in thought."[56] A similar fate is suffered by Stach Wilczek, a freed Polish peasant and aspiring industrialist. When he sells his land to a Jewish manufacturer named Grünspan who wants to expand his factory system, Grünspan ridicules Wilczek for being smart "only up to 40,000 złoty," for he would have willingly paid even fifty thousand złoty if only Wilczek had been a smarter negotiator. Wilczek, humiliated, "wandered around Łódź for entire days, submerged only in kombinacyas that sought to harm the manufacturer . . . in his money pockets." He begins to look into the conditions under which a factory belonging to Grosman, another Jewish manufacturer, had burned down, thinking he could arrange to have the same thing done to Grünspan's factory. He goes into business with Maks Bauman, son of a German manufacturer, and they build a huge factory that produces cotton scarves to compete with Grünspan's factory. In the eyes of the other God-fearing Poles in the novel, Wilczek's eventual transformation into an industrialist like Grünspan makes him an "amphibian," a "wild animal," and a "nihilist." Adam, the Polish nobleman for whom Wilczek had milked cows as a young farmhand under serfdom, notices Wilczek's "degradation" and comments, "Under the nobility he had happiness and God, but now, it seems to me that only the devil will be happy."[57] The invisible hand of the market has molded Poles into scheming creatures who answer to the new capitalist gods rather than following the Catholic, feudal, nationalist path of Polish self-determination. They have co-opted organic work for personal, not national, preservation.

Rather than being seduced by the kombinacja of industrial capitalists, the characters in Bolesław Prus's novels harness kombinacja in a delicately subversive way. In *The Returning Wave* (1880), a novel also set in industrializing Łódź, Gosławski, an exploited Polish factory worker, imagines other realities when his German employer is not looking: "Sometimes washed over with sweat he hung his hands on the gears and pondered that in his thoughts, usually filled with movement and kombinacja. . . Maybe he would cease to work if . . . he read a sign with the inscription 'Gosławski's Mechanical Workshop'!"[58] In *The Doll* (1890), set in Warsaw in Congress Poland, the protagonist Stanisław Wokulski, born into Polish nobility, is exiled to Siberia by the tsarist regime for having participated in the January Uprising. After he is freed, he travels penniless to Bulgaria, where he makes millions as a venture capitalist by supplying materials to the Russian army during the Russo-Turkish War. His clever enterprise of making money off the tsarist regime that exiled him wins him admiration among Polish characters who call him a "genius" with the "gift of kombinacja" (*dar kombinacji*) and a magical way of "working out brilliant ideas."[59] Wokulski has a double-consciousness of himself as "two men . . . one quite sensible, the other a lunatic."[60] Unlike Reymont's characters who are lost in a dreamlike state of kombinacja, Wokulski embraces his liminality and strategically navigates his transitory, apparition-like existence expertly, across physical borders, old and new regimes. In Prus's world, kombinacja complements the idea of organic work that posited creative, strategic solutions as a form of engaging in politics, or as the character Ignacy Rzecki puts it: "Politics depends on kombinacjas, which emerge from the arrangement of things."[61] When strategically harnessed in the mind, kombinacja could lead to self-determination—personal, political, economic. Wokulski represented this archetypal patriotic trickster, a new Polish masculinity with multiple selves who could benefit from the spatial, economic, and political schisms in the modern age. It became a new form of agency.

Stefan Żeromski warned against the master's ability to co-opt this agency. *Labors of Sisyphus* (1897), set in two rural schoolhouses in post-1864 Congress Poland, explores the gray zone of kombinacja as a form of conscious resistance and subconscious submission. In Owczary, where teachers enforce Russification with an iron fist, the Polish children playfully use kombinacja to distort reality and temporarily liberate their minds through magical realism. When Marcin Borowicz, the son of a fallen nobleman, sees his Russian teacher with big glasses, "by a process of strange associations of impressions . . . he *wykombinował* that the teacher resembles a huge fly."[62] Thinking is a form of resistance. In the other school, Klerykowo, Russification is much subtler. When Mr. Nogacki, a Russian teacher of Polish descent, teaches arithmetic, "there was something in Mr. Nogacki's curriculum that forced the boys into thinking in Russian. He required fast, immediate, lightning-fast kombinacja, elastic phrases that he coined, formulas of speaking, which he admired and which he drilled in, rammed, squeezed into their minds and into their memories by means of moral terror."[63] When co-opted by power in scheming ways, it is impossible to tell whether the exercise of kombinacja serves to resist power or to bolster it. Only at recess did the boys reclaim kombinacja through their bodies, using their "own elements of horsing around with the perceptiveness and strength of *kombinowania*."[64] The aesthetic expression of random bodily movements was itself a way of resisting bodily composure, order, and submission. When Bernard Zygier, a self-taught student of Polish literature who has been expelled from a school in Warsaw for his anti-Russian activism, joins their class, he starts a secret reading circle where he introduces the boys to Adam Mickiewicz's poetry. Nationalism reawakens within them, but we never know if they fully break the spell of Russification, partly because Żeromski died before he finished the novel. It remains unresolved whether the Sisyphean task in the novel was the futile attempt by Russia to harness the Polish mind or the Polish mind's futile quest for freedom from Russification.

It is no coincidence that kombinacja existed in the realm of Polish masculinity. Women's kombinacja was portrayed as a symptom of the "bad" kombinacja, with foreign influences wreaking havoc on the fabric of Polish society. Prus, the very author who made rule-bending Wokulski into a national hero, demonized the "monstrous kombinacja" (*potworna kombinacja*) his female characters displayed by publicly flirting with lovers in violation of social convention.[65] In 1875 Józef Chełmoński, the painter whose later work depicted male peasant enlightenment under beautiful blue skies, painted *Woman's Summer*, depicting a young peasant woman who appears possessed, lying with her body contorted in the middle of what looks like a failed crop, reaching up toward ominous clouds. Polish feminist author and "fantasmal lesbian" Narcyza Żmichowska was an outlier.[66] This French-educated founder of the underground women's rights group the Enthusiasts (Entuzjastki), helped organize the January Uprising and later faced imprisonment by the Russian military for plotting to assassinate the Russian tsar.[67] Though a national advocate for independence, her writing subversively furthered Polish women's sexual liberation in a masculinized, heterosexual, Catholic, Polish society. *The Heathen* (1846), a romantic novel about a heterosexual relationship, was a thinly disguised fictionalized account of her real-life lesbian encounters with Paulina Zbyszewska. (She confessed to her friend Bibianna Moraczewska that she had "sinned heavily" with Paulina and stated that to "make love like that isn't seemly, hence after the evil comes the punishment.")[68] She knew that some readers would understand what she alluded to while others would miss the point. A series of letters Żmichowska wrote to her romantic interest Wanda Żeleńska between 1859 and 1876 reveal how the word *kombinacja* evolved in her own imagination. Before the January Uprising, she used it in a normative sense (e.g., to mix), but after the insurrection, her usage became much more Westernized and sometimes served as an ostentatious display of worldliness. She praised someone as having "God's kombinacja" (*boża kombinacja*) for taking the risk of educating women in defiance of social convention, of desiring to "wykombinować" a rendezvous with another woman, and attempting to "skombinować" lower book publishing costs to increase the profit margins of her book.[69] Żmichowska conceptualized and practiced kombinacja in various ways to hack into masculinized and heterosexual Polish society on and off the page.

Ultimately, it was the outbreak of World War I, not elite-driven organic work, that led to the reconstitution of the Second Polish Republic in 1918.[70] As colonialism receded from an independent Poland, the idea of kombinacja as resistance against the partition lost its luster, but the work of the intelligentsia in bringing the revolutionary potential of kombinacja to the forefront of the Polish imagination was not lost. During interwar Poland between 1918 and 1939, gay artists and writers in the modernist Young Poland movement applied Żmichowska's legacy of kombinacja to gay rights. It was a family inheritance in a way. The novelist Tadeusz Boy-Żeleński, the most outspoken gay and women's rights activist at the time, was Wanda Żeleńska's son. In 1930 he published her letters with Żmichowska and exposed their relationship not out of malice but to give lesbian writers and thinkers a history in Polish society. Likewise, he adopted Żmichowska's method of alluding to homosexual acts, letting the reader's mind color in the details, as in this statement in his novel *Flirt with Melpomena* (1920), where it is unclear if his intoxicated subject is stealing money or pleasure from his neighbor's pocket:

> Today, the "New Human" [*nowy człowiek*] buys a ticket, accepts a morsel of spiritual nourishment without any large inquiry, whichever one they give him, goes to a restaurant and drinks through it with beer and as he is lulled by the sounds of a waltz his thoughts seriously wander onto matters, *kombinując* deep possibilities of lowering his hands into his neighbour's pocket engaging in possibly the least criminal activity.[71]

In *How to End Women's Hell?* (1932), Boy-Żeleński's female characters devise creative kombinacjas (sodomy, abortion) to avoid out-of-wedlock pregnancy.[72] The novelist Stanisław Ignacy Witkiewicz, rumored intimate companion of famed Polish-British anthropologist Bronisław Malinowski, used the same allusion in his novel *Narcotics*, about the erotic kombinacja (*kombinacji erotycznych*) that fantastically emerged in his psychedelic trips on various drugs.[73] In 1938 the celebrated bisexual author Witold Gombrowicz critiqued heterosexual love as a "hellish kombinacja" (*piekielna kombinacja*), a devil's scheme to fetter the world to a rigid "system" where the "dog chases and frightens the cat, and the cat chases and frightens the dog, and they both chase one another madly, relentlessly in a circle."[74]

In the interwar period kombinacja was not part of a hidden movement against an external enemy like a foreign occupant or capitalist, but the beginnings of an internal revolution within the Polish republic of imagination. Women's and gay rights activists were beginning to publicly question the organization of Polish society around Catholic-defined, heterosexual, and masculinized spaces. However, this effort was abruptly thwarted when the Nazis invaded Poland and World War II broke out in 1939. Boy-Żeleński was shot to death by the Nazis along with two dozen others in the 1941 massacre of Lviv professors. Gombrowicz ended up in Argentina. The rest destroyed their work, fled the country, or went missing. The literature went dead silent. Kombinacja disappeared along with it.

Shadow King of the Soviet World

Toward the end of World War I, two revolutions swept across the Russian Empire. Open revolts against Tsar Nicolas II's brutal regime that had produced massive military deficits, chronic food shortages, a toxic atmosphere of political repression, and jarring class divisions culminated in the Russian Revolution of 1917. A provisional government replaced the tsarist regime, but then another coup in October 1917, led by the Marxist Vladimir Lenin, overthrew it and brought the radical Bolsheviks into state power. Lenin's newly formed Soviet Russia immediately sought to build a postcapitalist world, a "quintessential Enlightenment utopia" ordered by a rational and scientific state apparatus.[75] That global revolution was quickly thrown into question when Bolsheviks failed to seize power in the Polish-Soviet War (1919–1921) while their domestic policy of war communism, which prioritized the provisioning of Red Army troops, had already starved six million Russian peasants by 1921. Soviet realities quickly overshadowed Marxist dreams.

Massive peasant revolts across Russia threatened Bolshevik rule. In response, Lenin introduced the New Economic Policy (NEP), ending war communism and restoring state capitalism. Starving peasants who had been forced to sell all of their mandatory quota yields (*prodrazvyorstka*) to the state would be allowed to sell some yields for profit. Traders dubbed "Nepmen" could operate private businesses (e.g., stores, pharmacies) and provide services (e.g., transportation, construction) that supported state enterprise. Amid Bolshevik fears that he had sold out the revolution to capitalism, Lenin consoled, "Wherever there is small-scale production and free exchange, capitalism will appear. But need we fear this capitalism if we control the factories, transportation systems, and foreign trade? . . . [W]e need have no fear of this capitalism."[76] He defended his policies using his *kto kogo* (who will vanquish whom) principle: Soviet Russia would strategically harness capitalism before co-opting it.[77] A resurgent capitalism in 1923, however, worried Lenin. He confessed to delegates that Nepmen were coming in through "many doors of which we ourselves are not aware, which open in spite of us and against us."[78] Lenin's long-term vision did not make clear which strains of capitalism, if any, would benefit the Soviet project. Laws were equally schizophrenic: one constitutional clause from 1918 disenfranchised private business owners while a 1923 law in the criminal code allowed them to exist.[79]

Lenin's death in 1924, the NEP threat to the Soviet command economy, and Bolshevik calls for a return to the revolution all created another power vacuum, which precipitated the rise of Joseph Stalin. This shrewd and power-hungry tactician knew the battle for the formal power of the state was waged on the fields of informality. Although NEP had revived the economy—studies show that in 1925 and 1926 government officials and proletariat made 36–40 percent of their purchases from Nepmen—this "new bourgeoisie" had no place in a collectivized and industrialized Stalinist Russia.[80] When Stalin rolled out his First Five-Year Plan in 1928, the purges of the Nepmen commenced. In a speech at the Sixteenth Congress in 1930, he invoked Lenin's *kto kogo*: "Either we will overcome and crush them, the exploiters, or else they will overcome and crush us, the workers and peasants of the USSR—that's how the question stands, comrades."[81] Pretending to continue Lenin's legacy, Stalin never formally repealed NEP, and well into the 1930s he denied that it had been abolished.[82] He wanted to give the illusion that it was workers' and peasants' ideologically driven tactical strategies—not his own policies—that eliminated capitalist elements from Soviet society. Stalin's twisted exercise of state power relied not only on the visible legislative, bureaucratic, and political arms of the state but also on the invisible purging of capitalist elements that threatened Stalinization. He promoted the impression that the Nepmen's disappearance was part of the natural course of the socialist revolution.

Stalin's trickster tactics to eradicate the Nepmen capitalists inspired a new antihero, similar to Prus's Wokulski, in interwar Soviet literature. Ostap Bender—"The Great Kombinator" (Velikii Kombinator)—in Ilya Ilf and Evgenii Petrov's cowritten novels *The Twelve Chairs* (1928) and *The Golden Calf* (1931) is a rogue who hunts for individualist treasures in a collectivizing landscape during NEP.[83] Already bored of building socialism by 1928, this self-described "son of a Turkish subject," sporting a white-top seaman's cap and a long scarf wrapped around his neck, dreams of making millions so that he can escape to the white sandy beaches of Rio de Janeiro. He travels across the wilderness of the Russian provinces to out-con an underground millionaire named Alexander Koreiko who has been posing as the lowest-ranking employee in the city of Chernomorsk's Department of Finance and Accounting, earning forty-six rubles a month. Written when Stalin's socialist realism policies mandated that all art promote a socialist agenda, the Ilf and Petrov novels subversively used Stalinist themes to expose the blurry line between corruption and resistance in Soviet Russia. "Good" kombinators, like Bender, "respected the criminal code," whereas "bad" kombinators like Koreiko, "waited for capitalism" and used deception and spectacle to get what they wanted. This new form of Soviet agency rested not in law, but in the ability to out-trick the other.

The Golden Calf is worth examining in detail for what it suggests about the place of kombinators in Soviet Russian popular culture in this period. Significantly, it achieved such notoriety that details of its plot became well known even to people who had not read the book. Whereas Westerners would not typically compare their life experiences to those of a character in a Dickens novel, in Soviet society, and in Central and Eastern Europe generally, people reference literary characters in their recollections of personal crises. In effect, writes Vieda Skultans in *Testimony of Lives* (1998), events on paper are used to justify the existence of events in reality.[84] *The Golden Calf* powerfully drives home this point. In the wake of the Russian Revolution, Koreiko has made his first millions looting abandoned aristocratic homes, gorging on their luxurious herring reserves to sustain himself. After a brief stint in prison, he poses as a Soviet food supply official during the Russian famine of 1921 and makes millions diverting state supply trains headed for the German Volga region and selling state typhoid medication, sugar, and food on the black market: "Every crisis that shook the young economy worked in his favor; every loss of the state was his gain. He would break into every gap in the supply chain and extract his one hundred thousand from it. . . . Koreiko never doubted that the old days would return. He was saving himself for capitalism."[85] Yet with every million he makes, inflation turns it to dust, so he has to constantly find new profit ventures. When Soviet authorities become suspicious, Koreiko escapes to the vast provinces of central Russia. There, he spots another opportunity at the construction site of a state power plant located alongside a scenic gorge. He persuades the state managers to give him seed money so he can raise funds for the project by selling postcards with photographs of it. His successful postcard sales eventually divert all the money from the construction project into Koreiko's adjacent printing press. When a high-level commissioner comes to investigate, Koreiko has already left. He moves on to another scam and never gets caught. This is Koreiko's modus operandi until Bender learns of his hidden millions.

Seizing Koreiko's fortune is Bender's key to funding his dream to escape to Rio. But Bender is no thief. A chameleon of an extraordinarily creative nature, Bender circumvents Soviet law without breaking it: "I revere the Criminal Code. I'm not a bandit. I'm a highly principled pursuer of monetary instruments. Mugging is not on my list of four hundred honest methods of taking money, it just doesn't fit," he claims.[86] Instead of stealing, Bender crafts scenarios so that what he wants to acquire is gifted to him. He carries around a Gladstone bag with a Kiev police hat, Indian turban, high priest poster, doctor's coat, stethoscope—all the necessary tricks to acquire pocket money. Skilled in the dark art of double-speak and double-consciousness, he morphs identities, effortlessly switches between monarchist and Bolshevik speak, and manipulates the political symbols of both regimes, thereby exposing their superficiality with equal measure. To fund his way to Chernomorsk, he poses as the son of revolutionary hero Comrade Nikolay Schmidt to win over a government official who supplies him with rubles and meal vouchers. In the guise of a Freudian psychoanalyst, he offers to heal a monarchist haunted by Soviet dreams in exchange for a place to store his car. As a moonshine expert, he gives two bootleggers from Chicago traveling across central Russia a secret recipe to take back to Prohibition-era America, for a fee of two hundred rubles. As a Soviet activist traveling by car across the provinces with a Soviet banner, he naturally accepts villagers' offerings toward the cause of Soviet automobile production. At last, as "director" of the bogus Bureau for the Collection of Horns and Hoofs, he uses the perks of his office to acquire stationery and stamps so that he can start a case file on Koreiko's underground enterprises and later blackmail him with it for a million rubles.[87] (However, because his bureau becomes so entangled with the state, the state later adopts it and renames it the State Horn and Hoof Association.) Bender's scheme to blackmail Koreiko ultimately fails, and his nemesis escapes again. Eventually, Bender finds him on a newly constructed Turkestan-Siberia Railway and relieves him of a million rubles. The like-minded kombinators become friends and part amicably. Koreiko, who had been burdened by his millions, "becomes more easy-going and amenable," and finds another job as an accountant.[88] Bender, however, ultimately loses his fortune while escaping to Romania and returns to Russia wearing a monarchist Order of the Golden Fleece medal of chivalry, vowing to bravely live out his life as an apartment manager. This is a remarkable ending because Bender uses the symbolism of chivalry from the tsarist regime to accept his fate as a Soviet citizen. He lives out the rest of his life as what Alexander Zholkovsky in *Text Counter Text* (1996) calls the "dream-genre's listener interpreter," blending the symbols of the old and new orders, simultaneously bolstering and subverting them but never fully giving in to the promises of either.[89]

The Ilf and Petrov novels became instant classics and ran through twenty editions in interwar Soviet Russia before the state officially banned them in 1948.[90] They tapped into a Soviet reality: every citizen had to be a Bender or a Koreiko to survive shortages and repression. Everyone had their own "Gladstone bag" of masks they wore for the authorities to evade the state's gaze, feed their families, and ensure their safe passage into the next Five-Year Plan.[91] Superficial declarations of loyalty to the revolution, masking one's identity, creating fake enterprises to divert state funds, nominating front men, hiding property and valuables from scrutiny, and siphoning state resources were a part of everyday life. In *Russia and Soul* (2000), Dale Pesman writes that *kombinatsiia*, a planned sequence of events that resulted in a tangible profit, became a fundamental component of how Russians acquired scarce resources to which they were not legally entitled or could not acquire in a state store.[92] A Stakhanovite worker who went well beyond the state plan at work and won accolades also rallied her *blat* (personal networks) to secure food and resources through informal channels.[93] Just like Bender's front men, who hunted for stationery for the Hoofs and Horns bureau, informal procurement agents called *tolkachi* (expediters) promoted the functioning of the "official" economy by acquiring raw materials, machines, and funding for real and fictive state enterprises.[94] In *Charms of the Cynical Reason* (2011), Mark Lipovetsky argues that the "Soviet trickster serves as the most important symbolic manifestation of the informal economy and of the blat social network insofar as they serve as the foundations of the Soviet society."[95] Kombinatsiia empowered Russians to transgress the claustrophobia of Stalinism and find agency in one's own hunt for resources rather than waiting for them to appear through official state channels (though not turning them away when they did). It was this collective filling in of systemic loopholes through kombinatsiia on all scales of the Soviet state apparatus and its command economy that ironically unified Russians across all classes and political inclinations.[96] With the characters of Bender and Koreiko, Ilf and Petrov captured this subversive individualism.

The novels also introduced a new political discourse for masking and unmasking deviance. The criminal code in interwar Russia had no laws against impersonating officials; thus, elites held multiple identification cards with different military and political affiliations to score state supplies, land a state position, or access "soft money" funds.[97] After the novels came out, phrases like "Horns and Hoofs" (Рога и копыта) and "Children of Lieutenant Schmidt" (Дети лейтенанта Шмидта) became popular Russian colloquialisms that referred to shady persons or suspicious enterprises. They caught on because they filled a need for a way to talk about corruption. These phrases could be used to check the power of local elites and competitors who usurped limited resources. For example, folkloric depictions of the Russian Revolution often portrayed Lenin as a trickster who usurped power through devious means, and Stalin as another trickster with unlimited thirst for power, manifested in his excessive expenditure of human lives.[98] Exercising kombinatsiia connected individuals to their leaders' magical grip on power. Whether or not they were good or bad tricksters was unclear, but that was exactly the point, for ambivalence could be quickly tweaked to reflect the level of trust between storyteller and audience. The state *also* used this discourse. At nearly every major state initiative in the 1920s and 1930s there were disruptions: protests, including women's protests (*bab'i bunty*), murders of collectivizers and collaborators, acts of vandalism and so forth, but the state-run media either did not report the events or spun them as "wrecking" or "sabotage" that could be solved only with more socialism.[99] Possession of the discourse meant control over the purging process, whether it was the state calling out saboteurs or a peasant woman gossiping about a corrupt official or neighbor kombinator to purge him from the pool of competition for limited resources on a collective farm. The key to becoming a Soviet citizen was not to believe the propaganda per se but to master this discourse and know when to deploy it. It was one thing when a man practiced kombinatsiia to feed his children and something completely different if someone called him out as a kombinator who overstepped his share.

In *Magnetic Mountain* (1997), historian Stephen Kotkin argues that it was exactly the intersection between the "grand strategies of the state" and the "little tactics of the habitat" that led to a distinctly "socialist civilization." Through "petty maneuvers and modest stratagems," Kotkin adds, "the basic outlines of the new socialist society made themselves manifest . . . socialism was not only built but lived by people—individuals with hopes, fears, a capacity for survival, and no small amount of inventiveness."[100] The paradoxical function of kombinatsiia as the tool of both the powerful and the weak supports this view because no matter what one's rank, everyone lived in the ecosystem of socialism. There was no escape. However, rank largely determined the scale and scope of one's maneuvers. The shadowy trickster tactics of Lenin and Stalin, *kto kogo*, the contradictory and incomplete legal code, purges that left no paper trail, and the forging of fictive realities through socialist realism all represented deceptive ways the state and its elites attempted to gain economic and political power. Meanwhile, because of the harsh Soviet realities of scarcity, the unclear role of capitalism in Soviet society, and the state's own ghost statecraft in usurping power, the rise of the kombinator popularized and valorized the everyday tactics many considered necessary. The kombinator diverted state funds and created new resource flows in a state and Soviet economy that was still in the process of formation. In this case, "informality" did not exist on the margins of a failing Soviet economy or under the turf of an already-established formal economy but, paradoxically, was constitutive of a series of practices that were key to not only creating the myths and imaginary of Soviet power but also bolstering its economic and political foundations in the 1920s and 1930s. This blurry line between the state and informality evolved into a Soviet model of modernity held together by order (command economy, propaganda) and disorder forces (blat, tolkachi, kombinatsiia) coexisting together, supporting and wrecking the state simultaneously, and reforging self and society in a Soviet Russia.[101] A Soviet criminal code riddled with contradictions about the legality of private enterprise allowed one Russian's "informal" economy to be another Russian's "formal" economy. The difference between formality and informality was in the eye of the beholder. The overall impact was not revolutionary: people's resource flows were too entangled in the state system for them to completely destroy it. In the 1980s Lenin's NEP policy of state capitalism returned in the form of Mikhail Gorbachev's perestroika and glasnost reforms.[102] The shadow kings of the Soviet world never escaped the system they had built. Revolution came from elsewhere in the Soviet bloc.

I, Kombinator

In *The Republic of Imagination* (2014), novelist Azar Nafisi writes that "the first thing a totalitarian mind-set does is strip its citizens of their sense of identity, rewriting their past to suit its goals, and rewriting history to serve its ends."[103] In the wake of World War II and the fall of the Iron Curtain upon the Soviet bloc a new kind of kombinacja literature and mentality emerged, one geared not toward building a bright future but toward protecting history from the tyranny of forgetting and historical revisionism. Postwar narratives of kombinacja represent the historical repossession of the self against encroaching totalitarian rule of the mind. They simultaneously retell the past and critique the present. The authors—war survivors, exiles, émigrés—rely on the written word, oral history, and the physical proof of their bodily wounds to tell their stories about the double-edged sword of wartime kombinacja. They speak out of a compulsion to reconstruct a people and country that no longer exist, out of an emotional need to grapple with the tremendous consequences of war and genocide, and out of a determination to warn humanity against going down that path again. The kombinator speaks. What is fascinating about this literature is that it encompasses memoir, fiction, and ethnography—including this one. There are sometimes no clear winners and losers. The key to survival in concentration camps, ghettos, and sites of forced labor obligations was finding creative ways to circumvent the state. Keeping imagination alive was the ultimate form of resistance against war and genocide. The memory of resistance becomes just as important as the method of resistance.

In his memoir *Survival in Auschwitz* (1958), the Jewish Italian writer Primo Levi writes that *Häftlinge* (prisoners) like himself survived Auschwitz by illegally dealing a third-rate tobacco called Mahorca: "The traffic is an instance of a kind of 'kombinacja' frequently practiced: the Häftling, somehow saving a ration of bread, invests it in Mahorca; he cautiously gets in touch with a civilian addict who acquires the Mahorca, paying in cash with a portion of bread greater than that initially invested." "Whosoever does not know how to become an 'Organisator,' 'Kombinator' . . . soon becomes a 'musselman'—a walking cadaver," he wrote.[104] Ryszard Friedmann, a Polish Jewish Holocaust survivor, also recounted that he had to "skombinować" makeshift shoes to survive the winter working as a forced factory worker in the ghetto. Even though German signs warned workers about the punishments for "sabotage," Friedmann realized that he would freeze to death without shoes. He traded half of his breakfast portion in return for smuggled steel scraps from one of the steelworkers in the camp. He evaded his work schedule by pretending to be sick and used the time to cut pieces of rubber he had siphoned from the factory floor. Then a prisoner-cobbler sewed his shoe together in exchange for a bread ration. After Friedmann had successfully carried out his kombinacja under the Nazi radar, he fantasized about scaling up his tactics: "The idea of committing sabotage on a large scale fascinated me," he wrote.[105] Levi and Friedmann's narratives put their kombinacja in a positive light: devising creative solutions to find food and warmth was the key to life, and survival itself was the ultimate resistance to the Nazi genocide of the European Jews.

Erica Tucker's ethnographic study of postcommunist memories of the war reveals a similar theme of equating a successful kombinacja with survival. Janina, who was a Polish Home Army (Armia Krajowa) hospital worker during the war, recalled to Tucker that after the Warsaw Uprising was crushed by Nazi forces in 1944, the hospital had to "wykombinować . . . to avoid our wounded and young people, especially girls . . . being taken to Germany to camps. . . To this end we came to the conclusion that despite the fact that this is a Home Army Hospital . . . we would try to make it a Red Cross hospital." They distributed bootleg Red Cross identification cards and the scheme was successful. None of their patients was deported to concentration camps because the German officers were afraid to gamble with bodies under the aegis of an American-supported humanitarian effort.[106] Of course, whether this was due to kombinacja or not cannot be verified; however, Janina's recollections pinpoint her conscious and organized effort to use deception to disorient the German officers. It is undoubtedly a successful kombinacja tactic she would have passed down to the next generation.

But survival can bring its own burdens and consequences, and the kombinacja stories reveal the open wounds and internal conflicts within the survivors' souls. Other recollections warn against those kombinators who profited from suffering. Art Spiegelman's graphic novel *Maus* (1973), based on his father Vladek's experiences as a Polish Jewish Holocaust survivor, portrays the dark kombinator figure represented by cousin Haskel, who was the chief of the Jewish Police in the Srodula ghetto in Sosnowiec. Vladek recalls, "Always Haskel was such a guy: a kombinator. . . A guy what makes *kombinacya*, a schemer . . . a crook." Vladek recounts that once when he was roughed up by a Gestapo officer in the ghetto and showed the officer his identification card, the officer said, "Go on your way then, and give Haskel my regards." Vladek comments, "*Such* friends Haskel had." The Gestapo liked Haskel because he lost a lot of money to them in the card games they played. When the deportations to Auschwitz began, Vladek bribed Haskel with a diamond ring to arrange for him and his wife, Anja, to escape, but even though Haskel also accepted jewelry from Anja's parents, he never arranged an escape for them, and "right away they went to the gas." Vladek recalls that "Haskel was happy to take from father-in-law the jewels—but the risk to save them, this he was not so happy to take." Haskel never suffered the consequences of his actions, at least not in Vladek's account. According to Vladek, he married the Polish judge who had hidden him in her house during the war and enjoyed a nice life afterward, even receiving remittance packages from Vladek, who lived in Brooklyn. Grief-stricken Anja, however, committed suicide shortly after the war.

Vladek adds that Haskel's younger brother Pesach, also in the Jewish Police, "was also a kombinator." He illicitly sold cake to fellow Jews in the ghetto, boasting that his wife, Rifka, had baked it with flour his officers had looted from Jewish households after their owners had been sent to Auschwitz. Those who lived in the ghetto had not seen cake or even bread for years, and they lined up with their meager earnings to buy it at the elevated cost of seventy-five złoty a slice. That evening, however, those who had bought the cake became "sick as dogs," for it turned out that instead of putting flour in the batter, Pesach had poured in laundry soap "by mistake." Vladek notes that even in the interwar period, Pesach and Rifka "found always schemes." They evaded paying high taxes on their resort hotel in Zakopane by telling their guests to hide whenever the inspectors came. One time Rifka had not made enough desserts to cover all the guests, so they yelled, "Inspection!" Half of the guests hid, and in the end, "Pesach had enough desserts left over even for the next day!"[107] The injustice was not that the circumstances of war brought out kombinacja in Pesach and Rifka but that they used the circumstances of war to carry out kombinacja against friends and family. Vladek's kombinacja stories taught his kin how to identify such practices and be cognizant of their consequences for family, community, and country.

During my interview with a German woman in Bursztyn named Krystyna, Zofia recalled a similar breakdown of trust among neighbors when she told the story of her father's kombinacja under the Generalgouvernement in the Kielce region of south-central Poland during the Nazi occupation. Her parents owned a twenty-hectare farm that they had purchased with money they had earned as factory workers in Chicago in the early twentieth century. Since her father spoke American English, in Zofia's recollections, he was able to pass as more Western and curry favor with German officials. Their family was forced to produce agricultural quotas for the Wehrmacht instead of being sent to work as forced labor in Germany. But of course, to survive, they also had to sell their yields on the black market. Zofia told Krystyna how her father evaded the Germans by having buyers come to pick up the produce at night. One time, however, German officials came unannounced to inspect the farm. Her father went to the credenza to get his carefully kept receipts and showed them to the officers. It all checked out. The receipts were all correct, meaning that her father did not divert the Germans' share of his yields toward his own profit, but then the officers inquired about his selling on the side:

They ask father, "You sold that last night?" and father says, "I sold it." "And did you sell a pig?" "I sold it. The winter is coming," he says, "I have to buy my children warm shoes, warm covers, warm clothes, because we all work—I have to put on warm clothes and eat well because we all work." And he came up to father and said "Good Boer!" Because he had [resources] for the state, for himself, and for his entire family. And father [later] said, "Well, someone here told on us pretty well."

She went on to say they thought it was a Silesian named Sajda, a Nazi collaborator who sat on a rock at the side of the road and surveilled everyone and everything. Her father told the entire family that if Sajda or anyone else ever asked who had come to visit them that afternoon, they were all to respond that it was family from America, not officials. He did not want Sajda to profit from the information, potentially further endangering their status with authorities and relations with their buyers. Her story revealed the tensions between the good kombinators like her father, who only sold on the side when he met his yields for the Germans, and the bad kombinators like Sajda, who sat waiting to profit from someone else's slip-up.

State-censored kombinacja stories from this period take on a more politicized tone. Bohdan Czeszko's novel *A Generation* (1951), set in Nazi-occupied Warsaw in 1942, tells the story of a young Polish intellectual named Jurek who attempts to get into the Warsaw Ghetto in search of loot to sell on the black market. A Gestapo officer stops him at the gate and states, "'I know you, kombinators. You enter, gather goods and walk out a different gate. You leave me out in the cold. I know you, kombinators." The guard finally lets Jurek through on the condition that "With the goods you come back the same gate, you understand.'"[108] Czeszko was one of the leading socialist realist writers of the postwar period and a major presence in the state-sponsored Polish Writers' Union (Związek Literatów Polskich). This scene depicting kombinators as collaborators demonstrates how memories of wartime kombinacja were co-opted by pro-Soviet Polish elites to portray the "old regime" of Polish intellectuals as morally bankrupt, because they collaborated with Gestapo officers to profit from riches plundered from Jews. Controlling kombinacja narratives about the wartime period was a way for socialist elites to shame this kind of opportunistic individualist maneuvering and make clear that it had no place in a socialist society.

Kacper, the retired official I interviewed who ruled Bursztyn with his father Houdini throughout the 1940s and 1950s, was a forced laborer under the Generalgouvernement and had a similar story to tell, but from a different perspective. In his memories of kombinacja, he used it "to hurt the Occupant, the German":

> Before the war, one did not hear about that word at all. I think that this word was used in Poland the most often during the time of Hitler's occupation. One did not feel like working normally for the Occupant, right? So they *kombinowali,* to survive it with family, but not to work oneself too much. I lived during Occupation. I also worked then and I also carried out [*wynosiłem*] from time to time. And I would have gotten a bullet if they caught me because I worked in the Wehrmacht warehouses. But people did not have calcium carbide [*karbid*]. The lamps were not electric back then, so I stole calcium carbide! In a 100

kilogram barrel, and so for that, I received either food or I carried it out (to sell on the black market) and my director knew about it, but he was a German who also needed food for his family because they also had it difficult under the Occupation. I delivered for him eggs, I delivered meat of some sort. Simply like that! And Poles got used to it [kombinacja].

He portrays his collusion with the German guard and director of the warehouse in a positive light, indicating that everyone suffered from the war, slaves and their masters alike. However, what is curious is the distinction he makes at the end between the practice of kombinacja during the war and kombinacja activity in the postwar period under Soviet rule in Poland. Having of course portrayed his own kombinacja in a sympathetic light, he then snaps back into "official" more critical mode about the Poles' postwar kombinacja against the Soviet-backed Polish regime. Fidelis used a similar rationale. He told me that kombinacja did not exist in the interwar period (although from my research I know that it did) because there was no need for it: "Maybe it existed, but usually not. Maybe it would have been in some higher spheres, maybe they kombinowali, but people between themselves, they simply did not kombinowali because there was no need. Everything was privatized and, secondly, when I had money and wanted to buy something, just like today, I went and bought it, and that was that." It existed only in the times of extreme shortages: Nazi and Soviet occupation. This idea, of wartime kombinacja as hurting the German occupant and then carrying over to similar conditions of occupation in the postwar period under Soviet rule, was politically dangerous at the time for the Soviet-run government, because the Polish state wanted Poles to believe that the socialist revolution in the postwar period was a natural evolution of Poles' own desires to build Stalinism on their turf. Thus, wartime kombinacja stories emerged as tiny time capsules containing alternative historical narratives and experiences. They evolved into educational tools that taught the next generation how to survive under occupation.

Finally, kombinacja as a discourse for preserving the memory of how people survived during war became a powerful means for marginalized groups to pass down survival lessons to the next generation. There is a certain power that comes from sharing these lessons and thereby controlling one's own history. These kombinacja solutions were not in the highbrow discourse of literary circles or in the grasp of the Catholic Church that dictated them as a particular kind of ideology like "organic work"; they were a strategy and discourse accessible to all that exposed how ordinary people, the ones who do not make it into the history books, overcame enormous obstacles. Kombinacja stories were part of an oral history that could not be censored by the state. Kombinators represent the political unconscious in a given society, and tracing their unique position can shed light on the invisible logics that may have no representation in any formal political platform but that form an important part of people's relationship with the state, the legal system, and the progress of any transformation.

Notes

1. The word *combination* is derived from the Latin *combinare*, "to join two by two." It is also worth noting that *socialism* comes from the Latin *sociare*, meaning "to combine." Bevir, *Making of British Socialism*, 14.

2. "A full and accurate report of the proceedings of the petitioners against a bill intituled [*sic*] 'A Bill to prevent unlawful combinations of workmen': with the speeches of Lord Holland and of counsel and a full abstract of the act, etc." (1800), p. 17. LSE Selected Pamphlets (1800).

3. Whatley, "'Fettering Bonds'"; Thompson, *Making of the English Working Class*; "Strikes and Lock-Outs," *Morning Post* (London), January 21, 1854, 1–2; "O'Connell and Combinations." *Lloyd's Weekly London Newspaper*, February 25, 1844, 1–2.

4. Thompson, *Making of the English Working Class*, 198.

5. Marx, "Chartism," 130.

6. Whatley, "'Fettering Bonds,'" 160; Clark, *Struggle for the Breeches*, 139.

7. Thompson, *Making of the English Working Class*, 503.

8. Whatley, "'Fettering Bonds'"; Thompson, *Making of the English Working Class*; "Parliamentary Trades' Combination Committee," *Operative* (London), November 11, 1838, 1–2.

9. George, "Revisions," 173.

10. 6 Geo. 4, c.129 ("Abstract of the New Act Relating to Combinations of Workmen" 1825, 1–2).

11. George Howell. "Working Class Movements of the Century VII." *Reynolds's Newspaper.* October 4, 1896. Issue 2408: 1–3. 19th Century British Library Newspapers. British Newspapers 1800–1900. British Library Online: http://newspapers11.bl.uk/blcs/. Accessed December 2, 2011.

12. "O'Connell and Combinations."

13. Ibid.

14. "Strikes and Lock-Outs."

15. Thompson, *Making of the English Working Class*, 123; Gray, "Law of Combination," 336.

16. Thompson, *Making of the English Working Class*, 496–97.

17. "News of the Day," *The Poor Man's Guardian* (London), October 5, 1833, 1.

18. "Trades Unions," *Morning Chronicle* (London), June 9, 1834, 1–3.

19. "Minutes of Evidence before the Select Committee on Combinations of Workmen," *Northern Star and Leeds General Advertiser*, September 15, 1838, 1–3.

20. Ibid.

21. "A Short Address to Workmen, on Combinations to Raise Wages," *Sheffield Independent, and Yorkshire and Derbyshire Advertiser*, February 4, 1832, 1–3.

22. Ibid.

23. "Combinations Defended: Being a Commentary upon, and Analysis of, the Evidence Given before the Parliamentary Committee of Inquiry into Combinations of Employers and Workmen. 1838," LSE Selected Pamphlets (1839), 1–64.

24. Ibid.

25. Ibid.

26. "Strikes and Lock-Outs."

27. Paine, "Rights of Man," 280.

28. Smith, *Wealth of Nations*, 95.

29. Marx, *Poverty of Philosophy*, 125.

30. Ibid., 124–25.

31. Ibid., 124.

32. Ibid., 121.

33. Marx, "Chartism," 131.

34. Ibid., 123–25.

35. Ibid., 125.

36. Marx, "Chartism," 130.

37. Marx, *Poverty of Philosophy*, 123–24.

38. Ibid., 126.

39. Ibid.

40. "The Union of Capital and Labour," *Northern Star and National Trades' Journal* (Leeds), January 24, 1852, 1–2; "The Wages Question," *Bradford Observer*, September 29, 1853, 1–3; "Strikes and Lock-Outs"; "Economic Effects of Combinations of Capitalists and Labourers." *Bradford Observer*, July 4, 1874, 1–3.

41. Mill, *On Liberty*, 17.

42. Ibid., 300.

43. Ibid., 121.

44. "Metropolitan Gossip." *Sheffield & Rotherham Independent*, November 24, 1860, 1–3; "Conspiracy, and Protection of Property Act 1875," chap. 86, 1–8, National Archives, http://legislation.gov.uk; "Economic Effects of Combinations of Capitalists and Labourers"; "The Labour Parliament," *Northern Echo* (Darlington, England), September 5, 1891, 1; "National Association of United Trades," *Northern Star and National Trades' Journal* (Leeds). December 28, 1850, 1–3.

45. Dicey, "Combination Laws," 531; Roll, "Review," 108; Cain, "Railway Combination," 623; "The British Trades' Congress," *Freeman's Journal and Daily Commercial Advertiser* (Dublin), August 30, 1898, 1.

46. Holmgren, *Rewriting Capitalism*, 7–8, 55. For example, Joseph Conrad's father took part in the January Uprising.

47. Davies, *God's Playground*, 2:13, 364; Ingbrant, "In Search," 43; Holmgren, *Rewriting Capitalism*, 8.

48. Kieniewicz, *Emancipation of the Polish Peasantry*, 186–87; Davies, *God's Playground*, 2:44–45.

49. Stauter-Halsted, *Nation in the Village*, 204.

50. Holmgren, *Rewriting Capitalism*, 11, 160, 177.

51. Nafisi, *Republic of Imagination*.

52. Felski, *Gender of Modernity*, 11; Ingbrant, "In Search," 35, 38, 40.

53. This mirrored historical reality. Davies, *God's Playground*, 2:107; Wisse, *Modern Jewish Canon*, 141.

54. Reymont, *Ziemia Obiecana*, 1:345–46.

55. Ibid., 55.

56. Ibid.

57. Reymont, *Ziemia Obiecana*, 2:355.

58. Prus, *Powracająca fala*, 21.

59. Prus, *Lalka*, 1:38.

60. Prus, *Doll*, 222.

61. Prus, *Lalka*, 2:182.

62. Żeromski, *Syzyfowe prace*, 4.
63. Ibid., 51.
64. Ibid., 78.
65. Prus, *Lalka*, 2:67.
66. Izabela Filipiak, "Fantazmatyczna lesbijka w Europie Środkowej na przełomie XIX i XX wieku," *uniGender* 1, no. 2 (2006), http://katalog.czasopism.pl/index.php/UniGENDER_1_(2).
67. Materka, "Women in 1848," 3544.
68. Phillips, introduction to *The Heathen*, xxvii.
69. Żmichowska, *Narcyssa i Wanda*, 64, 155, 322.
70. Davies, *God's Playground*, 2:107.
71. Boy-Żeleński, *Flirt z Melpomeną*, 8.
72. Boy-Żeleński, *Jak skończyć z piekłem kobiet?*, 7.
73. Witkiewicz, *Narkotyki*, 37.
74. Gombrowicz, *Iwona*, 28.
75. Kotkin, *Magnetic Mountain*, 364.
76. Lenin, *Polnoe sobranie sochinenii*, 43, in Ball, *Russia's Last Capitalists*, 277.
77. Siegelbaum, introduction to *Stalinism*, 2.
78. Lenin, *Polnoe sobranie sochinenii*, 44, in Ball, *Russia's Last Capitalists*, 160.
79. Kotkin, *Magnetic Mountain*, 515n6.
80. Ball, *Russia's Last Capitalists*, 164.
81. Tucker, *Stalin in Power*, 87.
82. Kotkin, *Magnetic Mountain*, 515n7.
83. Zholkovsky, *Text Counter Text*, 254.
84. Skultans, *Testimony of Lives*, xiii.
85. Ilf and Petrov, *Golden Calf*, 51.
86. Ibid., 132.
87. Ibid., 15, 74–77, 69, 143.
88. Ibid., 280.
89. Zholkovsky, *Text Counter Text*, 254.
90. Fitzpatrick, *Tear Off the Masks!*, 268, 299.
91. Ibid., 270; Lipovetsky, *Charms*, 38.
92. Pesmen, *Russia and Soul*, 204. She does not "date" when this process began, however.
93. Lipovetsky, *Charms*, 20–34, 42.
94. Ibid., 45.
95. Ibid.
96. Ibid., 48, 211; Fitzpatrick, *Tear Off the Masks!*, 152.
97. Fitzpatrick, *Tear Off the Masks!*, 279.
98. Abrahamian, "Lenin as a Trickster," 26.
99. Siegelbaum, introduction to *Stalinism*, 11–12.
100. Kotkin, *Magnetic Mountain*, 154; Siegelbaum, introduction to *Stalinism*, 20.
101. Lipovetsky, *Charms*, 43.
102. Ball, *Russia's Last Capitalists*, ix.
103. Nafisi, *Republic of Imagination*, 65.
104. Levi, *Survival in Auschwitz*, 80–89.
105. Friedmann, *Szlak obozowy*, 66–67.
106. Tucker, "Conspiring with Memory," 283–84.
107. Spiegelman, *Maus*, 116–20.
108. Czeszko, *Pokolenie*, 34.

3   Recovering Territories

ON ITS WESTWARD march toward Berlin in March 1945, the Red Army equipped the Soviet-backed Polish state with the military capability to enforce the Polonization and Sovietization of German and East Prussian lands east of the Oder and Neisse rivers. The Soviet-backed Polish Committee of National Liberation (Polski Komitet Wyzwolenia Narodowego) divvied up the new western frontier into administrative regions and populated each with ministers of reconstruction, finance, agriculture, and economic aid. The Polish Workers' Party (Polska Partia Robotnicza) set up political cells and rural offices; the Red Army occupied German estates and began their conversion into Soviet state farms called *sovkhozy* that would be integrated into the Soviet Council for Mutual Economic Assistance (Rada Wzajemnej Pomocy Gospodarczej). By the time the Red Army's First Belorussian Front victoriously hoisted the Soviet Victory Banner over the Reichstag after the Battle of Berlin in May 1945, Stalin's shadow colonization project was in full swing. And it succeeded. Germany's lost eastern lands, later ceded to Poland as a "prize of war" at the Potsdam Conference in July 1945, were renamed the Recovered Territories (Ziemie Odzyskane), the cradle of Polish national identity that Stalin-backed Polish communists had recovered from a millennium of German colonization.[1]

Stanisław Mikołajczyk, prime minister of the London-based Polish government-in-exile, opposed the colonization of German lands on the grounds that Poland's eastern territories (*kresy*), which included cultural capitals like Lwów and Wilno, still needed to be saved from annexation by Soviet Russia.[2] The Federal Republic of Germany also disputed the Soviet land grab. Jakob Kaiser, chairman of the West German Christian Democratic Union, which rose to power in the postwar era for its staunch opposition to the border changes, claimed that the Oder-Neisse line "is not a German, not a Polish, not even a Russian solution; it is a Bolshevik solution. What we need is a European solution."[3] Although much of the initial colonization project had occurred without the authorization of international law, the legality of the cession, and how international law ought to be interpreted in the first place, continued to be the subject of ideological debate between the Soviet bloc and the West for the duration of the Cold War. As the pro-Soviet Polish scholar Władysław Dobrzycki pointed out, the Recovered Territories were the "ideological battle ground between eastern socialism and western capitalistic Europe" and a "political test of the sturdiness and the resilience of leftist politics against those of the West."[4]

As the Iron Curtain descended on Poland, the PPR worked steadfastly with the Soviet military to swap the German population for a Polish one in what became one of the "greatest demographic upheavals in European history."[5] Four hundred thousand Germans living within the postwar borders of Poland perished while fleeing to or being sent to Germany west of the Oder and Neisse rivers.[6] Polish communists referred to this as a necessary physical and historical "cleansing" (*podporządkowanie*) of the German territories for the resurrection of the Polish state on the frontier.[7] The Soviet-funded PPR advertised itself as the only party with the resources and organizational capacity necessary to carry out such a massive resettlement campaign. It sent settler crews to occupy German villages, cities, and landed estates, to scout terrain, to assess war damage, to establish resettlement arrangements, to organize local administrative units, and to fill militia, medical, and transportation posts for population control. The State Repatriation Office (Państwowy Urząd Repatriacyjny) organized free transport, food distribution, shelters, pharmacies, medical care, and train tickets. The Polish Western Committee (Polski Związek Zachodni) took care of educating settlers and government volunteers on the "political, societal and economic meaning of the resettlement." By November 1945 the Ministry of Recovered Territories (Ministerstwo Ziem Odzyskanych), headed by Władysław Gomułka—First Secretary of the PPR—had centralized the administrative, technical, and political apparatus of the new state.[8] Seizing the western frontier meant seizing the political reins of the postwar Polish state. All the communists had to do was sell themselves and the frontier to the Polish public.

The Polish Workers' Party rolled out a massive propaganda campaign to sell the idea of the Recovered Territories as Poland's new land of opportunity to war survivors returning home from concentration camps and forced labor camps, many of whom had been forced into labor for years on those very lands. Fully aware that the Polish public would not buy into the idea of a Soviet Poland, Polish communists pushed what is known as the "Piast myth." According to the Piast myth, the Recovered Territories were part of Poland's lost El Dorado, a land once ruled by the Piast dynasty (AD 960–1370) that became the cradle of Polish national consciousness after Piast ruler Bolesław Mieszko I converted to Christianity in 966 and precipitated the birth of the early Polish state called the Kingdom of Poland in 1025. After Mieszko's death, the Piast dynasty never fully recovered the entirety of the Polish-German borderlands. Pomerania and all of northern Poland fell to the Kingdom of Germany by 1147, and Mieszko's boundaries would not be "recovered" until these special historical circumstances in the postwar era. The PPR invited Poles to become citizen "pioneers" (*pionierzy*) who would populate the German lands and return Poland's cities, churches, and castles to the mother country. Colorful PPR propaganda posters were adorned with messages like "To the Odra River border for our fathers' land and prosperity," "In the

West, Land Awaits!," "We are protecting the Oder AD 1106–1946." The messages accompanied images of *pionierzy* with knapsacks over their shoulders, marching from the squalor of prewar Poland toward quaint German farming estates.

The Piast myth was not a Stalinist invention. It originated in nineteenth-century partitioned Poland during the organic work movement, when nationalistic Polish scholars living under the German partition of Poland began to counter German colonial research called *Ostforschung* (research on the East). *Ostforschung* was using "science" to legitimize the idea that the Germanization of Central and Eastern Europe (*Drang nach Osten*) was inevitable. *Drang nach Osten* (literally "Drive toward the East") resembled the Manifest Destiny ideology of colonial settlers in the United States. Polish geographers countered German researchers by claiming that the German plains "naturally" ended at the Elbe River, and the western border of the Polish plains "naturally" ended at the Oder River. In response to German researchers who claimed that Germanic tribes had settled those lands before the Slavic tribes arrived as "migrants" from the east, in 1914 Polish archaeologist Józef Kostrewski presented data in support of the opposite finding. Both Polish and German researchers conveniently ignored the fact that both Germanic and Slavic tribes had settled the lands during the Bronze Age and the idea of a homogeneous nation state did not reflect the diversity of those tribes across the Central and Eastern European plains. During World War I Polish geographers hoped Poland would receive territorial gains and published atlases (banned by Germans) showing Polish borders that included the Silesian and Pomeranian regions. After the reconstitution of Poland following World War I, the idea gained supporters in the scientific community. The University of Poznań, Western Slavic Institute, Polish Western Union, and Silesian Institute all pushed for geographic and ethnographic research into what they considered "Germanized Polish" populations like the Silesians, Kashubians, and Mazurians living in Poland's "lost lands."[9] The concept of the Recovered Territories entered the political domain in October 1938, when President Ignacy Mościcki issued a presidential decree that made a territorial claim to reincorporate the Silesian region (under Germany) into the Republic of Poland.[10] The PPR consolidated all of those fragmented territorial claims made by various nationalist scholars and politicians into a single territorial claim, including a new one—East Prussia—that blurred Polish nationalist dreams of recovering their lost lands with Stalin's geopolitical aspirations. Co-opting the nationalist past was key to a Polish-Soviet future.

Unlike in partitioned Poland, where the intelligentsia used art to nurture spaces of nationalist resistance against the foreign occupants, the new generation of scholars in postwar Poland became aligned with the Soviet project—some by force, some by choice—and contributed to the production of "state-sponsored historical memory" of the new frontier.[11] The total destruction not only of the Polish intelligentsia but also of the institutions they led in the interwar period created a scholarship vacuum that was filled with pro-Soviet institutions and state-sponsored scholarship. For example, in 1934, geographer Maria Kiełczewska published a normative ethnographic study, *Typologies of Village Settlements in Pomerania*, using on-the-ground fieldwork and methodological rigor with references and citations.[12] Her study was published by the Baltic Institute (Instytut Bałtycki) in Toruń, which funded many such ethnographic studies about Polish, Kashubian, and German settlements in Pomerania.[13] However, after the war, the Baltic Institute was incorporated into the state-funded Western Institute (Instytut Zachodni) in Poznań, which, in turn, published old findings with a new political flair to offset the brain drain and lack of experienced researchers in the postwar academic landscape. In 1946 Kiełczewska and a coauthor republished her findings with the Western Institute under the title *The Oder-Neisse Is the Best Polish Border*. They applauded the return of the "maternal lands of the Oder-Neisse" because "their place is only in the organism of Poland," and they zealously provided extra maps with the Polish roots of former Polish settlements even farther *west* of the Oder and Neisse line, lamenting the fact that Poland had been unable to reclaim this region. The Polish state, in their view, had done the best it could at that point in history.[14] Scholars like Kiełczewska, who dedicated her interwar life to meticulous scientific research, had to wildly distort it with political rhetoric if they wanted to continue their work.

Scholars became puppets of the state, manipulating science to validate the Piast myth. Archaeologists located ancient "Slavic sites" in the territories dating back to 10,000 BC. Geographers veered into the mystical realm, "proving" the western frontier situated Poland's state boundaries in the "right" geographic location and asserting the "new world of objects and phenomena" would inspire a new generation of art and scholarship. Linguists determined the real Polish roots of German village names that had to be recovered. Economists argued that "recovering" simply formalized the Poles' westward migratory patterns into the German east and that the high reproductive rates of the Polish "rural proletariat," had "strengthened the ranks of the Polish autochthonous population in the German eastern provinces" since the nineteenth century. Historians critiqued "mistakes" of prewar, capitalist, Polish policies that focused on eastern colonization, not westward expansion.[15] "This territory was the cradle of the Polish State and here, one thousand years ago, a consciousness of Polish nationality was born," and "we are not here to colonize but to return to the fatherland based in historical traditions," they argued.[16] Not one scholar who focused on the idea of recovering 103,000 square kilometers of German territories tackled the more immediate problem of Stalin's annexation of 180,000 square kilometers of Poland's *kresy* lands.[17] "Cleansing" the history of German identity from the territories also encompassed cleansing the Polish mind of false histories. In 1946 the journalist Edmund Męclewski argued that a true and proper history of Poland had yet to be written and that the recovery of a true Polish tradition of (socialist) agriculture on the territories would require "education of political concepts" through "cultural politics and propaganda."[18] Elites contributed to the knowledge production of a socialist Poland with a new western frontier closer to Western Europe, rather than a capitalist Poland with an old eastern frontier closer to the Soviet Union.

And it worked. The Piast myth became a wildly successful propaganda campaign. It captured Poles' long-standing desire to be seen as Westerners, situating them closer to the geographical heart of Europe. In the National State Council's (Krajowa Rada Narodowa) famously rigged "Three Times Yes Referendum" (3×TAK) held on June 1946 that "democratically" proved Poles' acceptance of Soviet reforms like the nationalization of industry and agriculture, a majority of Poles voted in favor of the Oder-Neisse line, even according to the official results released in 1989, which showed that an overwhelming majority rejected all the other reforms. Eager to enact their revenge and be compensated for Nazi atrocities that had destroyed their lives, the last thing on people's minds was whether making historical claims on swaths of land that had been in German possession for a millennium was ethical or legitimate. The theme of "recovering" identities, was of course, something every Polish war survivor experienced on a personal level. The survivors had to recover their own sense of self, their lost childhoods, their dead scattered, their communities reeling from the shell shock and horrors of war that had transformed them into unrecognizable creatures willing to do anything to survive. The war-ravaged nation needed an imaginary paradise and the German El Dorado satiated that desire.

Reality, however, soon began to deviate from myth. Ethnic Polish pioneers who migrated voluntarily to the Recovered Territories inherited an apocalyptic "Wild West" (Dziki Zachód). Breslau, Stolp, and Stettin had been bombed to shreds. Fields were not filled with livestock and harvests but with mines and artillery. Farms were empty as a result of a combination of wildcat pillaging and official looting of agricultural machinery and food.[19] Neither villages nor cities had running water, electricity, gas, or public transportation. Many migrants returned home. While the propaganda posters with quaint German farms beckoned war survivors, in reality, the State Repatriation Office (PUR) settled ethnic Poles into farms and homes still occupied by the German and East Prussian owners ("autochthons") awaiting expulsion. It also retained indigenous ethnic groups like Kashubians, Silesians, and Mazurians, who did not neatly fit the fixed identity of the Catholic, ethnic Pole but were deemed Polish enough to remain in the new borderlands on the ideological premise that they were old Slavic groups that had been forcibly Germanized for centuries and that they too would recover their Polish identities.[20]

As the PUR resettlement process continued throughout the mid-1940s, ethnic Poles realized that they would not be the only nation recovering the cradle of Polish national identity. As per the resettlement policy to "Polonize the West and pacify the East," joining them would be forcibly "repatriated" anti-Soviet Belarusians from Poland's annexed eastern territories, forcibly resettled (and pacified) nationalist Ukrainians from the southeastern Polish-Soviet Ukraine border, Jewish Holocaust survivors, liberated Siberian gulag prisoners, refugees from the Greek civil war (1944–1948), and other "wildcat" settlers like the Roma, Czechs, Lithuanians, and Slovenians who found themselves in the territories after a circuitous search for a new home after the war.[21] "Polonization" had as much to do with creating new Soviet Poles out of the seters as it did with settling the lands with ethnic Poles. By collectively recovering a Soviet-engineered "Polish" heartland, the Slavic settlers would become a unified pan-Slavic society on the new western frontier of the Soviet bloc, ready for deployment against German revanchism.

The Second Serfdom

Władysław Gomułka envisioned that recovering Poland's lost lands would have the "impetus of a social revolution."[22] Ten percent of the territories were populated by Junker landed estates, owned by the aristocratic class, that stood as the symbol of German and East Prussian colonial domination of Poland's lost lands. During the war, Junker estates doubled as Nazi labor camps, using Slavic labor to produce agricultural yields for the Reich. En route to Berlin in 1945, the Red Army "liberated" the camps and executed any Junker aristocrats who had not yet fled the impending red wave. Gomułka envisioned that Polish peasants would band together to occupy Junker land, expunge the nobility, and redistribute the land as per the socialist agrarian reform, "to show the peasantry that the power of the PKWN could not be flouted." Workers' and soldiers' brigades would work together with the peasants to redistribute the land "to agricultural laborers and small peasants," not land-hungry "middle-sized farmers" whose capitalist leanings caused the need for a socialist agrarian reform in the first place.[23] By overturning the feudal Junker estates and the Prussian aristocratic caste, Polish peasants would break free of their historical chains of dependency: "Polish small holders and landless peasants no longer need to go to Germany in search of seasonal farm work, to toil at wages for capitalists and junkers [*sic*]," a pro-Soviet scholar promised.[24] But Polish communists could not count on the Polish peasantry to rise up against the Junkers. Instead, they sent over a thousand peasant activists to occupy German Junker estates in the less populated areas of the territories to perform revolution. By 1947 Minister of Industry Hilary Minc claimed, "The Polish State has superseded German capitalists. Polish peasants have superseded German 'Junkers.'"[25] In my investigation, I discovered a different reality: what was supposed to be a socialist revolution against feudal oppression turned out to be a revival of feudalism in the service of the socialist revolution.

The Red Army had already converted the Junker estates into 4,357 Soviet state farms, totaling more than 1.9 million hectares, and linked them with the Soviet supply chains (Rada Wzajemnej Pomocy Gospodarczej) to feed Mother Russia.[26] But who would work the fields? The influx of skilled Polish labor into the territories was slow. In fact, in late 1945, the state delayed the German expulsion so that the state could use Germans to complete the spring sowing on the state farms.[27] When Władysław Gomułka was asked in March 1946 how the effort to "cleanse the Recovered Territories of German elements" was proceeding, he responded, "We evacuate the 'nonproductive elements' first. In the late phase, it is the German workers in our employ who go. There is also a possibility of retaining a small number of qualified specialists whom we cannot replace." The state formalized this classification system. "White category 1" consisted of low-skilled German workers who would quickly be replaced by Polish workers; "blue category 2" were German workers who had to train Polish workers first before being expelled; "red category 3" workers were specialists whose expulsion would have to be authorized by the authorities. While members of the first two categories were granted personal security and the right to retain their residences, private property, and good working conditions, those in the third category became "an odd kind of forced laborer" who "lacked freedom of movement but enjoyed relatively good pay and treatment."[28] Sixty-five thousand of these German specialists would be retained by the state, effectively making them Poland's first proletarian workers.[29] Germans would be forced to convert their homeland into a Polish one as a way of exacting reparations for Nazi war atrocities.

In the village of Bernstein (later Bursztyn, where my grandparents ended up), German flight from Slavic rape and forced labor began in March 1945, when the Eastern Front was approaching. The PPR and KRN Polish administration had already arrived to take over the German government offices, schools, and businesses from the Red Army by June, before the border was formally approved by the Potsdam Conference. Tensions were high. Three war enemies—the Germans, Poles, and Russians—all descended upon Bernstein, and naturally took turns torturing and killing one another. Poles had no patience for German resistance: "Those who did not comply were arrested by the Polish militia and beaten. So the Poles tortured [a German villager] in the basement of the militia station to death."[30] To avenge that torture and killing of a German civilian, the German baker "persuaded" the Soviet commander to kill the three Polish militia men. And he did! Then, to avenge the murder of the torturers, the Polish militia incarcerated the German baker in Stolp while the Red Army appointed a Russian woman to take over the bakery—a vital lifeline for everyone. Episodes of retaliatory violence added up. By the time the German priest was expelled in June 1947,

Figure 3.1. German Junker estate, and later Soviet state farm where Krystyna's family worked. Photo by author.

he had recorded the death of sixty civilians and more than two hundred unresolved cases of missing persons.[31]

Krystyna, one of a handful of German women who now live in Bursztyn, told me about her family's experience during the transfer of power. She recalled that she had been born into a German peasant family that lived and worked on a German Junker estate five kilometers north of Bursztyn (then Bernstein) (see figure 3.1). Toward the end of the war, Ukrainian forced laborers rose up against the Junker estate owner and awaited the arrival of the Red Army in March 1945. The Red Army liberated them and murdered the Junker aristocrat by the gazebo behind the mansion. But the Ukrainian forced laborers left for home and there was no one to work the land except the Germans. Once the army began to transform the Junker into a state farm, it put Krystyna's father, an experienced tractor operator, to work, while Krystyna was sent to work in Bursztyn's Russian-run bakery:

KRYSTYNA: Then, you had to work. So then, we all received this cup of soup for dinner and a piece of bread. Every day we had to. We only worked and those who did not work got nothing.

EDYTA: So it was forced labor?

KRYSTYNA: It was forced, yes. But I am not saying anything, because father had
             it good. He was a tractor operator and he knew how to do every-
             thing, whatever it was. So once, when we were on the fields, we look
             and the Russians are coming after my father. Everyone says, "Look,
             they are taking your father now. They will kill him!" But they took
             him to Lipowo [state farm] because there was no tractor operator
             there and they gave him a horse so that he could go every day on the
             horse to Lipowo to work, and there were Russian women there. One
             Christmas Eve the Russian women came and brought my father
             such a huge circle of butter and there were pierogis, which we had
             never seen. Inside the pierogis was cheese. I say that when father
             was with us the entire time, we had it good. Then in 1948 that one
             Russian said that I have to go to the barn to milk the cows. I say,
             "I don't know how to milk the cow," and he says, "How do you not
             know how to milk a cow? Your sisters are younger and know," and I
             said, "I did not know how to." So he gave me a note and said, "Go to
             Bursztyn to the Russian bakery and give them this," and so I went.
             We had to bake bread for all of the estates all night. We transported
             it in the morning. And so I say, I had it very good—this was until
             the Russians moved out of here [in 1949].

The Soviets had it very good with German forced labor to carry out their colonization project. Germans received 75 percent of the standard food ration, and their
wages, if any, were often garnished to fund commune reconstruction projects.[32]
The downside of hiring incoming Slavic workers was that they felt entitled to
bonuses, wages, and decent working conditions. Many of them had to be trained,
whereas the Germans already knew the land and how to farm it.[33] Jan and
Elżbieta, a Kashubian couple who in 1946 sought employment on the state farm
where Krystyna's father worked, said the employment and settlement of Polish
workers did not begin until after the Soviets transferred the farm over to Polish
administration in 1949. Even then, German specialists were allowed to relocate to
an adjacent state farm and set up a colony complete with a German schoolhouse
that lasted into the 1950s.[34] The state became addicted to unpaid labor.

    Once the Junkers were secured with Soviet control and German labor, the
PKWN moved swiftly to bring socialist agrarian reform to the rest of the frontier
villages. The July 1944 agrarian reform that authorized the state to expropriate
Polish farms with more than fifty hectares of land within Poland's prewar borders was expanded to include the expropriation of German farms with more than
one hundred hectares of land in the Recovered Territories.[35] In the old provinces
peasants were beginning to resist the socialist reforms because there was not

enough land to go around to meet the reform goals. Communes of five hect-ares of land started to run out, and so the state started redistributing two- to three-hectare land grants with promises of more land to come after the agrarian reform was completed in the Recovered Territories. Many peasants did not want to wait for German land, nor did they want to leave their villages for promised land on the new western frontier. In response, the PKWN appointed land re-form commissioners with "dictatorial powers" in every county who expropriated larger farms. They parceled out the land into 250,000 farms with an average of 1.9 hectares, and 347,000 farms that averaged 5.4 hectares. By October 1945 the reform in the old Polish provinces had been declared "completed," and the state turned to carrying out the PKWN reform in the Recovered Territories.[36] There, the communists had the opposite problem: too much land. In September 1946, the PKWN passed another land reform specific to the new provinces.[37] Pioneers were entitled to seven to fifteen hectares of German land and up to twenty hect-ares for dairy farms, which meant that in the Recovered Territories, the state sought to create exactly the powerful and mobilized class of middle peasants that it had sought to expunge in the old provinces.

Although the first PKWN agrarian reform was intended for peasants, the first settlers to receive German land were Poles who had served in the Red Army and the Polish People's Army (Ludowe Wojsko Polskie). In late 1945 before full-scale agrarian reform began in the new provinces, more than fifty-six thousand German farms had already been redistributed to two hundred thousand army members and their families.[38] The first officials to arrive in Bursztyn, for example, took over the largest landed estates, between twenty and forty hectares in size, for themselves—more land than anyone else had in the village and a blatant devia-tion from the pattern of agrarian reform. This wild redistribution of German land resulted in the creation of a Polish-Soviet landed military caste in the territories who seemed to believe themselves to be above the law they were in charge of enforcing. The greater access to land enjoyed by the elites created an atmosphere in which those who were acting on behalf of the state got to pick which laws they would adhere to. Meanwhile the settlers they oversaw were expected always to answer to the law.[39] By controlling agrarian reform, elites were able to assert their territorial and emerging class domination.

The agrarian reform policy was set on establishing a permanent middle-peasant class (with roughly five to eleven hectares of land) in the territories that would have farms large enough to produce for the growing proletarian classes in the cities. One problem with this vision was the sandy soil of the Pomeranian lands in the northern part of the Recovered Territories, near the dune formations along the Baltic Sea. Bernstein's soil was also sandy and unfit for agricultural production without the intensive use of fertilizers and chemicals. Like the Po-meranian region it had previously been considered better suited for industries, like Bernstein's paper plant. The Red Army, however, had looted and destroyed factories, machinery, building materials, railways, and workshops, stripping the landscape of its industrial capital. While only 8 percent of the land around Bernstein was arable when the Red Army arrived, by 1947, more than half (around five thousand hectares) had been nationalized for commune and Red Army use. The rest was parceled into land grants for 142 peasant proprietors, 93 of whom received land grants of between five and twenty hectares.[40] Slavic settlers who were allotted new land grants also received land titles called *Akt nadania*. These documents prohibited them from selling or abandoning the grants, or employing outside labor to work them. This "locked" peasant families into their land and middle-peasant class status regardless of the quality of the land, where that land was located, or whether the settler families even had any previous experience with farming. In Bursztyn, most settlers received parceled plots of farms that had previously been owned by Germans, but many of the parcels were kilometers apart and inaccessible by foot. My maternal grandparents, Zofia and Konrad, for example, inherited eleven hectares that had been owned by Germans, but the parcels were far apart and the authorities denied their request to reduce their land grant to seven hectares. They had to pay taxes on the entire land grant. Zofia and Konrad cultivated only the seven hectares they wanted to keep, while some of their neighbors simply abandoned their land grants altogether and fled to Słupsk, where they disappeared among the proletarian masses serving the new factories. Władysława, who came from a Polish worker family in the interwar period and had no experience working in agriculture, became a liminal worker-peasant: she used her connections to secure a waged job in the city and shuttled back and forth to her land grant in Bursztyn, paying the taxes with her city wages.

Others were not as fortunate. Bursztyn's first peasant settlers shared vivid stories of "working off" (*odrabiać*), a type of corvée they called the *szarwark*, an unpaid labor obligation they had to perform as a labor tax to the state in exchange for the land they had been granted through its agrarian reform program. This labor tax consisted of performing unpaid services for the state like shoveling snow off the roads, planting trees, transporting wood out of the nationalized forest with one's private horse and wagon, and cleaning up and harvesting state fields. I found this perplexing at first because the elimination of feudal institutions was a defining feature of the Marxist-Leninist revolutionary agenda. In 1905 Lenin had chastised the Polish Socialist Party's early agrarian reform program in Congress Poland, which sought to abolish the szarwark, for attempting to fulfill only the "minimum demands" of Marxism, those that embraced "the struggle against remnants of serfdom as the basis and content of the present-day peasant movement."[41] Rather than abolishing feudalism through the socialist revolution, the state revived feudalism to solve labor shortages for its state project in the early state-making period.

In the broader scheme of history, feudalist revivals have occurred whenever there have been pervasive labor shortages in agricultural work, whether caused by war, famine, or peasant resistance.[42] During the First Five-Year Plan in 1929 Soviet Russia, Stalin passed legislation that revived the feudal corvée system, called the *barshchina*, which included a range of smaller labor and cartage obligations called *trudguzhpovinnost'*, burdening the independent peasantry and collective farm workers (*kolkhozniks*) with the responsibility of fulfilling the state production plans. The 1929 law that introduced corvées initially required rural Soviet officials to compensate peasants for fulfilling their obligation; however, subsequent laws in 1931 and 1932 conveniently omitted compensation requirements. Nonetheless, the *barshchina* was not enough, and the state moved to diversify the pool of obligations so that Soviet officials had access to more feudal tools of control. Another law in 1930 obligated peasants to provide labor brigades and horses for timber felling and timber rafting in the winter to meet state logging plans. While the corvée system empowered rural Soviet officials to channel peasant labor to meet certain state plans that otherwise would not have been fulfilled as a result of labor shortages or a resistant peasantry, they often abused that power and channeled peasant labor to fulfill other plans that had no legal framework. In the Soviet system, legislation that did and did not exist equally empowered the officials. Leila Fitzpatrick calls this tangled system of legal and illegal feudal obligations in the making of the Soviet state the "second serfdom."[43] And it set a precedent for Soviet state making on the Polish frontier.

To the Polish settlers, the szarwark did not represent Stalinist development per se, but a Soviet continuation of the German *Scharwerke* they had been forced to perform under Nazi occupation. The German *Scharwerk* (*schar* meaning "crowd" and *werk* meaning "work") was a feudal obligation that magistrates and municipalities had imposed on the German peasantry from 1280 until the German Empire's abolition of serfdom in 1848. German peasants had been forced by law to provide unpaid services for dignitaries and the state. This included plowing, harrowing, cutting grain, mowing grass, chopping wood, running errands, fixing bridges and roads, hunting dangerous animals, constructing fortifications, performing military service, working as border guards, feeding and managing hunting dogs during dignitaries' hunts in the forests, and hauling grain, wood, hay, manure, or building materials. The only way to get out of a *Scharwerk* was to pay a fine and find a replacement peasant. Peasant disputes erupted when authorities attempted to impose new and heavier obligations.[44] Nazis revived *Scharwerke* after their invasion of Poland in September 1939 and imposed them on the Poles in the Generalgouvernement. Poles had to deliver goods, ferry people, do construction work, clean, tend German graves, repair roads, clear away snow and clear railway tracks, deliver construction materials, serve as night watchmen, and so forth. They could "legally" opt out only on the condition that they put forward replacements; however, foot-dragging, feigning illness, and choosing lighter *Scharwerke* like transportation instead of road repair were common. Men delegated their women and children to complete their *Scharwerk* obligations for them while they produced food in the fields. Suspected saboteurs were fined, beaten, arrested, or had their land expropriated. About 75 percent of the adult Polish population had "toiled involuntarily on various official projects" in Nazi *Scharwerke,* and those memories of ethnic and class domination were still raw in the minds of the settler population, who had to perform what they called szarwarks for their own state officials in the Recovered Territories.[45]

Houdini, the military official who had been in charge of the resettlement process, became the military arm of the commune who rallied the peasants into the szarwarks. Zofia recalled that Houdini's brigadiers canvassed peasant homes telling them, "Tomorrow you have to go to the szarwark." Usually, pregnant women, children, and the ill were exempt, but when there were severe labor shortages, they even "rallied the women." These were orders (*nakazy*), and thus "every person had to go and to work it off." When I asked her what would happen if one resisted the call to go to the szarwark, she responded: "You know, he had to. . . . If they ordered it, people went." In cases of replacements, authorities "did not care where you got the money from, what they cared about is that you had to work yours off and that is that." Houdini "observed everything and walked around and looked" over the operation while his brigadiers patrolled them:

> And sometimes if someone did not want to work, then they had this measuring stick, which they traced out the meters and "You must do it." Because there were some who even were tricking everyone [into extra work] in the szarwark because, "You work and I will stand!" and "I will bounce around and will not do work—but you work! I am telling you, when there was that szarwark, there was that Houdini, let him rest with God in peace, he is long dead, but he was such a kombinator! And a liar!

Zofia called Houdini a kombinator because she felt she had been tricked into forced labor, that the idea of the western frontier was a lie. Shoveling a road for free while a brigadier with a measuring stick stood above you and forced you to work is no one's idea of freedom, and especially not to a peasant pioneer who answered the state's call and migrated to the West to recover Poland's lost El Dorado. Winter szarwarks were the grimmest. Anna, a Ukrainian peasant who was forcibly resettled by PUR in 1947 as part of Operation Vistula, recalled, "There were szarwarks, because back then, when there was winter, they shoveled by hand because there were no plows. To Słupsk itself there was a szarwark and people shoveled snow, working the road. And how? For free! We worked. Yes!" At about eight o'clock in the morning, each peasant received a shovel, lined up, and was presented with a state warrant (*nakaz*) that explained the work to be completed in an area that went from Bursztyn past the state farms to the edge of the commune boundary eight kilometers to the northwest. The brigadier then outlined the plot to shovel for each peasant. No food was provided. "They gave us nothing! No food, no drink, because when one went to work it off then he took a sandwich of some sort." When more plowing was involved, the day was extended past two o'clock in the afternoon, and if snow fell the following day, the peasants were rounded up again to repeat the szarwark. At the end of every szarwark day, all the peasants signed their names on Houdini's list to indicate that they had "worked it off," and then the list disappeared into the Kafkaesque corridors of the commune.

While Bursztyn's peasants vividly remembered the szarwarks, and Houdini's role in them, I could initially locate only two records from 1947 in the local archives in which rural authorities "unanimously agreed" to "rally Germans into szarwark labor," shoveling snow and ice in the winter and clearing fields in the autumn to prepare for the sowing period.[46] There was no mention of peasant szarwarks. Even Kacper, the son of Houdini who had enforced szarwarks in Zofia's recollection, confirmed to me that they once existed in Bursztyn:

> There were szarwarks. The peasant farmers were burdened with the szarwarks, if one had to go somewhere, or something, one had to bring one's wagon and horse, and they [authorities] were taking advantage of it. It was written out, that this many had to be done within a year, and how many times one could take advantage of it. And we took advantage of it.

Yet there was scant archival evidence of such a widespread state practice. After an unsuccessful search of Poland's postwar legislation, I delved into the Polish legal journal *Monitor Polski*, where I finally found this phrase: *świadczeń obowiązkowych w naturze (szarwark)*. It revealed to me that the state referred to szarwarks as "obligatory payment-in-kind."[47] When I returned to the archives, I found that in November 1946, provincial (*powiat*) government authorities ordered Bursztyn officials to requisition "payment-in-kind" (*świadczenie w naturze*) labor from Germans and settlers. Rather than linking those feudal obligations with German *Scharwerke* or the Soviet model of collectivization as practiced in 1930s Soviet Russia, it used the legal precedent from a 1935 Polish law that authorized the state to require "straightforward labor on foot and with machines," including the building and upkeep of roads, performing public water system repairs, building government structures, cultivating wastelands, and planting trees in fields. Officials could force peasants and Germans to perform unpaid labor in massive projects.[48] All rural officials, military personnel, and wage earners who theoretically did not produce on agricultural land (even though in Bursztyn they were the largest land owners) were legally exempt from obligation. Below is the commune's breakdown of how many days of labor each peasant was obligated to repay to the state as determined by the size of his or her land grant:

1–5 hectares: 1 day/year with wagon and horses; 3 days on foot.
5–10 hectares: 2 days/year with wagon and horses; 6 days on foot.
10–15 hectares: 3 days/year with wagon and horses; 9 days on foot.
15–20 hectares: 4 days/year with wagon and horses; 12 days on foot.[49]

While the state used the size of the land grant to calculate each peasant's "labor tax," the penalty of missing work was the same for all. If a peasant could not perform the labor, he or she was mandated to pay three hundred złoty per missed szarwark day and a one-hundred-złoty penalty for renting a labor substitute (this was called *Scharwerkgeld* in the German system).[50] Archival records show that Bursztyn's officials counted the szarwark by how many złoty the peasants had "saved" the commune, but the values were arbitrarily chosen. In 1947 a peasant who worked a full day with only a wagon and one horse saved the state 240 złoty, but the savings increased to 400 złoty if two horses were used. In 1948, 619 szarwark days on foot saved 123,800 złoty. There was no indication as to how much budgetary money there was in the first place or which projects the saved money actually went toward. The accounts also reveal that in 1947, the nationalized state forestry division volunteered 7,760 szarwark days from its waged forestry workers at a value of 1,552,000 złoty to the commune.[51] Even though by law the szarwark applied only to non–wage earners, the account reveals that the commune began to establish relationships with nationalized workplaces to help meet its goals. When a resistant peasantry withheld szarwark labor, directors of forest enterprises volunteered their own waged workers to szarwarks. Those who controlled the arms of the state began to exploit this feudal labor institution by shifting waged workers to meet state goals.

In addition to the szarwark obligations, the budgetary records revealed an entire system of ethnically stratified feudal taxes imposed on the Germans and the Polish peasantry. During the 1945–1946 fiscal year, German families "donated" 149,949 złoty to the commune's budget as part of an obligatory feudal tithe called a *danina*, which had no legal precedent that I could find, but was nonetheless used to force money out of Germans toward new state projects like opening Polish schools. The following year, they paid an additional *danina* of fifty złoty per household for no given reason.[52] Likewise, Polish peasants who migrated voluntarily to the territories were saddled with "enrichment taxes" (*wzbogacenie*), implying that they were greedy land grabbers amassing property to add to what their families already owned in central Poland. Others like Zofia were burdened with an additional "F.O.R." tax, for which I found no legal definition or translation. Repatriated Belarusians and forcibly resettled Ukrainians paid no taxes, on the grounds that they had received their land "in exchange" (*w zamianie*) for the land lost in the east. Possibly, the Polish peasantry was saddled with additional taxes to make up for an entire tax-exempt group of settlers, as well as for the Germans who fled or were expelled from those lands. This ethnically stratified tax code that penalized the Polish middle peasantry set "the stage" for the Stalinist theater of purging rich peasants (*kułaks*) and collectivizing agriculture.

In "Corvée, Maps, and Contracts," Martha Lampland writes that in 1950s postwar Hungary cadastral maps from the 1850s, used originally to determine taxation of the peasantry, and later by the Nazis to establish tax brackets, were employed by the Soviets to identify class enemies during Stalinist purges of capitalist elements from the villages.[53] In the Recovered Territories, however, kułaks were not a group of wealthy peasant farmers who had lived on those territories for centuries and accumulated wealth at the expense of the poorer peasants. Rather, they had been actively recruited by PPR propaganda to settle the German lands as "pioneers," and they were settled by PUR on land grants that abided by the agrarian reform rules. Peasants like Zofia and her neighbors who received more land from the commune during the agrarian reform were burdened with more szarwark labor, even though they had no say over how much land they received from the Germans who had vacated it, or how much to cultivate; they could not legally abandon, rent, or sell the land. Rural authorities had a vested interest in creating and preserving a class of middle and large peasant farms so that the owners would be responsible for more feudal obligations for state plans and projects. This helps illuminate why the authorities did not want peasants abandoning, selling, or downsizing their land grants: doing so would have jeopardized the szarwark system the state needed to consolidate its economic and political apparatus on the new frontier. The Polish peasants who had been lured to this land by the Piast myth felt that they had been tricked, chained to the land they had come to recover and saddled with feudal obligations.

The szarwark system opened the floodgates for numerous other feudal labor obligations the state imposed on the peasantry and the Germans, some of which were dictated by law and others of which had no legal foundation. In 1947 the state passed an even more exploitative legal requirement called "neighborly help" (*pomoc sąsiedzka*).[54] This labor arrangement had been practiced informally by propertied peasants in interwar central Poland. During harvests (*omłoty*), peasant neighbors voluntarily pooled their tools and reciprocated labor on one another's private farms. This way, they did not pay for farmhands. At the end of the working day, the host threw a party with food and drink. Then the hosting family reciprocated by sending the same number of people from its farm to help with their neighbors' harvests. Through this mutual-aid system, peasants secured unpaid labor that boosted profit margins; the system also allowed them to own more land than they could physically harvest with their family unit, so they could produce enough for family consumption and sell the surplus on the market. Neighborly help was supposed to be practiced by peasant neighbors who owned similar amounts of land and shared the same socioeconomic status. During the Nazi occupation, Polish women often continued the system of neighborly help to survive during labor shortages and to preserve a sense of community. Studies of a similar arrangement in Germany called *Bittarbeit* argue that while it strengthened peasants' class status, it was also problematic, especially in contexts where peasants would perform unpaid labor in exchange for a landlord's or state's "protection" rather than reciprocal labor on their own farms.[55] While the postwar state wanted to diversify the kinds of feudal obligations officials could impose on a resistant peasantry, the power of rural officials to exploit this traditional arrangement led to tyranny. In diversifying the kinds of feudal obligations officials could impose on a resistant peasantry, the postwar state empowered rural officials to exploit this labor institution to meet state goals.

The 1947 "neighborly help" law revived the practice as a type of feudal bondage.[56] Peasants were legally obligated to pool their labor and machines during sowing, plowing, and harvest periods as a form of uncompensated neighborly help, to assist both fellow neighbors and the state. Mutual aid relieved the commune's budgets. Unbeknownst to the peasants, their participation, or lack thereof, was secretly monitored by rural officials.[57] Peasants were also responsible for plowing, sowing, and harvesting the commune's nationalized fields. Although a "neighbor," the state did not "reciprocate" or compensate their unpaid labor.[58] In the autumn of 1947, commune archives reported that through neighborly help, peasants had planted one thousand hectares of grain on commune land. The 1947 law also authorized officials to channel peasant brigades to other communes facing shortages as they saw fit.[59] Although I did not see any record of it in Bursztyn's archives, Jadzia, a Belarusian peasant whom PUR had repatriated to the territories as a "Pole" from Poland's eastern borderlands annexed by the Soviet Union, recalled that she had been transported with other peasants to fields where they were forced to plant thousands of tree saplings to create entirely new "nationalized" forests— in return for a bucket of potatoes. Peasants, already burdened with szarwarks for public works projects, had to help their "neighbor," the state, by sowing its fields and planting its forests. A 1948 law exempted military personnel, commune officials, administrators, and other party authorities from the neighborly help requirement, thus creating a caste system split between those who dictated what work needed to be completed and those who did all of the work.[60]

Moreover, authorities abused that power by requiring "neighborly help" on their own private farms while using their state authority to relieve themselves from having to reciprocate it. Aneta and Bohdan, a couple from Ukraine who arrived through Operation Vistula in 1947, worked and lived in a state forestry division composed of about a dozen homes on Bursztyn's outskirts. Polish, Ukrainian, and Kashubian forestry workers populated the settlement. The commune allotted each worker family a home that had belonged to Germans and a worker garden (*działka*, less than one hectare) on which the family grew crops and livestock to supplement their wages. Workers were also entitled to material goods (*deputat*) like wood, clothing, and food, provided by the state forestry division. Usually, men earned wages working full-time for the forestry while women stayed home. Cezary, a German Kashubian who had lived in German Pomerania before the border changes in 1945, was the state forestry director (*leśniczy*) who lived among his workers in the forestry settlement with his wife, Anna, a seamstress who sewed for private customers. Aneta and Bohdan recalled that Cezary treated his farm as an extension of the workplace. In addition to working in the state forestry division as regular workers, both men and women in the division were expected to "work off" (*swoje odrobić*) Cezary's allotment garden and offer domestic services to his wife in exchange for the release of their wages and material entitlements. This feudal labor arrangement is similar to the German *Gesindezwangsdienst* (servants' compulsory service), which required employees to perform unpaid tasks on their employer's property.[61] Aneta recalled to me and Zofia her experience of "working off" and "helping out" (*pomagać*) on Cezary's property:

ANETA: The human back then had to fucking work one's ass off—children, cow, house. And one even had to work at Cezary's house, for a good healthy relationship, for free.

EDYTA: Why? What was that?

ANETA: "The director's worker"! The worker had "to work one's [labor obligation] off" [*swoje odrobić*] at the director's [house]. He did not pay!

EDYTA: Meaning that one worked in the forestry, but also had to plow his land?

ANETA: One worked the land which the director had just like us and one helped him, worked it, and every woman helped [*pomagała*].

ZOFIA: Hmmm [pensively].

EDYTA: So it was privately done?

ANETA: Just Mrs. P. [a German Kashubian] did not help out.

EDYTA: And so one had to help?

ANETA: Well, you know. If one did not want to, then one did not want to—

ZOFIA: Yes.

ANETA: But if one wanted to live well with them, one went to help.

Cezary kept the forestry's state barns and horses on "his property" and treated them like his own. Therefore, when Aneta and the Ukrainian women came to clean the barn and the horses (when they were not cooking for Anna, washing the couple's clothing, and entertaining their guests), it was impossible to tell whether they were doing it for the "state" or for Cezary. Aneta, Bohdan, and the other workers eventually "broke free" of these obligations after a series of events in which Cezary and Anna revealed "bourgeois inclinations" by bragging to people in their home village about having Ukrainian servants in Bursztyn. When the workers revolted, Cezary illegally sold his house to another Kashubian, Fidelis, who succeeded him as the forestry director, and fled the village with Anna. Incredibly, Aneta and the workers relied on socialist discourse to free themselves of feudal chains and purge the bourgeois trickster from their settlement.

Cezary's story brings to mind Jerome Bloom's study "The Rise of Serfdom in Eastern Europe," in which he writes that a common misconception about serfdom is that the serf was bound to the soil, when in reality "the deepest and most complete form of serfdom was precisely when the lord was able (as he often was) to move his peasants about as he wished, transferring them from one holding to another, converting them into landless field hands or into household servants, or even selling, giving, or gambling them away without land."[62] This is precisely what happened in Bursztyn: state officials exploited feudal institutions to force workers, peasants, and Germans into building the nascent command economy.

Fidelis, who still lived in Cezary's old house, claimed that the labor obligations that had no name were the most brutal form of exploitation. Absolute power was exerted not by the rule of law, which would have made it accountable to the law to some degree, but by raw power exercised by the masters over their subjects. His words come to mind whenever I think about Orzeł's story. In late 1944 Orzeł was the first Polish KRN official to arrive in Bernstein and take hold of the reins of the Polonization process. He settled in with a German family on a forty-hectare farm in the northernmost part of the village, which linked to the road that led to the city and was adjacent to the Junker estate farm that Krystyna's father worked on as the agriculture specialist. Orzeł's colonization effort began at the household level, where he made the German owners who shared their home with him into his laborers. When I interviewed the ninety-four-year-old, his daughter Bożena had to repeat some of the questions on account of his poor hearing:

ORZEŁ: I lived with Germans.

BOŻENA: And you ate together.

ORZEŁ: And why not!? They [Poles and Germans] ate together.

BOŻENA: Together they ate, together they worked. They [Germans] helped [*pomagali*] you out too.

ORZEŁ: They worked for me—The landowner [*gospodarz*]—all the Germans.

BOŻENA: They worked for money or for food or a bit of both?

ORZEŁ: There was no money, only food. We had cereals [*zboże*]. The Rus-
                sians gave us cereals. There were entire fields filled with potatoes.
                In mounds, we took the potatoes. There were potatoes and later, we
                planted potatoes. We gave milk to the Germans. And to them all,
                we gave potatoes. One had to give them food. The Germans who
                were living with us, they had two children. One had to feed them.

Domestic colonization was perhaps one of the blurriest feudal institutions. What
were the Germans doing? A szarwark? Neighborly help? In Orzeł's view, he was
helping the Germans survive by employing them in return for food, but did the
Germans see it that way when a Pole marched into their home, declared himself
the landowner, and turned them into laborers on their own farm in exchange for
food? Even when Bożena tried to soften the arrangement by calling it "helping,"
he asserted that it was "working," as if they had to work in exchange for food.
Orzeł said that the early postwar period was ruled by a "quasi-government" (*pół-
rząd*). It was a world in which he could be both a colonizer in charge of expelling
the Germans and a cohabitant in their very own homes. He could be a socialist
official redistributing land from the German bourgeoisie as well as the largest
"landowner" in the village who worked his own German laborers. Survival of
the early Polish elites relied not on following the myth of the Recovered Territories but on navigating official and unofficial identities and discourses to secure a
bricolage of German and Russian resources to keep them fed and in power. The
Wild West was Orzeł's chessboard.

In *The Agrarian Sociology of Ancient Civilizations* (1909), Max Weber described unfree domestic labor obligations as the vestiges of corvées.[63] In Bursztyn
the domestication of German labor had no legal precedent like the corvée system
as far as I could find, but it was very much a widespread and accepted practice.
While employing domestic labor was prohibited on German land grants, because
the state interpreted the practice as a continuation of capitalist agrarian relations,
an exception appears to have been made for German labor. Incoming settlers
who entered German homes with Akt nadania documents and settled in with
the former German owners, also made the Germans into their farm laborers.
Everyone I spoke to had "his" or "her" or "our" Germans (*nasi niemcy*). Domestic
arrangements varied on a case-by-case basis. There was no rubric for negotiating
labor and resources between two peoples who had just fought a brutal war. Zofia and Konrad, for instance, took over the executive authority of Frau Agathe's
farm. During our discussion with Krystyna, whose father worked for the Red
Army, Zofia delicately explained how she supported Frau Agathe and employed
Heinz as a farmhand:

They were poor. They had huge poverty. We came here, then my husband
brought a cow because two children had already been born. Upstairs lived

Frau Agathe. She was such a good woman. How much I liked her! She said that she worked in a hospital in Słupsk in the children's division and she came to me, I had a cow, and we helped her out a lot because I felt bad for her children. She had a son, Heinz, he milked our cows, and he said that he will sleep here and I said "good." I always gave them milk, about three liters a day.

Of course most Germans did not wait for the new Polish settlers to decide their fates. In some cases, German owners, fearful of being looted by gangs, sent the Polish settlers to Słupsk to sell their valuables on the black market for a commission. Many Germans also took an active role in searching for jobs and strengthening reciprocal labor arrangements in order to secure food for themselves and their families. Mein Gott, the German woman in Bursztyn who still lives in the house in which she was born, explained to me how the women in her family worked at Polish and Russian settlers' homes:

Later, I went to work for a Polish household. I cleaned there and worked there in the house. I received food for it. And my father later worked in the forest for the Poles when they took people into the forest (for szarwark). My mother and sister worked for the Lew family, in the house. The Lew family had a store. Sister took care of their children and mother cooked. So that was something. My grandmother went to one woman because she always had to sew for those Russians. She said to grandmother, "Come cook for me. I will give you food and you can take some home with you."

Who ended up in the Germans' houses was determined by the luck of the draw. Some settlers who had suffered Nazi atrocities were thirsty for revenge. Jagoda, a Belarusian peasant who had been repatriated with her husband in 1946 to the village of Podwoda, about ten kilometers south of Bursztyn, recalled in alarm that one of her Polish neighbors tortured the female German owners of the house they moved into:

There were the types who lived here three houses from ours. When the Germans were around, they [Poles] came from Toruń and they harnessed the Germans to the plow, to the wagon, and worked with them! And they dragged them and tortured them! Poles! Yes! It was not everyone. And those young German women were innocent! They did not murder people. They tortured those women.

When it comes to postwar feudalism, the devil is in the details, told through memories, fractured archives, laws that did not exist, and whispers. The Polish-Soviet authorities revived feudalism to fund socialist projects and meet pervasive labor shortages resulting from the flight of the German populace and the slow influx of skilled Polish laborers to the lands. What was supposed to be a socialist revolution on the frontier became a feudal revival. Just as they had done with the

Piast myth, the Polish communists revived and revamped pre-1945 practices and ideas to create continuity with the past in a way that helped construct a socialist future, even though this was a type of socialism with little basis in the Marxist-Leninist tradition. Officials became the largest landowners and did as they wished with the peasantry, imposing labor and tribute obligations as a way of solving labor shortages. They conformed to the principles of the socialist revolution when they were politically pressured to do so by the state apparatus, but they delved deep into the tool kit of serfdom to keep local control of the peasant population in a way that suited their private needs. There was not much deviation from this serf-like structure of life, except that the new power was the socialist state; serfdom was adapting to the state, and the state was co-opting it to gain control over the territories. Upon arrival, peasants realized that instead of pioneers who would oust the Germans from their lands, they were to be serfs, coerced alongside the Germans into feudal obligations for the state. Exploited by the state, they in turn exploited Germans to meet their subsistence needs. Thus, Zofia's tirade against Houdini the "kombinator" and the discrepancy I found between peasants' memories of the "szarwark" and the state's records of its "payment-in-kind" activities were not accidental. Mutual feelings of being "tricked" into forced labor by state authorities marked an important moment when the Slavic peasantries forged a "common thought of resistance," a new political discourse that rejected the state's language and set the stage for peasant resistance against the trickster Polish-Soviet state.

The Polish *Heimat*

Mychajlo, a Ukrainian peasant who had been forcibly resettled to the territories in the Operation Vistula campaign of 1947, resided with his sister Ula in the largest two-story German home along Zofia's street. In 2009 their house was a time capsule. Inside there was no electricity, no plumbing. The foyer was still adorned with dusty German-era wallpaper with orange flowers that had suffered its share of leaks and stains over the previous sixty years. Mychajlo had not destroyed the German furniture, unlike other Polish settlers on the street who had decided to domesticate the state policy of "cleansing" and burned the clothing, furniture, linen, toys, books, paintings, documents, photographs, and political banners that had belonged to "their Germans." In Mychajlo's opinion, vengeful burning was "a pain inflicted on Hitler," but an expression of hatred nonetheless. Himself a victim of ethnic cleansing carried out by the Polish government, Mychajlo knew how a single flame could spark a conflagration of hatred. A German professor had once lived there, he recalled proudly, as if the man had been his son. His frozen home gave Mychajlo a transient persona, as if he were the temporary custodian for a German family away on an extended vacation. The house revealed no evidence that he and Ula were connected to it. Many villagers' homes were dotted with "German-era" (*poniemieckie*) furnaces, wallpaper, paintings, crosses, photographs, credenzas, and even timber framing. Such remnants gave homes a unique aesthetic quality and a link with the German past. These homes each told stories of a family's settlement experience with the Germans, their struggles with the state, and their feelings about the border. They preserve memories of cleansing that the archives omitted.

Two houses down from Mychajlo lived Jadzia, a peasant who had been repatriated in 1946 from lands that had been part of eastern Poland before the war. German-era objects around her property, like her fence and furnace, recalled the time when she stood up to Houdini's overreach of power into the domestic sphere. At that time Houdini lived with his wife, Ela, and their son Kacper down the street in Mychajlo's home, which was conspicuously the largest house on the street. There, in the front yard, he kept a large cage filled with many tiny birds. This military man relished denying freedom to birds and peasants like. But the birdcage was a public display of bourgeois tastes and perhaps even a Warsaw upbringing. Who Houdini was, or where he came from, nobody knew. In the commune archives, Houdini was listed as a military official who was paid wages by the Communist Party, but in the minutes of the commune meetings, he identified himself as a *robotnik* (worker) who was *bezpartyjny* (without a party). In one instance, he was referred to as the tax collector.[64] He seemed to be a man who was straddling many different identities. But above all, he was seen by the peasants as an outsider who held a tight grip on state power and was accountable to no one.

Jadzia recalled that Houdini was a master looter. He sent his son Kacper and other men to each house on the street and presented the peasant settlers with official state orders authorizing them to seize for the state all valuable German furniture and valuables like porcelain or silver. When his men arrived at Jadzia's house, she refused to comply, stating that the items were her "entitled German-era property" that she had received "in exchange" for all her losses in the east. She insisted everything she had received with the house belonged to her, not the state. Whether or not these were official or fabricated state orders remains a mystery. According to gossip, Houdini was reselling furniture on the black market near the German border and pocketing the profit. When Jadzia and Zofia spoke about these episodes, they portrayed Houdini and his cronies as using state power to trick the peasantry.

Mein Gott, on the next street over, provided a different angle to this furniture story. She said the state redistributed the furniture to incoming settlers as a bonus for choosing to become workers instead of peasants. German furniture was valuable not only because of its craftsmanship but also because the settlers owned no furniture. All of them wanted a wooden desk, credenza, or table to furnish their homes. This was the age before mass-produced furniture. Access to furniture became a "perk" that the state provided to incoming settlers who signed up to the Communist Party or who accepted proletarian jobs on the state farm, in the state forestry, or in the administration. This was confirmed by a Belarusian settler who said that when the state settled her on her designated farm, the state farm director permitted her to go to the state farm warehouses and pick out whatever furniture she needed for her home. Settlers might even have received furniture as a reward for providing valuable information or for joining the voluntary Citizens' Militia (Milicja Obywatelska). A settler who became a postal worker boasted that she had been granted access to German furniture simply because the state official recognized her from a forestry partisan group they had both (supposedly) fought in during the war back east. Anyone who was classified as a worker or had connections to the nomenklatura networks was a beneficiary of the "redistributed" German furniture. Redistribution of German furniture created early patronage relationships.

Whoever gained access to German capital owned the frontier. According to one archive from 1946, a peasant settler stood up during an open quorum meeting demanding that officials return the German-era potatoes they had taken from his land grant without his permission. The officials refused because, as one of them put it, "the potatoes were German-era and they were redistributed to the poverty-stricken during the unpaid sowing action."[65] The official reframed the seizure of his potato crop as a redistributive measure, even though the peasant himself was poverty stricken and there was no mention of such a program in the archives. Top-down redistribution of food was also a problem. When aid packages arrived from the United Nations Relief and Rehabilitation Administration (UNRRA), rather than redistributing them to the people for whom they were intended, officials served the herring at banquets for new communist recruits. Władysława, who shuttled back and forth from the city to the village, said that her contacts in Słupsk were *powiat*-level officials who brought home boxes of UNRRA aid. In contrast, the only thing Zofia and Jadzia received from the aid packages was inedible "monkey lard" (*małpi smalec*). In another instance, Houdini mixed up "winter barley" with "summer barley," causing massive barley crop failures. The gossip was that he'd sold the real stuff at the border. Whether or not this gossip was true is unclear. What it reveals is that peasant and state confrontations over capital defined the boundaries between private and public spheres, the gray area between the private and state sectors. Official looting in Bursztyn drove a deep political wedge between villagers who were and were not employed by the state. Disputing the legitimacy of Houdini's official looting (*szaber*) of furniture, crops, and buildings was one way that peasants exposed the corrupt and self-interested face of the socialist revolution and state power.

Official looting based on orders from the government to seize food, furniture, agricultural machines and tools, industrial material, literature, typewriters, sewing machines, radios, pianos, and anything else of value on the black market was a pervasive practice across the Recovered Territories.[66] When I spoke to Motylek, a Polish communist official who worked in the early postwar period, about the early days of state making in the commune, he said that he had been allocated "a very small budget and one had to kombinować so much, so that everything played right, so that everything would work out fine, for there to be help at school." He said he had bought a German carpet on the black market with state money to ensure that the new state school director had a carpet in her new office to highlight her new role of state authority. The material trappings of the state had to come from somewhere. The officials needed desks to write their orders, and the militia needed a carpeted room in the basement of the commune police station to interrogate enemies of socialism. Villagers ironically called this interrogation site "on the carpet" (*na dywanek*) because their poor treatment by local authorities was done with bourgeois flair. Yet it was these very human inclinations for comfort that drove rural officials to preserve and prolong the state of dystopia rather than working on the socialist utopia they had signed up to create. And this was their downfall, for the peasantry began to counter officials' centralization of German wealth by hiding and retaining German capital within their private homes. Hiding or preserving German valuables in their households, away from the gaze of the state, was a way for settlers to resist the collectivization of space. They began to experiment with the state's "blind spots" as well as the possibilities of the domestic sphere as a site of resistance against the state.

The villagers, as I have mentioned, all intentionally retained German artifacts, or *gotyks*. Weronika, who had been repatriated as a "Pole" from East Prussia, explained to me that "a *gotyk* is a type of memory gift [*pamiątka*]. . . . One can neither chop it, nor take it. It must stand." Recently, when her daughter wanted to chop up German antique furniture to use for firewood—a common practice even today!—Weronika stopped her, saying, "It is not mine, it is not yours, so let them stand!" Zofia described her gotyk as a gift. When the Germans were being deported from the territories, the commune ordered each of the new settlers to transport "their Germans" to Słupsk, just like they transported wood out of the forest with horse and wagon. Her husband Konrad refused. When she was parting ways with Frau Agathe, Agathe gave her a large black-and-silver cross as a "memory" gift that stands as the centerpiece of her dining room (see figure 3.2):

> Frau Agathe gave me a cross in two parts because, "What am I going to give you for keepsake?"—because they were leaving for the Oder. I said, "I do not want anything because I will remember you anyway." They were good people. And she took out the cross but in two pieces the cross was broken in two, right? I said, "Who broke your cross?" [and Agathe replied,] "Russian! He took it

Figure 3.2. Gotyk cross Frau Agathe gave to Zofia before her expulsion to Germany. Photo by author.

from me, threw it and stomped on it!" He stomped on it. I took the cross. Love, I have it to this day. There was this one whose name was Giera, a welder who came over and he was from Warsaw. And I tell his wife about it and he listens and he tells me this: "Zofia, give me the cross. I will weld it for you. But I will shorten it." Because it was longer. He says, "It is so destroyed that I have to shorten it, to cut it evenly." Whenever I look [at it], I see Frau Agathe and those Russians who are stomping on it.

The gift of German property was more meaningful than the right over German property bestowed by the state. Zofia's story of how she was given a cross and then "recovered" it is her way of telling the border narrative of the territories. While the state was promoting revenge and expulsion, Zofia and the German family practiced reconciliation and transnational reciprocity through multiple gifts. They acted like a fictive extended family who "co-managed" the farm. Zofia took good care of the old German property while the German family stayed in close contact throughout the socialist period. The German family sent packages and money, and even visited in the 1970s. Zofia's story exposes how settlers informally "recovered" the territories from the Germans through the preservation of these artifacts. Rather than settlers representing the state's conquest of the state territories, the gotyk symbolized the family-based transmission of property into the ownership of the settler families who would treat the property well. Gotyks were proof of an alternate history, proof that Germans had once been the owners and that Poles were "custodians" of that lost identity. They are a border narrative that advocates porosity, co-ownership, and reciprocity, not revanchism.

The choice to retain, discard, or hide German-era objects in their homes said a lot about the settlers' sense of "belonging" to the territories. The more I stepped into villagers' homes, the more I noticed variations of Zofia's artifacts—even plastic replicas! It is as if the replicas functioned as talismans, providing a form of protection. The gotyks and their replicas offered a way for villagers to legitimize their stay in the territories in the midst of restitution battles fought between Poland and Germany that are still being waged to this day. The gotyks preserve the spaces that give life to German nostalgia, *Heimat*, a term villagers often use to describe Germans' sentiments toward the lands. *Heimat* is short for *Heimatgefühle* or "feelings of home."[67] Many of the original settlers have used gotyks as a physical insurance policy for a "recoverable past" should the German owners ever return.[68] Moreover, the gotyks, especially those made of porcelain or silver, held black market value. If they had to escape the lands, a German antique would likely help them curry favor along the way. Settlers like Mychajlo, Ula, and Weronika who perceived the German-Polish border as temporary refused to invest in their "German" properties.[69] They thought about the border in a much broader time frame than the "end of the war" or the "end of socialism." Stefania, a Ukrainian peasant who was one of the original settlers, told me she keeps a special room just for the German family to stay on their old property. Aunt Kinga, who has never met the owner of the house she occupies, takes special care of a German apple tree in her backyard. In the 1990s the German owners' daughters returned to the house and wanted to taste the apples from their childhood. When Kinga showed them the tree and gave them the apples, the women cried. The tree is collapsing, but Kinga and Alfred take special care of it and have propped up the branches "just in case" the Germans visit. Gotyks are passed down as family heirlooms—I even have one, Frau Agathe's silver jewelry box, given to me by my mother. Whether they are transferred or purchased as replicas, the gotyks represent a responsible, ethical stewardship and a respect for the German Heimat. When I think about the power of the gotyk in opening up German feelings of the Heimat, I think of Krystyna and her German books.

Gotyks are artifacts of ideological alterity that marked the domestic "front" against the Sovietization of everyday life.[70] Almost all of the interviewees possessed a gotyk, but the stories behind each item represented individualized human bonds and economic relations with Germans. All stories shared a common feeling about the overreach of the state into domestic life, something the state could take away from them. While official looting of the furniture represented the state's collectivization of materials and space, the unique gotyks represented villagers' individuality.[71] They commemorated "unofficial" contexts in a contested past. Their narratives represent "refracted meanings" from the dominant ideological discourse about recovering the frontier.[72] That gotyks remain in villagers' homes reveals that recovery is never a one-way street or political project with a beginning and an end. It is never "over," nor is the future "secure," no matter what any state may promise, especially in Poland. What the gotyks tell me is that the furniture raids sparked the nascent formation of an alternate narrative about the state that did not coincide with the polarizing Piast myth or the celebrated role of the Soviet-Polish authorities in ushering in a new postwar era of Polish self-determination. The forcible seizure of household furniture was an episode that to the settlers represented the state's intrusion into private life, and the gotyks are physical remnants of what became emerging spaces of resistance against the Polish state.

Villagers arrived to recover a lost civilization but instead found themselves lost in a new socialist one. The immediate postwar period was a perpetually chaotic state of protosocialism. The question of why villagers overwhelmingly omitted the term *kombinacja* from what looked and sounded like a landscape of resistance is curious and warrants investigation. It cropped up on only two occasions, once when Zofia called Houdini a kombinator because he tricked labor out of the peasants during the road szarwarks, and once when Motylek said he had used kombinacja to acquire a carpet for the school.

In the immediate aftermath of the war, people truly believed in the Piast myth, including the intelligentsia who had kept a degree of separation from the state and had been critical of foreign occupation as it had been during the nineteenth-century partitions. The Polish villagers saw themselves in line with the political project of recovering Polish lost lands and believed in the logic of the German expulsion. But when they arrived in the lands by force or by choice, they experienced a certain degree of disorientation upon encountering the many ethnic, linguistic, and national groups that lived in their newfound communities. Isolation from their families, networks, and capital back home also played a role, in that the new pioneers did not have established discourses or spaces in which to voice their concerns. To some, Germans became their family, and there is still a great deal of shame, guilt, and silence about Poles' benefiting from the German expulsion. To create a collective resistance, they would have to overcome hatred toward their wartime enemies. This happened during szarwarks and furniture seizures. The peasantry in Bursztyn had a new enemy and scapegoat—Houdini— whom they could use to create a common antistate discourse against the emerging nomenklatura class that was taking over the reins of redistributive power across the commune lands.

The "formal" apparatus of the state was still in its nascent stages. Orzeł, the KRN commune official who founded Bursztyn, himself called it a "quasi-government." Motylek, the PPR official, relied on the black market to create the material makeup of the state. In *Rebuilding Poland* (1997), Padraic Kenney writes that the postwar period on the frontier was one of "negotiation" between the settlers and those who represented the state. The identity of the "authorities" was unclear; compliance "was not automatic" and "control was incomplete."[73] The idea of what was "formal," and the loopholes around it, was beginning to surface, but it was also polysemous. The PKWN was passing legislation and reforming it at an astonishing speed, without friction. There was a time lag between the legislation on paper (which only officials read) and its on-the-ground reality (which only officials implemented). Villagers did not "see" the laws. This disjunction empowered the commune officials who could delay or selectively decide what to adopt without legal consequence. There was much room for unregulated activity because even if the state was defining itself through law and on paper, the actual application of the law and the regulation of economic activity were largely missing. To know how to exercise kombinacja, as demonstrated in the previous chapter, one must know how to work around the system, but without a clear system with loopholes, there was no framework for deviance. It was unclear what could and could not be done. In fact, the absence of laws empowered officials to seize control of the frontier.

Resistance was carried out in a completely new terrain of struggle: networks. Max Weber's definition of the state as a "relation of men dominating men" most accurately describes this new state of play.[74] "It was a government, but it was nothing. Whoever won, [others] lost," recalled Weronika, a repatriated refugee from former East Prussia. Anna, a Ukrainian peasant, defined the state itself as a "couple of families" rather than as an institution that regulated economies, passed laws, and redistributed property. Irena, a Polish seamstress who received expensive watches and scarves when she sewed for the Red Army stationed at the nearby state farm until 1949, nostalgically remembered that the state was "like one family." When I asked Zofia if her husband had ever belonged to any of the political parties, she responded that all of the peasant parties "were incestuous! Cousins!" In hindsight, I think she may have literally meant that the political parties were headed by members of the same family. Those who benefited from this "family" looked back on it nostalgically, whereas those who got the short end of the stick remembered the families that exercised state power using patronage networks. Although the Soviets formed a colonial presence, they clustered in Junker estates, out of view, and used German labor. The everyday face of the state was a small group of well-connected families. Villagers related to the state through their allegiances or through vendettas with the families who represented the "state." Gossip about encounters with those families was a discourse about the state.

Villagers as well as state officials became experts at using creative tricks to do what they felt necessary. Contriving exceptions to the rule was not just an anti-state effort, but a key theme and strategy through which the Polish state emerged from the ashes of war. On the national level, Polish state authorities in Warsaw adopted the Soviet state model to create their own path to socialism (with no collectivization at first). The Minister of the Recovered Territories, Władysław Gomułka, was a known trickster who never fully declared his allegiance to Joseph Stalin and fought to find a "Polish way to socialism," a move that led to a 1948 coup against him as secretary-general of the Polish Workers' Party (Polska Partia Robotnicza). Certain strains of these trickster tactics were nationalistic. Instead of expelling the Germans to "recover" the homeland, regional authorities used German labor to repair infrastructure and secure the first proletarian workers in their nationalized state workplaces. On the local level, emergent nomenklatura domesticated capital and labor and used state power for private gain. They helped the state secure political and economic power on the frontier, but undermined its legitimacy in the process. Disconnecting from the authorities "up there" in the higher echelons of the state was, oddly, a way for authorities to demonstrate antiestablishment leanings and assert their Polishness to obtain some modicum of legitimacy from a segment of the population. This created the perfect amount of confusion and "space" for growing private enterprises and eventually for kombinacja that helped "fix" these misalignments. Bending rules became everyone's modus operandi.

Socialism in the Recovered Territories was built on the foundations of feudalism that mixed Polish, German, and Soviet variants at different points in time. Villages were ruled by father-son teams; commune officials granted themselves landed estates and secured cheap German labor for them; forestry division directors treated workers as their own domestic laborers. The state was defined not by the rule of law from Warsaw but by familial networks. Party officials did not always carry out state policy, and peasants who resisted state law were not always acting against the spirit of the socialist revolution. Workers' and peasants' silent revolts against individual commune officials had little to do with the actual socialist revolution; rather, they were directed against the trickster tactics of officials with bourgeois leanings. Settlers who represented the state apparatus and those who did not manipulated space, resources, and labor to ensure their family's subsistence needs were met. Perhaps this *was* the making of Gomułka's Polish road to socialism. The kombinacja silence was the silence before the storm of Stalinism that would dramatically transform the frontier and unleash the kombinator within.

Notes

1. Dulczewski and Kwilecki, "Wstęp," 7; Davies, *God's Playground*, 2:562; Pagel, "Rathsdamnitz," 800–811.

2. Mikołajczyk, *Rape of Poland*, 41.

3. Szaz, *Germany's Eastern Frontiers*, xiii.

4. Dobrzyski, *Granica zachodnia*, 190.

5. Davies, *God's Playground*, 2:563.

6. Snyder, *Bloodlands*, 405.

7. See Pollak, *Rola Ziem Zachodnich*.

8. Dulczewski and Kwilecki, "Wstęp," 6–9.

9. Kulczycki, *Belonging to the Nation*, 23.

10. Dziennik Ustaw 1938, Numer 78, Pozycja 533, Dekret Prezydenta Rzeczypospolitej z dnia 11 października 1938r. o zjednoczeniu Odzyskanych Ziem Śląska Cieszyńskiego z Rzecząpospolitą Polską (Decree of the President of the Republic from October 11, 1938, on the reunification of the Cieszyn Silesian Recovered Territories with the Polish Republic), Dziennik Ustaw Rzeczypospolitej Polskiej, http://isap.sejm.gov.pl/VolumeServlet?type=wdu&rok=1938&numer=078.

11. Davis, *Memories of State*, 4.

12. Kiełczewska, *Rodzaje i typy*, 76.

13. Other examples are Hulewicz and Manthey, *Rolnicza spółdzielczość*; Dziedzic, *Rolnictwo Pomorskie*.

14. Kiełczewska and Grodek, *Odra-Nysa*, 22, 60.

15. Barcikowski, introduction to *Odzyskane*; Chojanski, *Słownik Polskich*; Kiełczewska and Grodek, *Odra-Nysa*; Ziółkowski, *Population of the Western Territories*; Męclewski, "Repolonizacja-programem"; Dylik, *Geografia*; Chmarzyński, *Pomorze Zachodnie*.

16. Kolipiński, "Economic Problems," 211; Barcikowski, introduction to *Odzyskane*, 7.

17. Yoshioka, "Imagining Their Lands," 274.

18. Męclewski, "Repolonizacja-programem," 10–14. See also Mitkowski, *Western Pomerania*, 5–6.

19. Kruszewski, *Oder-Neisse Boundary*, 115–23.

20. Ahonen and Stark, *People on the Move*; Thum, *Uprooted*, 53.

21. Brown, *Biography of No Place*; Gatrell, "Trajectories"; Kruszewski, *Oder-Neisse Boundary*; Zielinski, "Pacify, Populate, Polonise," 194.

22. Polonsky and Drukier, *Beginnings of Communist Rule*, 67; Korbonski, *Politics of Socialist Agriculture*, 83–84; Dulczewski and Kwilecki, "Wstęp," 9.

23. Polonsky and Drukier, *Beginnings of Communist Rule*, 67; Korbonski, *Politics of Socialist Agriculture*, 83–84; Dulczewski and Kwilecki, "Wstęp," 9.

24. Jędrychowski, *Recovered Territories*, 8.

25. Minc, "Recovery of the Regained Territories," 16.

26. Korbonski, *Politics of Socialist Agriculture*, 82–83; Jędrychowski, *Recovered Territories*, 8.

27. Korbonski, *Politics of Socialist Agriculture*, 83.

28. Thum, *Uprooted*, 84–85.

29. Kruszewski, *Oder-Neisse Boundary*, 67.

30. Pagel, "Rathsdamnitz," 811.

31. Ibid.

32. Thum, *Uprooted*, 85–86.

33. Ibid., 86.

34. Pagel, "Rathsdamnitz," 660.

35. Dziennik Ustaw z 1944, Numer 4, Pozycja 17, Dekret Polskiego Komitetu Wyzwolenia Narodowego z dnia 6 września 1944 r. o przeprowadzeniu reformy rolnej (Decree of the Polish Committee of National Liberation of September 6, 1944, on agrarian reform), 18–21, Dziennik Ustaw Rzeczypospolitej Polskiej, http://www.dziennikustaw.gov.pl/DU/1944/17/1.

36. Korbonski, *Politics of Socialist Agriculture*, 81–86.

37. Dziennik Ustaw z 1946, Numer 49, Pozycja 279, Dekret z dnia 6 września 1946r. o ustroju rolnym i osadnictwie na obszarze Ziem Odzyskanych i byłego Wolnego Miasta Gdańska (Decree of September 6, 1946, on the agricultural system and settlement in the area of the Recovered Territories and the former Free City of Danzig), 513–18, Dziennik Ustaw Rzeczypospolitej Polskiej, http://www.dziennikustaw.gov.pl/DU/1946/279/1.

38. Dulczewski and Kwilecki, "Wstęp," 9.

39. Polonsky and Drukier, *Beginnings of Communist Rule*, 67; Korbonski, *Politics of Socialist Agriculture*, 83–84; Dulczewski and Kwilecki, "Wstęp," 9.

40. Kruszewski, *Oder-Neisse Boundary*, 120; Stefan Żurawski, *Zarys Dziejów [Bursztyn]: Monografia opracowana z okazji 500-lecia [Bursztyn] i 40-lecia powrotu Ziem Zachodnich i Północnych do Macierzy* (Historical outline of [Bursztyn] on the fortieth anniversary of the Polish People's Republic: Monograph prepared on the occasion of the 500th anniversary of [Bursztyn] and the 40th anniversary of the return of the Western and Northern Territories to the Motherland) ([Bursztyn]: Biblioteka Publiczna Gmina [Bursztyn], 1985), 51.

41. Polish Socialist Party, "From Narodism to Marxism," clause 6.

42. Kolchin, *Unfree Labor*, 2.

43. Ibid., 134.

44. Cinnirella and Hornung, "Landownership Concentration," 138; Chodakiewicz, *Between Nazis and Soviets*, 50; Renate Blickle, "Frondienste/Scharwerk in Altbayern," *Historisches Lexikon Bayerns*, 2014, http://www.historisches-lexikon-bayerns.de/artikel/artikel_45466.

45. Chodakiewicz, *Between Nazis and Soviets*, 117.

46. Numer 2, 1946–1948, Protokoły z Posiedzenia Zarządu Gminnego (Minutes of the Commune Board Meeting), Gminna Rada Narodowa. Zarząd Gminnej w [Bursztyn], 16, Oddział Ogólno-Organizacyjny, 1–26, Wojewódzki Archiwum Państwowy w Koszalinie: Słupsk; Numer 4, 1945–1946, Budżet i sprawozdanie z wykonania budżetu od 1.X. 1945 do 31.III 1946 (The budget and the report on the implementation of the budget of October 1, 1945, to March 31, 1946), 1, Gminna Rada Narodowa-Zarząd Gminnej w [Bursztyn], Oddział Finansowo-Budżetowy, 1–61, Wojewódzki Archiwum Państwowy w Koszalinie: Słupsk.

47. Monitor Polski 1956 r., Numer 18, Pozycja 253, Artykuł 4, Numer 6, Punkt 1, Zarządzenie Finansów z dnia 13 lutego 1956r. w sprawie szczegółowego planowania pokrycia finansowego w zakresie inwestycji limitowych na rok 1956 (Management of finance of February 13, 1956, on the detailed planning of financial coverage for limited investments for 1956), 280, *Monitor Polski*, Dziennik Urzędowy Rzeczypospolitej Polskiej, http://www.monitorpolski.gov.pl/MP/1956/253/1.

48. Numer 1, 1946–1947, Protokoły z posiedzenia Gminnej Rady Narodowej, 1946–1947 (The minutes of the meeting of the Commune National Council, 1946–1947), 5–6, Gminna Rada Narodowa-w [Bursztyn], Oddział Ogólno-Organizacyjny, 1–74, Wojewódzki Archiwum Państwowy w Koszalinie: Słupsk.

49. Ibid.

50. Numer 14, 1953–1954. Protokoły z posiedzenia Prezydium Gminnej Rady Narodowej r., 1953–1954, (Minutes of the meeting of the Presidium of the Commune National Council, 1953–1954), 43, Prezydium Gminnej Rady Narodowej w [Bursztyn], Referat Ogólno-Administracyjny, 1–217, Wojewódzki Archiwum Państwowy w Koszalinie: Słupsk.

51. Numer 1, 1946–1947, Protokoły z posiedzenia Gminnej Rady Narodowej, 1946–1947 (The minutes of the meeting of the Commune National Council, 1946–1947), 72, Gminna Rada Narodowa-w [Bursztyn], Oddział Ogólno-Organizacyjny, 1–74, Wojewódzki Archiwum Państwowy w Koszalinie: Słupsk; Numer 3, 1948–1950, Protokoły i zarządzenia polustracyjne Zarządu Gminnego, 1948–1950 (Protocols and management requests of the Commune Board, 1948–1950), Gminna Rada Narodowo-Zarząd Gminnej w [Bursztyn], 3, Oddział Ogólno-Organizacyjny, Wojewódzki Archiwum Państwowy w Koszalinie: Słupsk, 1–46.

52. Numer 5, 1945–1946, Sprawozdanie z wykonaniu budżetu administracyjnego na rok 1945/46 (The report on the implementation of the administrative budget for the year 1945–1946), 20, Gminna Rada Narodowe-Zarząd Gminny w [Bursztyn], Oddział Finansowo Budżetowy, 1–29, Wojewódzki Archiwum Państwowy w Koszalinie: Słupsk; Numer 1, 1946–1947, Protokoły z posiedzenia Gminnej Rady Narodowej, 1946–1947 (The minutes of the meeting of the Commune National Council, 1946–1947), 11, 29, Gminna Rada Narodowa-w [Bursztyn], Oddział Ogólno-Organizacyjny, 1–74, Wojewódzki Archiwum Państwowy w Koszalinie: Słupsk.

53. Lampland, "Corvée," 17.

54. Dziennik Ustaw z 1947r., Numer 59, Pozycja 320, Artykuły 1–2, Dekret z dnia 12 września 1947 o pomocy sąsiedzkiej w rolnictwie (Decree of September 12, 1947, on neighborly help in agriculture), Dziennik Ustaw Rzeczypospolitej Polskiej, http://www.dziennikustaw.gov.pl /DU/1947/320/1.

55. Bücher, *Industrial Evolution*, 268–69; Kelen, "Reciprocity," 1296; Malinowski, *Diary in the Strict Sense*, 72.

56. Dziennik Ustaw z 1947r., Numer 59, Pozycja 320, Artykuł 1, Dekret z dnia 12 września 1947 o pomocy sąsiedzkiej w rolnictwie (Decree of September 12, 1947, on neighborly help in agriculture), Dziennik Ustaw Rzeczypospolitej Polskiej, http://www.dziennikustaw.gov.pl /DU/1947/320/1.

57. Numer 14, 1953–1954, Protokoły z posiedzenia Prezydium Gminnej Rady Narodowej r., 1953–1954 (Minutes of the meeting of the Presidium of the Commune National Council, 1953–1954), 86, Prezydium Gminnej Rady Narodowej w [Bursztyn], Referat Ogólno-Administracyjny, 1–217, Wojewódzki Archiwum Państwowy w Koszalinie: Słupsk.

58. Żurawski, *Zarys Dziejów*, 51.

59. Numer 40, 1947, Przebudowa Ustroju Rolnego (Rebuilding the Agricultural System), 66, Referat Rolnictwo i Reform Rolniczych, 1–72, Wojewódzki Archiwum Państwowy w Koszalinie: Słupsk; Dziennik Ustaw z 1947r., Numer 59, Pozycja 320, Artykuły 2–3, Dekret z dnia 12 września 1947 o pomocy sąsiedzkiej w rolnictwie. (Decree of September 12, 1947, on neighborly help in agriculture), Dziennik Ustaw Rzeczypospolitej Polskiej, http://www.dziennikustaw.gov .pl/DU/1947/320/1; Dziennik Ustaw z 1948r., Numer 11, Pozycja 89, Artykuł 1, Rozporządzenie Ministra Rolnictwa i Reform Rolnych z dnia 5 marca 1948r. wydane w porozumieniu z Ministrami: Administracji Publicznej, Ziem Odzyskanych, Obrony Narodowej, Poczt i Telegrafów oraz Leśnictwa w sprawie zwolnienia niektórych kategorii i posiadaczy gospodarstw rolnych od obowiązków świadczeń z tytułu pomocy sąsiedzkiej w rolnictwie (Regulation of the Minister of Agriculture and Agrarian Reform on March 5, 1948, issued in consultation with the Minister of Public Administration, Recovered Territories, National Defense, Posts and Telegraphs and Forestry on the exemption of certain categories of farms and holders from the tribute duties of neighborly help in agriculture), Dziennik Ustaw Rzeczypospolitej Polskiej, http://www .dziennikustaw.gov.pl/DU/1948/89/1.

60. Numer 40, 1947, Przebudowa Ustroju Rolnego (Rebuilding the Agricultural System), 66, Referat Rolnictwo i Reform Rolniczych, 1–72, Wojewódzki Archiwum Państwowy w Koszalinie: Słupsk; Dziennik Ustaw z 1947r., Numer 59, Pozycja 320, Artykuły 2–3, Dekret z dnia 12

września 1947 o pomocy sąsiedzkiej w rolnictwie (Decree of September 12, 1947, on neighborly help in agriculture), Dziennik Ustaw Rzeczypospolitej Polskiej, http://www.dziennikustaw.gov .pl/DU/1947/320/1; Dziennik Ustaw z 1948r., Numer 11, Pozycja 89, Artykuł 1, Rozporządzenie Ministra Rolnictwa i Reform Rolnych z dnia 5 marca 1948r. wydane w porozumieniu z Ministrami: Administracji Publicznej, Ziem Odzyskanych, Obrony Narodowej, Poczt i Telegrafów oraz Leśnictwa w sprawie zwolnienia niektórych kategorii i posiadaczy gospodarstw rolnych od obowiązków świadczeń z tytułu pomocy sąsiedzkiej w rolnictwie (Regulation of the Minister of Agriculture and Agrarian Reform on March 5, 1948, issued in consultation with the Minister of Public Administration, Recovered Territories, National Defense, Posts and Telegraphs and Forestry on the exemption of certain categories of farms and holders from the tribute duties of neighborly help in agriculture), Dziennik Ustaw Rzeczypospolitej Polskiej, http://www .dziennikustaw.gov.pl/DU/1948/89/1.

61. Blickle, "Frondienste/Scharwerk."
62. Blum, "Rise of Serfdom," 808.
63. Weber, *Agrarian Sociology*, 56–57.
64. Numer 13, 1953–1954, Protokoły z sesji Gminnej Rady Narodowej, 1953–1954r. (Minutes of the National Commune Council Sessions, 1953–1954), 7, Referat Ogólno-Administracyjny, 1–117, Wojewódzki Archiwum Państwowy w Koszalinie: Słupsk.
65. Numer 5, 1945–1946, Sprawozdanie z wykonanie budżetu administracyjnego na rok 1945/46 (The report on the implementation of the administrative budget for the year 1945–1946), 21, Gminna Rada Narodowe-Zarząd Gminny w [Bursztyn], Oddział Finansowo Budżetowy, 1–29, Wojewódzki Archiwum Państwowy w Koszalinie: Słupsk.
66. Thum, *Uprooted*, 127.
67. Bammer, "When Poland Was Home," 110.
68. Grossman, "Memory Objects," 142.
69. Mach, *Symbols*, 192.
70. Henare, Holbraad, and Wastell, "Introduction," 12; Buchli, *Archaeology of Socialism*, 24.
71. Grossman, "Memory Objects," 133.
72. See Humphrey, "Ideology of Infrastructure," 55; Grossman, "Memory Objects," 25.
73. Kenney, *Rebuilding Poland*, 29, 344.
74. Weber, *From Max Weber*, 78.

4 Magical Stalinism

In 1948 STALINISM arrived in Poland when a coup ousted Władysław Gomułka from power as the general secretary of the Polish Workers' Party (Polska Partia Robotnicza) and replaced him with Polish president Bolesław Bierut. Stalin, impatient with nationalist deviations from the Soviet model after his conflict with nationalist Yugoslav leader Josip Broz Tito that year, sought to remove Gomułka from public life and marginalize his socialist loyalists who wanted a "Polish road to socialism," one devoid of collectivized agriculture and Stalinized politics. With Gomułka out of the picture, Stalinist hard-liners like Hilary Minc scapegoated the *gomulkovshchina* doctrine, one that favored a slower transition from capitalism to socialism, as having encouraged the "battle for trade" by capitalist Poles who impeded the centralization of industry and agriculture during the Three-Year Plan (1947–1949). Shortages incurred by these enemies from the old capitalist regime could be reversed only by dekulakization (*rozkułaczanie*) and collectivization drives. In July 1950, at the Fifth Plenary Session of the Central Committee of the Polish United Workers Party, Bolesław Bierut sold a Stalinist vision: "There has never been and there is no more beautiful, splendid, more creative and inspiring aspiration in the history of man than the idea of the complete liberation of man from all oppression and slavery."[1] After the completion of this new Six-Year Plan (1950–1955), modeled on the Soviet First Five-Year Plan (1928–1932) that had nationalized agriculture and industry across the Soviet Union, all economic estuaries would finally flow into the collective sea of the Soviet command economy. Poland, renamed the Polish People's Republic after the passage of the 1952 constitution based on the Soviet model, would achieve liberation only through the adoption of Stalin's colonial utopia.

These were magical times for Poland. Soviet-style Stakhanovite propaganda in the Polish state media praised proletarian heroines (*przodownice pracy*) with superhuman physical power and strength of will who went above and beyond the state production plan out of zeal for the revolution.[2] Officials were encouraged and valorized for their ability to devise creative solutions to problems or sometimes even circumvent the law, all in the spirit of carrying out the revolution. In 1953 when the national authorities were recruiting men for the security apparatus, Vice Minister of Public Security Jan Ptasiński stated in a speech that the new recruits must have "operational kombinacja" (*kombinacja operacyjna*), meaning that they should be creative and flexible in their methods to absorb the shock of chaos wrought by Stalinist collectivization and nationalization, but in a way that expressed their loyalty to the state.[3] Curiously, years later, an analogous claim was made in the Russian context, when Leonid Brezhnev, general secretary of the Central Committee of the Communist Party of the Soviet Union from 1964 to 1982, was described as the "engineer of the soul of the party" and the "sober kombinator of the forces of power" that solidified his "stay at the Olympus of the Kremlin."[4] State kombinacja operating in the spirit of the revolution in Poland became critical to the exercise of Soviet power from the national to the local level of the state.

In the midst of this Soviet spirit possession, the cunning capitalist enemy (*wróg*), pulling Poland back into the abyss of backwardness and exploitation, would have to be purged from the nationalization of industry and agriculture. New socialist work discipline laws sought to oust the state enemies who lurked in state workplaces and who found private profit in "faulty production" (*brakoróbstwo*). A 1950 law led to the imprisonment of 44,440 workers (21 percent of all convictions that year) for leaving the factory during the workday, lowering production, absenteeism, and other "crimes" like drunkenness. By 1952, another 46,700 people were sentenced to labor camps (*lagry*) after being charged with vaguely defined "office crimes," "actions against the state monopoly," as well as "plunder and appropriation of public property."[5] Socialist property laws fined and imprisoned anyone who engaged in "self-proprietorship, or extract[ed] collective goods in any way." New workers recruited from the liquidated private sector and those who looked for employment "with an eye for social benefits" such as "cheaper apartment rent, electricity, fat coupons, etc." were especially suspicious of crimes against socialism.[6] These purges of capitalist elements had little to do with evidence of crimes or solving the postwar shortage crisis; they were intended to repress antistate thoughts and intentions. All new proletarians were required to report found resources, property, or materials to the state and transfer all workplace innovations to state ownership.[7] There would be no opportunities or space for accidental innovation and creative thought within the command economy. All shortages traced back to capitalist sabotage rather than faulty design in the supply chains; all state property, including proletarian bodies and minds, belonged to Father Stalin.

When Stalinist policies descended down on the Polish countryside, they refracted like beams of light hitting water. At the Fifth Plenum in July 1950, Hilary Minc, the architect of the Six-Year Plan, shared his vision for a "social transformation of the village" through a "transition on a voluntary basis from small, scattered individual peasant economy to a socialist, collective economy."[8] The collectivization of agricultural production would entail the creation of Stalinist state farms (*sovkhozy*), composed of agricultural laborers who lived year-round on them and received small land plots for subsistence, and collective farms (*kolkhozy*), formed out of independent peasant farms. To soothe reactionary fears against Soviet-style collectivization that entailed the mass expropriation of peasant property and political purges, communists rebranded the sovkhozy as state agricultural farms (*państwowe gospodarstwo rolne*) and the kolkhozy as agricultural production cooperatives (*rolnicze spółdzielnie produkcyjne*).[9] Collectivization however, was not new to the Six-Year Plan. In his 1948 Politburo speech to the Polish United Workers' Party (Polska Zjednoczona Partia Robotnicza), Minc had already called for an end to independent peasant farming riddled with "rich peasants," called *kułaks* (after the Russian word *kulak*). He called for small (*biedniak*) and middle (*średniak*) peasants to organize and collectivize their land to compete against these rural capitalist farmers wealthy enough to employ labor.[10] The widespread failure of early collectivization drives across central and eastern Poland led to the arrests of tens of thousands of resistant peasants and further food shortages. Kułak farmers abandoned their land for wage labor in the city and left it to state and collective farms to cultivate on their own account. To escape collectivization, they mutated into model proletarians.

Communists sought to purge the kułaks to satisfy Minc's Stalinist doctrine, but in reality, the state needed successful peasant farmers to produce food for the industrializing socialist cities. To keep kułaks tied to their land, Minc's reformulated Six-Year Plan included a compromise but with Stalinist political undertones: collectivized and uncollectivized peasants would be required to meet mandatory agricultural quotas, called *kontyngenty*, that incorporated the peasantry into the command economy's supply chains. Anyone with more than a hectare of land would produce unsubsidized milk, livestock, potato, and grain quotas that they would be mandated by law to sell to the state at fixed prices.[11] This quota system represented a new "fraternal cooperation of workers and peasants" that linked agricultural production in the villages with industrial growth in the cities. Whether they chose to collectivize or not, peasants' formal role would be to feed the new proletarian masses.[12] Uncollectivized kułaks who fared better than the rest would be subjected to higher taxes and state quotas. The transition to the quota system was challenging even for successful peasants who chose independent farming. In the autumn of 1952 tens of thousands of peasants who failed to deliver their quotas were arrested by the secret police across Poland.[13] Still, this flexible new path to collectivization in the Six-Year Plan allowed Polish agriculture in the southern and eastern provinces—which were not affected by border changes and where the peasants still owned their land from the prewar capitalist era—to retain its "private" character.

In the Recovered Territories, however, the beam of light pierced right through. Widespread collectivization ensued. State farms, converted from of German Junker estates, covered 10 percent of the total territory.[14] Some had been formed as early as 1945, shortly after the Red Army had marched through the German lands and rid it of the German aristocratic class on the estates. Bolstered by a Red Army presence, the communists were a much stronger force in the western territories than in the rest of Poland because of the enormous volume of resources the state had poured (and was still pouring) into the colonization process since the late stages of the war. Early settlers' cooperatives founded during resettlement that provided services like re-Polonization classes were perfect incubators for educating villagers about collective farms. The demographic makeup was completely different. Villages were more ethnically fractured and less networked than in the older Polish lands. People were still on the move; the expulsion was ongoing while new peasant settlers had not yet received their land titles. This gave the authorities the power to make tectonic shifts in land and people to fit a collective model, with the Red Army capable of stifling any resistance.[15] Peasants who had not yet been given their *Akt nadania* titles to the land distributed to them under the 1946 agrarian reform were coerced by their local officials into collectivizing their German land grants.[16] By 1952 the lands boasted two thousand collective farms spanning 486,000 hectares, which had been created out of more than fifty thousand peasant farms.[17] By 1954, nearly 76 percent of all collective farms in Poland were located in this region.[18] The Recovered Territories resembled Soviet Russia more than the rest of Poland.

Communists had to come up with a political justification to situate this widespread collectivization across the Recovered Territories in line with Minc's vision of "voluntary" collectivization in the Six-Year Plan. They attributed it to the fact that most of the peasant pioneers in the western lands were repatriated from the east where they had been exposed to the "higher" form of agriculture during Soviet collectivization drives in 1940–1941. Historical processes beyond peasants' control had already disconnected them from their "old methods" like using horse-drawn ploughs and primitive tools still used in the eastern and southern provinces.[19] After the successful Third-Year Plan (1947–1949), agrarian reform had solved petty property disputes in the western territories. Peasants were pacified. The modernization of villages with electricity, industry, education, cultural centers, roads, and railways was already "protecting them from capitalist exploitation by increasing production, elevating farming technologically, and elevating its welfare."[20] Peasants were evolved enough for the next stage of Soviet modernization.

If collectivization truly were voluntary, then how could pioneer peasants who had just arrived to recover the lost Polish western lands, many of whom were escaping collectivization in the east, reorient themselves so quickly to the east as Stalin's peasants? How could they come to terms with the reality that the very state that had just allotted them German land grants following the postwar agrarian reform—land that they themselves could not alter, abandon, or sell—was now waging dekulakization purges against their so-called capitalist enrichment tendencies? Was there any resistance? Were these peasants possessed by magical Stalinism? What kinds of benefits did collectivization provide for this newly formed peasantry? If collectivization was not voluntary, then how did the commune officials form collective farms?

Masquerade

Trying to understand the process of collectivization in a place like Bursztyn is like navigating history with a compass that has gone haywire. Flipping through local archives one day, I came across a peculiar document. It was an anonymous Commune State Council (Gminna Rada Narodowa) report from an August 1953 commune session in Bursztyn that officially announced the beginning of the mandatory quotas system. By then, Stalin had already died of a heart attack, Bierut had died of suicide or poisoning in Moscow, and the Ninth Plenum had already accepted the failures of nationwide collectivization and drawn up plans for a post-Stalinist agricultural policy. Dekulakization campaigns and the entire rhetoric of collectivization came to Bursztyn when everywhere else Stalinism was falling apart. Whether the state archives really marked the beginning of mandatory quotas in August 1953 or if this was a recitation of rhetoric by local officials under some kind of surveillance by higher officials is unclear from the text. The report, however, was special because it introduced quotas as a measure to purge the kombinators:

> The People's Republic is providing steps in the direction of shortening specula-tion, reducing black marketeers and disabling the enrichment of kułaks in the village by introducing mandatory quotas of grain, livestock, milk, potatoes, that have the objective of . . . holding up speculation and forcing of kułaks, kombinators and those peasants who are in this era, for the national economy, not meeting their citizen duties, and sometimes even their own farms, in the meeting of their duties within the State—We will not allow for this, for some dishonest citizens and speculators to disregard their duties to the State and to the legitimate and patriotic mass of peasants, in order to create difficulties in providing [food] for the cities.[21]

Astonishingly, it was the first and only mention of kombinacja in a state archive that I had ever seen from the postwar period. My survey of Poland's legislative journal from 1944 to 1989 revealed no specific laws against kombinators or kombinacja. Nor were there any theoretical doctrines about the role of the kombinator in Stalinist society that I could find. Indeed, I had come across soft power concepts like operational kombinacja and kombinacja as a state tactic to embed Stalinism in everyday life, but here was physical proof that the "bad" kombinator was a threat to the state. Here was this Ostap Bender figure from the Soviet novels wreaking havoc on the countryside; his capitalist antics had to be eliminated through these mandatory quotas. Stalinist ideology and its unraveling in Bursztyn was understood through this folkloric figure.

I also suspected that I knew the anonymous author of the report after I compared some linguistic quirks to that of a decorated local communist whom I interviewed during fieldwork. It was possibly written by Motylek, who had been the presiding officer in charge of representing the national interests and law of the state in the commune during the Stalinist era. Curiously, during our interview, he proudly recalled how as the presiding officer he had to dabble in the arts of kombinacja to ensure that the local state apparatus ran smoothly even on a very low budget. His kombinacja was dedicated to miraculously preserving the formal apparatus of the socialist state. Yet in the report, the kombinators were a scourge bunched in with the kułaks and the peasants! This contrasted with Zofia's memories of authorities like Houdini being the bad kombinators who distorted the socialist revolution by saddling peasants with feudal labor and tithes. How peculiar that the political discourse of kombinacja reemerged at the same time in villagers' memories and in the state archives, and as a means of both subverting and supporting socialism. What function did this practice and discourse play in the genesis of collectivization in Bursztyn? Was kombinacja a vestige of the capitalist past or was it key to the making of a Stalinist future?

Peasant memories of the quotas ran deep; they marked the first encounter with Stalinism. Radosław, a Polish peasant who lived in Podwoda village with his peasant mother, recalled that the very history of the territories began with the mandatory quota system: "Here, the formation of our Polish history is composed of agriculture. Oppression, mandatory quotas, every potato: 'Allocate to the state!,' pig: 'Allocate to the state!' And how heavy the fine was!" To the Polish peasantry, the imposition of quotas was a significant historical event because it brought back memories of the Nazi occupation, when they had had to produce such quotas for the Third Reich. The reimposition of quotas to supply food to the proletarian masses and the Council for Mutual Economic Assistance (Rada Wzajemnej Pomocy Gospodarczej) marked the moment of Soviet occupation in the countryside. However, to write about collectivization in Bursztyn is to suspend all notions of time. The chronology of historical events that occurred in the rest of the region and the country did not apply. Peasant and archive narratives did not always align, and history played tricks on the eyes. When the mandatory quotas started and ended when the collective farms began is still unclear to me. What matters is that in the peasant recollection, quotas came first, collective farms came second. Both materialized out of thin air, and few could recall how they really got there.

While mandatory agricultural quotas in Minc's Six-Year Plan were intended as a response to shortages wrought by failed collectivization drives in eastern and southern Poland and as a way to incorporate both collectivized and uncollectivized peasants into the command economy, in Bursztyn, mandatory quotas first arrived as economic blackmail: they were a way for officials to burden peasant pioneers, or so-called kułaks, with quotas, feudal taxes, and labor obligations as a means to pressure them to collectivize. Mandatory quotas were the halfway house between independent and collective farming. The state's dual introduction of mandatory quotas and the dekulakization drives occupied a distinct era in peasant memories when their lives teetered on the precipice of collectivization. By law, mandatory quotas applied to anyone, kułak or not, who occupied more than a hectare of land. So what function did the "kułak" purge play?

In theory, kułaks were rich bourgeois peasants who owned at least five hectares of land and were wealthy enough to employ labor on their farms. In these territories dominated by "middle peasants" with five to fifty hectares of land, everyone was technically a kułak, even the officials. The same officials who had distributed land to the settlers, allocated the largest parcels for themselves, and employed German labor on their own land were also the ones responsible for purging the kułaks from the territories. To align themselves with Stalinist ideology, many altered their land grants to slightly less than a hectare to exempt themselves from both the mandatory quotas and the kułak class category. Officials deployed the kułak rhetoric to claim land and labor for the state. They observed those who practiced superior extraction techniques and resource management, were productive, wore nicer clothes, "fared better," possessed an "economic mentality," owned three cows or two horses, and/or had multiple wagons. However, villagers recalled that there were no parameters for what made someone a kułak. Weronika, a Polish machine operator recalled her brother's shock at being called a kułak: "I am a 'kułak,' but I have poverty at home!" During interviews, peasants, who had arrived as pioneers, often repeated the phrase in disbelief, "And then they made us into kułaks!" Fidelis argued that the term was used by the commune to set economic restrictions on those who were a political threat to the officials or who could one day replace them. German workers who cultivated a half hectare of land and knew they were soon to be expelled from the country were burdened with quotas, enrichment taxes and tithes because they were so-called kułaks. Arena recalled that peasants like herself from the Ukrainian minority, who were forcibly settled by the State Repatriation Office (Państwowy Urząd Repatriacyjny) in a colony (*kolonia*) on the village outskirts, were called kułaks because their colony had rich soil and the commune wanted political justification for absorbing it into a collective farm. State officials played on ethnic tensions to create factions within the peasantry. Ukrainian and Belarusian peasants who received small land grants because they had arrived after many of the Polish settlers from central Poland were often promised party positions and other perks to turn against the Polish kułaks and form collective farms. The kułak rhetoric provided the local state with the political lubricant to jump-start the collectivization drive and make drastic shifts to land, labor, and capital that it had just redistributed through the postwar agrarian reform.

The irony of the dekulakization drive is that it repressed the very class of middle peasants that it depended on to meet mandatory production quotas. Polish peasants were already subjected to myriad bizarre taxes like the "FOR" (full name unknown) and "enrichment tax" (*wzbogacenie*), a penalty for settling the lands voluntarily out of opportunistic greed.[22] These "kułaks" that Bursztyn's officials themselves had created through the redistribution of German land grants were excluded from state agricultural credits and were forced to secure their own tools, fertilizers, and seeds. That they had to find their own capital to jump-start their state production plans was a form of taxation too. For instance, to meet the milk and livestock quotas, Zofia's husband Konrad returned to his home village in the Kielce region of southern Poland to bring back a family cow. He also returned with his father, who helped him demolish an abandoned German home and reconstruct a barn to hold the quota harvests. While many Polish settlers still had family connections to the old Polish lands, Ukrainian and Belarusian minorities had no chance of a return home and lacked the privilege of mobility to secure resources. While the dekulakization drives were intended to rid the village of farmers out to enrich themselves, it was actually the state that enriched itself the most by shifting the burden of subsidizing production onto the peasantry and sucking all capital out of independent farming.

Peasants saw the introduction of mandatory quotas and the "kułak" purges as the state's brutal colonization of independent farming in the Recovered Territories. One feature of this colonization was its irrational imposition of quotas without consideration for local ecological conditions. Each peasant family with a hectare of land or more had to produce fifty kilograms of grain and one hundred kilograms of livestock per hectare, regardless of the soil quality on their land, their family size, or the availability of seeds and other necessary machinery. Hiring outside labor was illegal on peasant farms because that was a sign of bourgeois kułak inclinations, and thus peasant families were chained to their land grants without wages or any other state subsidies to help pay for fertilizers and seeds. Peasants had to sell their cereal, potato, and livestock quotas seasonally and milk quotas weekly to the state. There were various rules about what counted as a quota. For example, peasants were forbidden to feed livestock twenty-four hours before selling them. Such rules were very constraining for resource-strapped peasants. Last-minute feeding of the livestock to reach the weight quota was much more cost effective for peasants than the amount of food it would take to grow the livestock to the required weight over a longer duration of time. A potato quota required months of hard labor to fulfill, but the payment that peasants received for it from the state was not worth more than a quarter liter of vodka (made out of low-quality processed potatoes) at the local state store. Fidelis called this irrational system "the plunder economy" (*rabunkowa gospodarka*), based on fast extraction and exploitation, not long-term sustainability.

Peasants transported their quotas on horse-drawn wagons to the newly constructed "Peasants' Self-Help" Commune Cooperative (Gminna Spółdzielnia "Samopomoc Chłopska"), located along the German tombstone road in Bursztyn. There, the GS workers weighed the quotas and state inspectors bought the quotas at fixed prices well below the market rate. After they sold their mandatory quotas to GS, the peasants then received a receipt, which they took to the commune headquarters down the street to clear their quota obligation balance. The GS consolidated the quotas in the commune and subcontracted some of the raw materials to the state's local processing sites to produce bread, butter, and meat, which were sold in the commune's state stores.[23] The commune then delivered the remaining quota further down the supply chain to the county level, which was pooled and delivered to the provincial level, then to the national level, and finally to the Council for Mutual Economic Assistance (Rada Wzajemnej Pomocy Gospodarczej).

The state's archival records of quota production are deeply troubling. A 1953 commune report in Bursztyn boasted that its peasants had "contracted" around 2 million złoty more quota value to the state than they had in 1952 (a date that conflicted with the previous report that supposedly introduced mandatory quotas in Bursztyn in August 1953) and that they had sold around 144,000 złoty more of their quotas to the state than in the previous year. It gave the false impression that the peasants wanted to give more than their quotas out of zealousness. It praised not peasants' ingenuity in meeting quotas, but the state's own successful efforts in "repressing speculation, lowering free marketeers, and disabling the enrichment of kułaks" that had increased quota yields and contributed to national development. To celebrate this achievement, the report claimed that the commune would increase peasant cereal and potato quotas by 10 percent for the following season.[24] The report's tone shifted dramatically when it came to the "lack of mass-political work" that caused peasants to meet only 60 percent of the livestock quota and only 21 percent of the milk quota in 1953. These shortages were caused by "resistant elements" (*elementy oporne*). Lacking education in socialist work discipline, peasants were "working how they want and [with] what makes them comfortable." The solution, it claimed, was to increase the number of pro-state "agitators" in the village to build peasant "trust in the Committee." Curiously, the report also attacked the workers at the milk quota points: "The milk purchase points are not controlled and workers are working in whatever way they fancy." Control, according to the commune, was the key to lessening shortages, as "the toleration toward speculators and kułaks will increase the audacity of enemy elements" (*wrogich elementów*).[25] Without stronger party leadership and a broader network of agitators, the commune report announced that the masses would further disconnect themselves from the state.[26] In the archives, the quotas were never meticulously logged, nor were there any serious discussions about solutions.

While the state archives recited the rhetoric of socialist modernization, quota production in Bursztyn did not eliminate or replace feudal obligations. Instead, officials used neighborly help as a means to pressure peasants to pool their resources to help the state workplaces in the commune meet unrealistic quota production plans. According to a new 1950 neighborly help law, the commune was legally obliged to compensate neighborly help in the form of labor, machine rental, or horse transport on commune land with rye.[27] (In 1959 neighborly help would formally become waged labor.[28]) However, that was not what happened in Bursztyn. There was one case in the archives where the commune had sent a brigade of peasant laborers to "help" the state forestry division meet its increased logging quota by transporting wood with their own wagons and horses.[29] At an open quorum meeting in 1953, a peasant, Czesław, stood up and demanded compensation to fix the damage that transporting wood had done to his wagon and feed for his horse that had nothing to eat. Another peasant, Bartłomiej, complained about a delay in receiving the barley crop that the forestry director had promised from the shared forestry-commune fields as compensation for the lumber export brigades. At the meeting, the forestry director responded that the peasants had told him they did not want the "expensive" barley. In Bursztyn, neighborly help did not entitle peasants to compensation as per the law; it only gave them access to state barley for sale, which explains why peasants did not want to pay for it. They were already performing double duty by producing quotas on their own farms and providing unpaid labor for quota production in state workplaces. In-kind compensation would have certainly helped peasants reinvest capital into their farms toward quota production. Officials played with lives by exploiting the interstices between the feudal and socialist systems to extract labor, time, and capital from the peasantry.

Open quorum meetings in 1953 and 1954 were filled with peasants begging authorities for quota reductions. Failed harvests landed families in poverty. Time and again, peasants' pleas to receive permission to abandon their land or pay lower property taxes were rejected. Instead of providing economic relief, officials called for more activism to mobilize peasants into neighborly help among themselves, meaning to help support one another through quota shortages.[30] This was both a poverty-reduction measure and punishment for not meeting the quota. Radosław's neighbor Zygmunt, a Belarusian peasant in Podwoda village, recalled that peasants faced "neighborly help" penalties for incomplete quotas. "If he did not give wheat or milk—there were a myriad of responsibilities. Those were the times that when one had a horse and wagon, one had to transport wood out of the forest because there was no storage. It was a responsibility to [transport] this and that amount, or the fine counted as this and that." Although the archives valorized the modernization of the peasantry when they met the quotas, the reality was that the state continued to use feudal obligations—"heavy fines," as Radosław put it—to punish the peasantry for deviating from state plans. There was even some talk among officials about confiscating and nationalizing farms that were altogether poorly productive; however, it was Houdini who pushed back during a January 1953 commune meeting between officials, claiming, "There ought to be no purging from the farms, that is the law. The farms have been given to the people as ownership and they are inheritable, and we will not liquidate anyone, because that is not our property, and whoever abandons the farms will be held accountable."[31] What compelled the most despised communist in Bursztyn to push back on forced nationalization of peasant land? It was one of those curious cases where peasants in the open quorum meetings wanted change to alleviate their misery while the leading communist pushed to retain the agrarian structure of independent farming. In doing so, Houdini may have been the last bastion of opposition to collectivization, but he prolonged the misery of those who truly could not meet the quota. People died. In Bursztyn's cemetery, there is an entire section of small graves of infants who never made it through these very sinister years of the early 1950s.

The kombinator figure was born out of these desperate conditions. Left without investment capital or state support, the peasants learned to perform magic tricks to meet the state's irrational regime of domination and spaces of mobility within the rigid structures of the command economy. "There was a lot of poverty, and so people had to use kombinacja. Everyone, everywhere," Zofia recalled. Evading the plan became the only way to stay alive. Peasants began to shift the burden of subsidizing agricultural production over to the state. To ensure that the state would subsidize its own production quotas, peasants stole potatoes and cereal harvests from the nearest state farm fields and sold them to the GS as their quota. They raised more beef than pork because cattle grew faster, did not consume farm fodder, and could "wander" onto the commune's fields to eat state grass. They purchased lower-quality produce on the black market, likely stolen from the state farms, and sold it to the GS while retaining and selling high-quality goods they produced on the farm for higher prices on the black market. They paid off inspectors to dilute the milk with water and accept pre-fed livestock at GS points. This was not unique to Bursztyn. Peasants all over Poland "juggled their deliveries, cheated on land records, or used judiciously placed bribes to keep local officials from becoming too curious."[32] How else were they supposed to replenish their livestock, fix their machines, and feed their own children for the next round of mandatory quotas? Peasants did not adopt kombinacja to destroy the quota system; rather, they deployed its strategies to meet their quotas and stave off starvation.

The rigidity of the mandatory quotas gave peasants a formal state system they could easily identify and work around through informal economic networks. A black market emerged not as a physical space in a market place, but as an archipelago of hiding spots. A lot happened at night. "They [peasants] had these 'receivers on the left' [*lewych odbiorców*]. They made plans, and he took the [meat] and left it somewhere, and then someone [picked it up] and it was this kind of kombinacja," Zofia recalled. Transactions did not occur on the spot. Rather, the peasant (or worker) left something somewhere "by chance" that was later "picked up" by the receiver. The seller and buyer were never together in the same location, nor did the payment occur immediately; rather, the arrangement could be consummated years later when the buyer wanted a favor from the seller, and so on. The state knew that peasants were selling higher-quality yields on the black or "free market" (*wolny rynek*), so it introduced a grading system by which peasants could sell their higher-quality produce for higher prices at the GS.[33] It also offered to buy any surplus quotas at those higher prices. The state called these prices "premium" (*premia*), but locals called it "free hand" (*wolna ręka*), because they were allowed only after the peasants had freed their hands of their quota shackles. However, peasants rarely sold their surplus to the state because there was rarely any surplus, and when it did exist, they wanted to control their own prices and forge economic relationships outside of the command economy.

The tentacles of the black market reached all of the spaces of the state's supply chain. Even if a peasant met his livestock quota, slaughterhouse workers fixed the scales at the GS and sold the meat on the black market to peasants who could not meet their meat quota, to hungry workers in the villages and the cities, and even to officials who also could not escape local conditions. A worker "stole and had these receivers [*odbiorcy*], and so he kombinował at work. He stole from the state and sold it cheaper over there and put the money into his pocket. And it was the state's because the state paid for the piglets, the livestock, no? And it needed to account for it," Zofia said. The black market in the GS became a feedback loop that nourished the worker and peasant villagers who lived in poverty. The real fraternal cooperation between workers and peasants was not in their efforts to produce for the socialist revolution, but in their emerging unspoken alliance in ensuring that villagers, not the state, had control over how much food stayed in the village and how much of it was exported to the RWPG.

Fraternal cooperation existed alongside mistrust and betrayal. Spontaneous inspections became common as the state and its Volunteer Reserve Militia (Ochotnicza Rezerwa Milicji Obywatelskiej) of villagers attempted to "find" these spaces of quota evasion. Weronika, a Polish peasant from East Prussia, recalled that she was frequently subjected to surveillance by local officials: "It was like this: one saved some for oneself, for the pigs, for the horse. And [one day]—when I was out farming!—he [official] came after me upstairs! And he looked around to see how much of the grain there was! I said, 'So you see, sir, I have to feed the horses, the pigs, sowing—what am I going to purchase with that later?!'" A Ukrainian peasant named Maria also recalled that a female friend with whom she was walking home after Sunday mass one afternoon announced an inspection and went upstairs to inspect Maria's attic for hidden harvests. When she found four tons of grain, she ordered Maria to sell it to the state. Others recalled how ORMO villagers (*ormowcy*) would come up to their windows and peer into their private lives, looking for infractions of the rules.

Commune officials too were under extraordinary pressure to adjust quotas to local conditions and to supply food to the industrializing cities with their proletarian workforces. Although forced inspections of peasant farms were illegal and subject to penalties, there were reports of officials imprisoning kułak suspects to confiscate their quotas. Motylek, the Stalinist official, explained the pressure to stay in line with forced threshing:

> There was a committee meeting where we would talk about the kułaks. There was this activist who held anger toward his neighbor and said that he was evading his quota. The commune had to force it out [*wymusić*] because he is a kułak, that he does not want to, he is defiant, and does not want to give away his cereals. And then what? The committee said to the Party leader: "You must organize people, machines, and force it out of him." And that peasant had already been imprisoned. The Ministry of Public Security [Urząd Bezpieczeństwa] had already imprisoned him. Yes, we had to thresh his farm. And even more so, I stood guard so that not one kilogram went "to the left" [*na lewo*]. We threshed the field clean and we weighed it in front of the committee board. We threshed eight quintals of grain but he had twelve as his quota. After the threshing, his wife comes up to me and says, "Presiding officer, can you, sir, give me a testimony? I have to take this to the UB so that maybe they can release him. We cannot give that much. If we give away those eight quintals, then what are we going to live off of?" I wrote it for the woman who went to the UB. They did not have an option, because I wrote, "Wrongly imprisoned, cannot untie himself [*wywiązać*] from this quota" and that he only had to return two quintals to the state. Six quintals he could save for himself for sustenance. Before they let him go, the prosecutor calls and asks: "Presiding officer, for what does the Polish state give you the stamp [of authority]?" I responded, "So that, so that, I would confirm, confirm with the stamp, the compatibility with the written word." So I thought that the UB would come for me, and lock me up! But bullshit! They did not come! They let the peasant go. He hugged me by the knees and thanked me!

State officials punished suspected peasants for evading quotas, but they too employed evasive and creative strategies to protect themselves and preserve power. "It seems to me that every individual should rule his own house—the legal structures had to be avoided but delicately," Motylek added. Indeed, archives from 1954 show that the state eventually responded to peasant pleas by decreasing their milk and potato quotas as well as leasing out state livestock to the poorest peasants to raise and then return to the state as their quota obligation.[34] But there was also another level of evasion at play: falsifying accounts. When Motylek told his county-level superior that the village had met 80 percent of the quota, he said, "How he hit his fist down on the desk! How the ink jumped from the casing and spilled all over the desk! I remember it like it was today! And he said 'What? 80 percent? You have to report you have 100 percent!' This is what discussions were like!" Falsifying quotas hid black market tracks because when commune and county officials claimed that they had reached the quota plan, the provincial and national authorities could not trace the source of the shortages. State officials adopted these evasive tactics to perform for the state even as they informally reformed it. The state archives became incredibly unreliable because they displayed socialist performance on paper rather than reality.

In hindsight, Motylek recalled to me: "The quotas were a bane for peasants. It was a bloody pillory that was mandatory. People were bloody agonizing about it and if it were not for the quotas, then people would have a different view of the entire government. Those quotas butchered those peasants. It was the worst torture!" The quota system that converted peasant farms into a state unit of production and parallel dekulakization campaigns that further repressed the middle peasants were tragic on many levels. They destroyed the Piast myth that branded the Recovered Territories as the land of opportunity and self-determination for the postwar Polish nation. They were carried out by the officials who were the largest landowners in the village and ultimately enriched the state. They destroyed the more resourceful middle peasant class whom the state needed to produce mandatory quotas. The political repression of the peasantry was a tremendous waste of state resources that could have been used to bolster quotas and keep peasants on farms, not in prisons. If peasants could have hired labor, managed their quota size, and received support from the state, the system would have been much more legitimate in their eyes and would have strengthened the command economy. Instead, the state's failures to reform fueled a nascent black market economy that evaded the state's gaze to feed the population. Memories of quota production feature prominently in peasants' recollections because quotas were a stepping-stone to collectivization and marked the peasants' collapse under Stalinism. However, they equally marked the moment when villagers resurrected the wartime strategy of kombinacja to alter their fates and fortify alternative resource flows that diverted raw resources and labor away from the Soviet "plunder economy."

Trickster States

According to reports in the commune archives, Soviet collectivization drives arrived in Bursztyn in January 1953, before the introduction of mandatory quotas in August 1953.[35] This chronology fit into the Six-Year Plan model, but not into the era of quota production prior to the formation of the collective farm so vividly remembered by the peasants and the former officials. A commune report of a meeting among officials from January 1953 recorded the minutes of a speech made by an activist named "W.M." from Słupsk's County Committee of the Polish United Workers' Party (Komitet Powiatowy Polskiej Zjednoczonej Partii Robotniczej) that laid out the grand vision for the collectivization program and the countryside's new role in the command economy:

> W.M. said that the Agricultural Production Cooperative is a farm with a higher level of production that gives benefits for the members of the collective and the State. In this way, the People's Poland gives the possibility of building a new life, a life that allows for the working peasant a better assemblage of material and cultural life. Villages that are established on the foundations of the Production Cooperative will eliminate the exploitation of small and medium peasants from the kułak elements and will strengthen the worker-peasant alliance, a foundation of the People's Authority in Poland. And we here in Bursztyn have the possibility of setting up an Agricultural Production Cooperative, so let us not waiver, and get to work, and the People's Poland will help us.[36]

After the speech, there were philosophical discussions about the function of the collective farm in the modernization of the villagers. Citizen Grabowski explained that these cooperatives were a "different technique for buttering people up [to labor], raising them anew." Echoing Bierut's rhetoric, Grabowski added, "The person who in his work employs the newest techniques and expertise, as well as in his private life, orients himself toward enlightenment and culture, and understanding its meaning, becomes a person who is enlightened and cultured. Everything is telling us that we cannot stay in a dead end, because we are entering into a new year of life that will lead us to new paths."[37] Collectivization was intended to level economic disparities among peasants and create a single peasant class earning wages on collective farms. By abandoning the backward methods of independent farming, peasants become modern. Citizen Jan, however, warned that there were forces at play that would jeopardize this enlightenment project: "On our terrain there are lurking many discrepancies [*rozbieżności*] in setting up an agricultural production cooperative and we will have to be more forceful in putting these people on the just path who are still hesitating."[38] Thirty-five percent of villagers supported collectivization, and an overwhelming "65 percent were enemy elements [*wrogi element*] that were only looking to intervene."[39] Then Houdini, the military official, suggested how the cooperative would take shape in the midst of these obstacles: "In these days, we will inform the people en masse and will set up the Agricultural Production Cooperative. And our efforts will probably come true, because on our terrain we have many active people on whom we can depend, who will enter the Agricultural Production Cooperative, and in their steps, others will follow."[40] Instead of waiting for the peasants to see the light, the commune would guide them into it. State activists would enter production cooperatives and persuade the hesitant peasants to "choose" to collectivize.

The voluntary aspect of collectivization was key because it both gave the peasants the sense that the production process would be in their control and placed the onus on them to come up with capital to fund the creation of the farm. Once peasants decided to collectivize, they would have to invite the representatives of the county's party committee and other official delegates to present their determination and receive permission to start up a collective farm.[41] Once they received permission to pool their land grants, they pooled monetary and in-kind shares like machines and livestock into a collective farm fund. They used that fund to buy or rent machines, seeds, and fertilizers from the commune to produce the farm's grain, flax, potato, linen, beets, livestock, and dairy quotas, which were adjusted annually by the centralized government.[42] They then sold them to the GS at prices fixed by the state, just as they did when they were independent peasants. They redistributed the profits as wages and pooled a portion to rent or buy more capital from the commune for the next production cycle. Ultimately, peasants' function as quota producers for the state did not change; they still had to pool their own resources to fund the quota production process. However, the collective farm model would link communes into the nationalized system of agricultural production much like the economically robust state farms nearby that received a seemingly limitless stream of agricultural capital from their centralized supply chains. It would provide access to state subsidies that members could use to buy state seeds, fertilizers, and pesticides, and they could rent agricultural machines. The greatest appeal of the collective farm, however, was that it would unburden peasants from the individual mandatory quotas and all of the other tax and labor obligations they paid to the state. Zofia and Konrad could finally relieve themselves of those eleven hectares for which they paid high taxes. Collectivization provided a path out of feudalism, but at a price. By relinquishing themselves of their independent farms, peasants would subjugate themselves to their corrupt officials, and subjugate the countryside to the cause of urban industrialization.

To execute Houdini's collectivization plan, officials recruited activists to travel across the commune lands and persuade (*namawiać*) its villages to collectivize. Fidelis, a forestry worker at the time whom Cezary, the forestry director, had recruited as an activist, explained to me how activists and their superiors recited the script of collectivization to peasants without believing in it:

> For the activist, it was the most difficult thing to set up those collective farms. Sometimes you needed to say what you needed to say in order to set it up. Anything to overthrow dissent. We talked about what they ordered us to talk about. "That this is good. That this is a collective! That it will be your ownership only! And that you will farm alone! That you will live just like now! That they will not be squeezing you with taxes! That you will pay to the collective! That they will

not take bread! You do not have to give away this and that!" We said it all! But the director and I, we talked among ourselves about the subject: "What? [Collective farms] will be even worse! The peasants are doing fine just as they are."

Fidelis was sent to villages where he was not easily recognizable. This gave the revolution a much more anonymous, collective feel, even though the activist was from a village a few kilometers away. In instances where he knew the peasant, Fidelis performed the state transcript before switching to the "hidden transcript":[43]

> I look at a peasant who lives there, is milking a cow on a Sunday after dinner. He was an elderly man, and we explain to him how it will be good, how this and that—and he knew us and we knew him! And he says later in the conversation, "Yes, gentlemen, you are right!" He says, "In the collective, the bread comes in three forms!" And we ask, "What type?" And he responds, "The bread is wheat, rye, and crappy!" And then he says, "But the crappy one is always plentiful! There is no wheat [bread] and the rye from time to time!" But we laughed! We were not going to tell the authorities that this peasant said it because they would have locked him up.

By not reporting peasant resistance, activists like Fidelis gave the peasantry the space to limit the collectivization process. At times their discussions ended in an unspoken "consensus" that the peasants would collectivize. Both sides knew, however, that this was only a performance:

> There was a kołchoz here in Podwoda; Bursztyn had a second one, and Byt, a third, but the rest held on [to land]. Those villages used kombinacja. Simply, they promised, "We will collectivize at such-and-such a time." Those establishing the kołchozy could then overlook it.

Peasants in certain villages realized that agreeing to collectivization actually diverted the state's gaze away from any "enemy activity" and gave them the space to drag their feet. Historian Andrzej Korbonski writes, "Very often joining a cooperative was the only way a peasant could save himself from constant harassment or jail and keep his land and livestock."[44] Belarusian peasants in particular who arrived from the east knew what was coming, for they had fled from collectivization drives after the Soviet Union invaded Poland's eastern borderlands in 1939. (Even though the state rebranded collective farms as "agricultural production cooperatives," during interviews, villagers called them *kołchozy* to emphasize their Soviet origins.) For example, in the Belarusian-dominated village of Podwoda, located several kilometers southeast of Bursztyn, peasants consented to collectivization but kept their individual property markers (*miedzy*) intact. They each worked their individual plots but pooled machines, labor, and fertilizers during major sowing and harvest periods to meet the "collective farm" quota. Their land was collectivized on paper but still independently cultivated in the fields.

Agreeing to collectivization did not always translate into work on that nationalized land. Many peasants agreed to collectivize when the activists came to their doors but then quickly abandoned their farms for city jobs, leaving the commune with their land but not their labor. While the collectivization drive sought to dekulakize peasants, the objective was to ensure that kułaks worked on collective farms. Abandonment was an interesting phenomenon as peasants chose to self-liquidate and proletarianize, but in such a way that they also burdened the commune by shifting their labor to the nonfarming state sectors. They resisted collectivization by choosing to live the life of a model proletarian citizen. Officials, many of whom were the largest landowners in the village, also played this game. A March 1953 report revealed that there had been complaints from peasants in a village called Bagno—which belonged to the Bursztyn commune—that the highest-ranking official of the GRN who pushed them to collectivize their land himself owned a large piece of farmland on which he had even employed Germans before the expulsion. He pooled his land into the collective, but because he was the official leading the dekulakization campaign against peasants, he exempted himself from working the land. Coincidentally, Orzeł, the official in Bursztyn who had forty hectares of land and had forced the German owners into labor on his farm during the postwar period, was in that delegation sent to Słupsk to confer with the county authorities about the Bagno issue.[45] (In that same report, the collectivized peasants of Bagno also called out the culture of corruption between uncollectivized peasants who bribed officials with vodka to relieve them of their quota and labor obligations. Bursztyn officials responded by sending out a teacher who would educate the "fearful" peasants on the meaning of the revolution.[46]) When it came to the collectivization process, it was very difficult to determine whether the peasants who delivered on their promise to collectivize were really the enemies that the dekulakization campaigns portrayed them to be, or whether they were in actuality guarding the socialist revolution from various strands of corruption.

Some villages were given no choice at all. In Byt one Belarusian peasant told me: "It was a *nakaz* [state order] to set up the kołchoz. It was a nakaz! But it was not 'who wanted' or 'who could,' but they took the agricultural equipment by force! I remember, they took the agricultural equipment by force! Because 'it was for the kołchoz'!" To create the Byt collective farm, the officials in Burszytn combined settlements and boundaries and expropriated abandoned or underused peasant agricultural buildings as they saw fit. A 1954 commune report noted that the commune incorporated its national land from the Land Fund (Fundusz Ziemi) into the Byt collective farm without adding the extra labor or capital to offset the extra burden on the collective farm workers (*kołchoźnik*).[47] So, not only was the Belarusian peasant forced to give up her land; she was also forced to work additional parcels of land that the state had nationalized and incorporated into the collective farm. Officials also used the collective farm structure as a catchall site to fix other societal problems. In a 1953 meeting report in Bursztyn, Tadeusz, an official, recommended that an entire colony (*kolonia*) on the village periphery occupied by sick and elderly peasants either be turned into a fourth collective farm or be incorporated into the adjacent state farm.[48] The nonchalance of the official, and the fact that no one questioned his ethics, reveals how zealously the commune approached the goal of plugging all eligible labor into the gears of the economy. Officials became chess players who shifted land, capital, and labor into arrangements that took the burden of subsidizing quota production off the commune (including themselves) and onto the collectivized peasantry or the nearby state farms. Those peasants who chose to collectivize soon learned that they had to work a lot more land than they pooled into the collective farm. The line between collective farm and gulag became blurry.

Bursztyn's collective farm was founded in March 1953; twenty-three peasants had signed up. Zofia was adamant about her choice to collectivize: "No one forced us to do anything!" she insisted. To her and Konrad, collectivization providedmuch needed-relief from the enrichment taxes, individual quota deliveries, interrogations, surveillance, and szarwark obligations. Before collectivization, these peasants worked daily on their land grants located at the end of the street that opened up to vast expanses of fields. When the kołchoz opened, Konrad walked down the same street and onto the same fields with his neighbors; but instead of working their private plots, they met with the director who distributed work assignments, went to the warehouse man to pick up their tools, were supervised by a brigadier who watched them work from a wooden watchtower to ensure that they completed their tasks, and were paid by the accountant after the mandatory farm quotas were sold for fixed prices to the GS. It was the first time that Zofia earned income, and she proudly recalls how a county-level official arrived to inspect the collective farm and complimented her on how meticulously she had organized the dry hay bundles "like matchsticks in a box." It was perhaps the only time she saw herself as anything like the smiling peasant woman in the colorful propaganda posters who was fulfilling the plan with a vast field of workers in the background. She was part of something larger than herself, and, as a woman, she was valued for her work not in the household but in a workplace (see figure 4.1). She was even recruited into the party, but Konrad, who had been interrogated "on the carpet" before, forced her to turn it down. There was something else Zofia said, however, that caught my attention. A day before giving birth to her fourth child in the autumn of 1954, this Stakhanovite worker recalled to me that she was "working off" her linen harvest obligation on kołchoz fields. It was a curious comment because collective farms were supposed to have eliminated feudalism.

Figure 4.1. The collective farm workers in Bursztyn. Zofia (top center), Jadzia (top right), and Konrad (third from right). Courtesy of Zofia.

Collectivization paved a way for peasants to free themselves from feudal debt, not clear it. Although most of Bursztyn's peasants agreed to collectivize their land, the state was not going to allow them to choose collectivization as a means to escape their feudal labor, tax, and individual quota obligations. A 1953 report stated that 33 percent of the member peasants farmed the land collectively, and the other 67 percent sowed the vestiges of their original plots to pay off their szarwark obligations.[49] Even after a peasant agreed to collectivize, he or she had to work off feudal debts to become a collective farm worker (*kołchoźnik*). Technically, collective farm land was a national entity; thus, feudal obligations like szarwarks and neighborly help that the state had used to tax the peasantry could be applied to it. Since most of Bursztyn's arable fields were clustered in the northern part of the village, all the different "stages" of socialism were playing out there simultaneously. In one section of the collective farm fields would be the collective farm workers working for wages; on another part of the field a large percentage of peasants would still be toiling away their feudal obligations on what had formerly been their plots (by then "nationalized"). This is likely where Zofia "worked off" her linen obligation to clear her individual quota, neighborly help, or szarwark debts to the state from the era before collectivization. Once the obligations were met, the *miedza*—a several-meter-wide grass marker—was plowed over and redrawn into two-hectare parcels they would be responsible for working as "collective farm workers" toward the collective farm quota. (This applied only to peasants who wanted to collectivize but still had outstanding obligations. Those few peasants in the village who did not collectivize "chose" to remain in the old feudal system.) While preaching the gospel of enlightenment and modernization, collective farm directors and commune officials slowed down the progress of collectivization to ensure that peasants paid off their feudal debts before their metamorphosis into collective farm workers.

Collective farm workers who cleared their individual quota and szarwark debts were freed from those feudal obligations once and for all, but the state did retain one institution of feudal labor that it was desperately addicted to: neighborly help. Mutual aid was still key to facilitating the state officials' movement of collectivized peasants and other agricultural laborers across the commune to deal with labor shortages and meet state plans. During a national potato beetle infestation in 1953, Bursztyn sent the collective farm workers and two hundred villagers as "neighborly help" to pick beetles off crops on other state and collective farms. However, increasing resistance against this exploitation of the collective farm workers began to challenge that system and pressure officials to make deals on terms they could not meet. In a commune meeting in 1954, officials complained that resistant collective farm workers were forcing officials to get "help" from the adjacent state farm to transport wood from the state forestry. It was an embarrassment to the state officials that they needed unpaid labor from elsewhere. To return the favor to the state farm, the officials claimed that they would send their peasants to help harvest the state farm's next potato quota.[50] (Whether these were the uncollectivized peasants or collective farm workers is unclear.) Officials preferred an enlightened peasantry that served them to a peasantry of collective farm workers that resisted feudal oppression. It is astonishing how much of early socialism and Stalinism was built by unpaid peasant labor. Modernization in Bursztyn meant never fully closing the doors on feudalism.

There was no golden age on the collective farms across Bursztyn commune. Problems with quota production were immediate. According to accounts from 1954, some grain quotas like that for Secale, a cereal grass, had no chance of completion because the commune never received the seeds to sell to the collective farm. Instead of each collective farm receiving its share of all of the quotas, the commune delegated different quotas to each of its four collective farms spread across nearby villages that belonged administratively under commune control. Some farms received all of a certain seed variety; others did not. Each focused on meeting one mandatory quota—usually grain—while showing enormous deficits in all others, like milk. The commune struggled to keep up with the quickly changing laws that determined annual quota prices, measurements of quotas per hectare, substitutions, and quota types. By the time necessary changes to the new quota law were made, another was passed that resulted in another reassembling of labor, capital, and space to adjust to the new rules. Some quota yields were decreased because peasants decided against buying or taking out credit to obtain expensive and harmful chemical fertilizers. They preferred cheaper, slower horses over expensive, more efficient tractors. In effect, production progressed at the peasants' pace and failed to meet the increasing quotas provided by the state.[51] (This was a widespread problem. Many communes never even received the paperwork that revealed their quota amounts for the season, and thus their "collective farming" consisted of collective farm workers producing quotas to feed themselves and their own livestock.[52]) The collective farm supply chains were broken. The only productive collective farm in Gwiazda met its quotas through a neighborly help arrangement with a nearby state farm, even though villages and state farms were different national entities.[53] No other collective farm in Bursztyn's commune could produce its state quota using its own devices.

In Bursztyn proper there were more acrimonious disputes about the management of the farm, which was rigidly controlled by the commune officials. At one commune meeting, Ignacy, a collective farm worker, stood up and expressed the farm workers' frustration regarding the amount of grain the farm had been forced to give away to the GS in the previous quota cycle. Ignacy stated that "a rational form of livestock farming is difficult in our conditions . . . especially since last year there was a weak grain harvest and we gave almost all of the grain for planned purchase, and this year we do not have anything to feed the pigs, since there are shortages of animal feed and there is nowhere to buy animal feed." He complained that the collective farm workers had asked the director of the GS in Bursztyn to sell them animal feed, but he had rejected their offer because he was holding them accountable for siphoning grain from the collective farm to feed their private pigs. Ignacy responded that a poor collective farm makes life difficult for the collective farm workers, who have to meet high quotas but make low profits and do not earn enough to pay their property taxes. Although they were collective farm workers, they still retained small parcels of land on which they produced food and raised livestock for subsistence needs, and they still paid taxes on that land. The state provided no poverty alleviation measures for the collective farm workers who had pooled most of their land into the farm and struggled to meet subsistence needs. Ignacy mentioned the injustice of this system: "On our lands peasant farmers who have several hectares only can raise one cow each, but allotment gardens [belonging to workers and officials] can have two cows, because they are not oppressed with such high mandatory quotas [in the collective farm]."[54] Collective farm workers like Ignacy were not rising up against the collective farm or commune, but they felt their economic needs and their need for access to resources were not being met by the authorities—which plunged them into poverty and encouraged rule breaking, like siphoning grain from the collective farm fields to feed their private pigs, as a desperate measure to provide food for their families.

At a later commune meeting in 1954, Teofil, a collective farm worker, complained that the commune often failed to pay wages on time, which delayed production and undermined morale. Collective farm workers began to refuse to perform neighborly help and other labor obligations for the commune as a protest against their poor treatment. He said to the officials:

> When [the commune] wanted to set up the collective farm, they drove around [persuading], but once they set it up, [they] left us to our own losses, and now they do not care to expedite their accounting process when collective farm members do not have anything to build up stock, there is no hay for horses, and this is having an adverse effect on the wood transport. This is why peasants are no longer taking part, because without hay they will not go [neighborly help] to transport wood [for the forestry].[55]

Officials, however, recast collective farm workers' pleas for additional support as enemy activity. In response, Wojtek, a commune official, stood up and stated that the collective farm in Gwiazda village was the only one that functioned well in the commune, "and the rest work however they feel like." In retaliation, another peasant representative from the collective farm in Bursztyn stood up and responded that "the caretaker of the collective farm members ought to be the party leader," and he threateningly invited Wojtek "to come to the fields to take a look, and try ordering [us] around." But Wojtek continued with his "argument" that the only reason farms were not functioning effectively was because "there are still these types of peasants, who approach mandatory quotas with strong resistance."[56] Shortages were not the symptom of a broken system but of economic sabotage. The commune officials thought it was the collective farm workers' responsibility to mobilize resources and labor, whereas the collective farm workers thought it was the commune's responsibility to supply them with capital. This exchange demonstrates that the commune officials knew how to manipulate the political rhetoric of peasant ownership of the collective farms to relieve themselves of the responsibility of fixing the problems on the farm. Neither officials nor collective farm workers wanted to dedicate any more resources than they already had to subsidize quota production. Scapegoating helped shift that burden and the blame.

Collective farm workers in the Byt collective farm in the commune revolted against these difficult conditions. In 1953 a party agronomist from Byt complained to the commune that two groups of workers had formed on his collective farm. Several workers who were fired from the farm had sought factory jobs, where they were paid higher wages, incentivizing the remaining members of the farm to drag their feet. Others abandoned their homes and sought work in the city, while the rest were stuck with their pooled land.[57] There was no "leader" to this resistance. The agronomist reported that peasants would do anything to avoid working on the collective farm to produce the quota, including setting fire to grain warehouses and barns, killing horses, breaking wagons and machinery, dragging their feet, and drinking on the job. All of these actions, he said, subverted quotas. In 1953 citizen Stanisław, from Byt village, complained in front of the open quorum in the commune headquarters that on that collective farm, the agricultural machines worked all year, except when the sowing began for the season. That was "enemy work" (*wroga robota*), he emphasized. Commune officials skeptically recorded collective farm workers' complaints that labor was slow because of hazardous working conditions with the new machines, confusion about quota plans, broken machines not being fixed on time, or a dearth of plows. Officials in Bursztyn logged incomplete quotas as the "gray heritage of capitalism that presented itself with resistance from old classes and masked enemy agents in workplaces."[58] What was missing from the commune reports and meetings was a clear and mature discussion of economic and scientific solutions that could increase quota production.

When Zofia and her neighbor Jadzia, also a pioneer peasant-turned-collective farm worker, reminisced about the collective farm in Bursztyn, they said the only reason kombinacja was allowed was because "the kołchozy were not like the kołchozy in Russia." Jadzia explained, "They planted seeds, took what they wanted, and gave the rest away to the state. It was like this, you see? It was not yet completely nationalized. They threshed, they talked, the bag of wheat they took to sell for a liter of vodka." Zofia added, "Because in Russia, you could not steal anything. They were real kołchozy." Half-broken collective farms gave the workers a lot more access to resources than the "real" collective farms in Russia. Broken collective farms allowed peasants and officials to maintain their agrarian livelihoods. Peasants adapted kombinacja to deal with the poor conditions on the collective farm. The most profitable ventures were the collective farm workers' dealings with peasants who were not collectivized. They sold collective farm livestock to them so that the latter would not have to deliver their highest-quality beef to the state, and others borrowed collective farm tractors to perform private services for the uncollectivized peasants. Most collective farm workers, however, domesticated the state property by feeding less fodder to the state livestock and diverting the rest to feed their own. They butchered the state livestock for private consumption and siphoned off the grain they produced for private storage to feed their families and livestock. Although there appeared to be some collective consensus that kombinacja was inevitable, kombinators did not always work in the interest of the collective. Zofia recalled that collective farm workers competed for access to limited socialist property, which contributed to the lack of trust among them:

> So, I want something from you and I will use kombinacja to take it, no? Or trick someone. Lie. That is kombinacja for oneself. It is this kind of kombinacja, and it was around in . . . the kołchoz. There was kombinacja or stealing,

or trickery between one another, or trick the state, and there were such kombinators—it was this type of kombinacja.

Zofia then recalled how Konrad once found two collective farm workers taking bags of grain and hiding them in the fields to pick up later that night in those secret hiding spots that the peasantry had already figured out in their black market dealings with the quota system. Instead of collaborating or reporting them, Konrad reprimanded them by stealing their bags. He took them home and fed the grain to the chickens so there would be no "trace" of theft. When Zofia and Jadzia talked about this incident, they called it "taking" (*brać*), not "stealing." This is important because they played on the state propaganda that collective farms belonged to the peasantry. If that was the case, then the peasants "owned" that socialist property, so by definition, how they split it up would not be "theft" if it was "their" property all along. Yet they understood that the kombinacja needed to be kept "invisible" from state surveillance. During the wheat harvests on the collective farms, Zofia recalled that the commune sent out watchmen to sit atop the wooden watchtowers and surveil the peasants. "There was such order, that 'God forbid something is stolen!' Because he was so just that he had to report that immediately and they imposed fines for it. That was not allowed!" She knew the "formal" rules. This just reveals how collective farm workers circumvented the state in their own interest but, like the officials, strategically deployed state political discourse to situate their actions within the creative spirit of the revolution.

Collective farm workers were not the only kombinators who benefitted from a broken kołchoz. Officials themselves carried out black market kombinacja, especially where there were "manipulable resources" that were either undefined by legislation or constituted a surplus to the obligatory quota plan.[59] A record from a commune meeting in 1953 shows that one party official, Jacek, accused another party official, Wojtek, of selling wheat from an abandoned peasant farm. Rather than giving it to the nearby Gwiazda collective farm to help fulfill its quota, he sold it on the black market to uncollectivized peasants still burdened by individual quotas. Wojtek responded that the robust collective farm had canceled its order to buy the wheat, so instead he had sold it to two village mayors and twenty "poor," uncollectivized peasants. The matter ended there, as the director of the collective farm in Gwiazda, rather than inquiring further into what his farm had lost, defended Wojtek and declared his collective farm as the best in the entire commune.[60] Questions like why Wojtek did not sell the wheat to Bursztyn's other struggling collective farms or what he did with the money were not pursued. (This existed across the agro-industrial divide in Bursztyn; a commune state brewer director was caught selling beer quotas on the black market rather than to GS local stores.) While officials like Motylek were writing reports about the "peasants, kombinators, and kułaks" on the prowl who were subverting

the socialist economy, peasant memories of kombinacja combined with other records in the archives show that everybody suffered from shortages and contributed to shortages by using the blind spots of the law and gaze of the Other to
secure socialist property.

Bursztynians reworked the Six-Year Plan to suit their economic and political
interests. The collectivization model centralized varied landscapes, economies,
and people under the structure of a "collective farm" but did not have the structural mechanisms to adapt flexibly to this variation. Although collective farms
shared a cookie-cutter administrative structure, they were built on diverse economic landscapes and became a bricolage of land, capital, and people. Because
the rigid structure of the collective farms did not have mechanisms to adjust to
the "uneven development of collectivization" between farms and on a regional
scale, officials continued to rely on feudal obligations to meet the state plan.[61]
Although not everyone had the choice to collectivize, everyone had a choice to
exercise kombinacja. This diverse practice emerged as a flexible response to the
lack of capital, delays in the distribution of wages, and the commune's continu-
ous breaking of the promises it made during the collectivization process. It was
not an attempt to find a solution to the structural problems plaguing the farm;
rather, kombinacja represented collective farm workers' individual attempts to
solve immediate subsistence problems. In doing so, they staved off starvation
and ensured that they could keep on producing quotas for the state. Keeping the
collective farm broken was certainly beneficial for everyone—the commune did
not have to do its job or secure resources for the farm, and the collective farm
workers did not have to exert labor to earn wages for which they were not paid
on time. "Taking" resources and selling them or incorporating them into their
domestic spheres was a way to avoid bigger confrontations with the commune. To
make ends meet, officials and collective farm workers both used different kombinacja tactics to leverage control over the flow (and pace) of labor and resources
between the household and the state supply chain. Thus, the strategy served to
stabilize the command economy, preserve the political power of the elites, and
lift collective farm workers out of poverty. Kombinacja emerged as the will of the
collective.

Enlightenment

Kombinators navigated the gaps between Stalinist myths and Polish realities.
Like Reymont's description of nineteenth-century Łódź subjected to the wave
of capitalist kombinacja that transformed the city, as the Soviet economic occupation spread across the commune, and the kombinacja powers of the Stalinist state became a more formalized entity in settlers' minds, so did the magical
kombinator alter ego. Like Ostap Bender in 1920s Soviet Russia, in Sovietizing

Bursztyn kombinators were opportunists on the prowl: they were on the lookout for food to divert from state supply chains and for opportunities to speculate on land and engage in black marketeering. The Soviet kombinator represented the awakening of a new kind of subjectivity vis-à-vis the state when villagers became increasingly aware of being under the powerful forces of Stalinist occupation. With no way out, kombinacja became a masquerade villagers performed as a deviation from their declarations of faithful support to Stalinism. Rather than engaging in outright resistance through political organizing or underground resistance movements, individual kombinators worked alone within the system, using magical tactics that both subverted and supported the state to tilt the balance of power in their favor, albeit delicately. The kombinator could be an official carrying out Stalinist law one moment and black marketeering the next, or independent peasants agreeing to collectivization with the intention of dragging their feet throughout the entire process. It was by playing along with the system when its gaze was directed toward them that kombinators could inflict the most damage when the system looked away. Whereas magical realism is about magic existing in plain sight in everyday life, magical Stalinism is about "magic" that influences everyday life but is not in plain sight. Villagers became magicians who played with the state's blind spots and began to create a transient subjectivity for the spaces and moments when the state's gaze was elsewhere. The struggle over labor and resources in the village took place in spaces no one could see: in the hidden meanings behind expressed intentions, in the interstices of regime change, in an archipelago of hiding spots at night, in discourses that shifted the burden of production upon the Other, and so on.

The rebirth of the kombinator persona sheds light on a critical moment in the history of magical Stalinism when the struggle over power in the village took place not in the open or through law, but in the blind spots of both the state and the villagers. What the other could not see became key to the expansion of both state power and the black market. Blind spots became spaces of resistance and oppression. By agreeing with the state, peasants, villagers, and elites alike could create different realities. Model workers diverted meat quotas to recipients using hiding spots across the commune. Activists traveled across the commune and performed the state transcript while privately agreeing with the peasants and letting them collectivize the way they wanted. Peasants collectivized up to the point where the collective farm was broken enough for them to siphon its resources. By engaging in kombinacja, villagers created their own Stalinist realities in the village: one on paper and another in the fields. Blaming poor production and broken supply chains on the liminal Other ensured that a real debate on how to make the system work better would not take place and also that no one would be held accountable for a broken collective farm. I wonder if anyone truly wanted a replica of a Russian-style kolkhoz.

After a postwar silence, the resurgence of the kombinator figure in the archives coincided with the villagers' memories of kombinacja during the same period of Stalinization. In a way, the "blind spot" was a Stalinist invention. The Stalinist state justified its dekulakization campaigns with the premise that it was searching for the ghosts of capitalism that lurked inside the realm of imagination—in ideas, intentions, and feelings residing in spaces the state could not penetrate. The state also encouraged a mythical vision of reality through propaganda campaigns and the doctrine of socialist realism, and that vision contrasted starkly with realities on the ground. In all likelihood, practices that were then identified as kombinacja did not begin in 1953; however, giving something or someone a name is also in itself a political act. The discourse of outing kombinators resembled a dekulakization campaign of pinning blame on the Other. Just like the kułak figure, there was no established definition of what characteristics defined a kombinator. Kombinacja might not have existed in the villagers' discourse if the state had not cracked down on economic miscreants. Brian LaPierre found a similar pattern with the term *hooliganism* (anarchism) in Stalinist Russia. Cracking down on hooliganism bred more hooliganism against the state.[62] The kombinator became a self-fulfilling prophecy; the state imagined him and he magically appeared. And in some ways, kombinacja was how ordinary people connected to the Soviet project and the magical powers of the Soviet state and its cultlike trickster leaders.

Another reason kombinacja might have reemerged was because people felt that they were under occupation. When Stalinist collectivization came to Bursztyn, peasants were confused. The commune had just praised them as pioneers of Polish nationalism and handed them Akt nadania ownership documents that formalized their settlement on the new land grants. Then those same officials called them kułaks, imposed agricultural quotas, and pressured them to collectivize. This was a massive breach of trust between settlers and the new authorities. Likewise, peasants from the east, some of whom had fled Soviet collectivization, also knew how Stalinism began. The example of the Belarusian peasants agreeing to Stalinism showed that they knew how to resist it by accepting it. I also wonder whether in the collective process of "recovering" Polish identity of the lands, the villagers collectively "recovered" their former memories of kombinacja under Nazi occupation. Kacper, a former village official, said that Poles adapted the lessons of kombinacja that they practiced during the Nazi occupation to the Soviet occupation of their country. They "learned during the German occupation, and then later, the same thing afterwards!" Perhaps the alignment of Stalinization with their past experiences of state oppression rekindled similar feelings of injustice and survival strategies. Perhaps in the immediate postwar period, kombinacja did not exist because peasants still felt they had opportunities for self-determination. Once the Stalinist dekulakization campaigns occupied their lives, they unleashed the kombinator within to create an alternative reality for themselves.

Kombinacja also became bundled in a broader politicized discourse. Language helped link villagers to alternate historical narratives. Villagers began to reject the formal language of the state, the language that falsely rebranded Soviet kolkhozy and sovkhozy as examples of a "Polish road to socialism." They pejoratively used the Soviet term *kołchoz* instead of *rolnicza spółdzielnia produkcyjna* (agricultural production cooperative) and the informal *chłop* (peasant) instead of the state term *rolnik* (farmer): each word choice emphasized the villagers' repressed condition and their rejection of the state's discourse of modernization. Although peasants claimed they were not "forced" to collectivize, the term *persuasion* (*namawianie*) is almost always used pejoratively, about someone trying to convince someone else to agree to something under false pretenses. The use of vernacular, rather than official, terms exposed the villagers' political dislocation from the state's development goals. It subversively emphasized the historical continuities of power dynamics between peasants and masters from the feudal period that persisted within the framework of Soviet-model agriculture. Only officials in interviews still used the "formal" terms. Although this might be a stretch, it is possible that using the term *kombinator* instead of *enemy* (*wróg*) also emphasized this historical figure as the hero rather than the perpetrator of capitalist bourgeois inclinations. Its use in discourse also helped chart the landscape of blind spots and resistance. Anyone who knew that kombinacja had been committed recognized that alternatives to the state economy were possible, without knowing exactly what had been done to produce those alternatives. The term was informative but simultaneously vague. It may have emerged as a unifying logic among the ethnic groups who arrived to the territories after the war. It became a practice and discourse they used to situate themselves relative to one another and the state. Kombinacja may indeed have been a collectivizing force, a way of linking people to each other without any formal or easily detectable traces of organization. They achieved enlightenment through magical thinking to survive shortages in Stalin's dystopia.

The resurgence of the kombinacja narrative in the archives and memories shows that the embers of resistance from the interwar and prewar periods never burned out during the period of collectivism. As people became more aware of "how" the state worked, they also became aware of its blind spots, in which it was possible to play, manipulate, and switch between sides. These sideline activities diverted the flow of resources that were destined for the city and helped strengthen agrarianism and localism. Kombinacja partially limited the penetration of collectivization and partially disconnected the village from the state's rural-urban supply chain. Villagers understood the context in which kombinacja could be revived or continued under new conditions. Once a certain threshold is reached, kombinacja is again deemed necessary for survival. Through this "beginning" or "rebirth" of kombinacja, which social science calls a practice of informality, we see how informality can change over time, be appropriated by different groups, and involve a critique of state power. These strategies can continue during regime change, can be transferred geographically, and can be relied on when conditions of the previous regime are unresolved by the new one. Informality has a history, a culture, and a life of its own.

Notes

1. Bierut, "We Are Building the Structure of Socialist Poland," 14–15.

2. Davies, *God's Playground*, 2:579; Fidelis, *Women, Communism, and Industrialisation*, 58; Gibney, *Frozen Revolution*, 227; Kenney, *Rebuilding Poland*, 206; Ludowski and Zawadzki, *Concise History of Poland*, 287.

3. Murat, "Promiscuous Pioneers," 26.

4. Onesti, "Portrait of a Generation," 143.

5. Fidelis, *Women, Communism, and Industrialisation*, 75; Kenney, *Rebuilding Poland*, 201.

6. Kenney, *Rebuilding Poland*, 193.

7. Dziennik Ustaw z 1950, Numer 20, Pozycja 168, Ustawa z dnia 19 kwietnia 1950r. o zabezpieczeniu socialistycznej dyscypliny pracy (Act of April 19, 1950, on securing a socialist discipline of labor), 219–21, Dziennik Ustaw Rzeczypospolitej Polskiej, http://www.dziennikustaw .gov.pl/DU/1950/168/1; Dziennik Ustaw z 1950, Numer 47, Pozycja 428, Artykuły 1, 2, 23, Dekret z dnia 12 października 1950r. o wynalazczości pracowniczej (Decree of October 12, 1950, on workplace innovation), Dziennik Ustaw Rzeczypospolitej Polskiej, http://www.dziennikustaw .gov.pl/DU/1950/428/1; Dziennik Ustaw z 1953, Numer 17, Pozycja 69, Dekret z dnia 4 marca 1953r. o ochronie własności społecznej przed drobnymi kradzieżami (Decree of March 4, 1953, on the protection of public property against petty theft), 110, Dziennik Ustaw Rzeczypospolitej Polskiej, http://www.dziennikustaw.gov.pl/DU/1953/69/1; Dziennik Ustaw z 1953, Numer 16, Pozycja 64, Dekret z dnia 4 marca 1953r. o ochronie interesów nabywców w obrocie handlowym (Decree of March 4, 1953, on the protection of purchasers in the course of trade), 106, Dziennik Ustaw Rzeczypospolitej Polskiej, http://www.dziennikustaw.gov.pl/DU/1953/64/1; Dziennik Ustaw z 1966, Numer 22, Pozycja 141, Rozporządzenie Rady Ministrów z dnia 14 czerwca 1966r. w sprawie rzeczy znalezionych (Council of Ministers of June 14, 1966, on things found), 200–201, Dziennik Ustaw Rzeczypospolitej Polskiej, http://www.dziennikustaw.gov.pl /DU/1966/141/1.

8. Minc, "Six-Year Plan," 37.

9. Agriculture production cooperatives were identical to the Soviet model, but the Polish communists rebranded them to give them a more Polish orientation.

10. Korbonski, *Politics of Socialist Agriculture*, 185.

11. Dziennik Ustaw z 1952, Numer 8, Pozycja 46, Ustawa z dnia 15 lutego 1952r. o obowiązkowych dostawach zwierząt rzeźnych (Act of February 15, 1952, on the compulsory supply of animals for slaughter), 81–82. Dziennik Ustaw Rzeczypospolitej Polskiej, http://www .dziennikustaw.gov.pl/DU/1952/46/1; Dziennik Ustaw z 1952, Numer 22, Pozycja 142, Ustawa z dnia 24 kwietnia 1952r. o obowiązkowych dostawach mleka (Act of April 24, 1952, on the mandatory deliveries of milk), 229–31, Dziennik Ustaw Rzeczypospolitej Polskiej, http://www .dziennikustaw.gov.pl/DU/1952/142/1; Dziennik Ustaw z 1952, Numer 32, Pozycja 214, Ustawa z dnia 9 lipca 1952r. o obowiązkowych dostawach zbóż (Act of July 9, 1952, on the compulsory deliveries of grain), 313–16, Dziennik Ustaw Rzeczypospolitej Polskiej, http://www.dziennikustaw

.gov.pl/DU/1952/214/1; Dziennik Ustaw z 1952, Numer 37, Pozycja 255, Ustawa z dnia 28 sierpnia 1952r. o obowiązkowych dostawach ziemniaków (Act of August 28, 1952, on the compulsory supply of potatoes), 429–32, Dziennik Ustaw Rzeczypospolitej Polskiej, http://www.dziennikustaw.gov.pl/DU/1952/255/1.

12. Numer 13, 1953–1954, Protokoły z sesji Gminnej Rady Narodowej, 1953–1954r. (Minutes of the National Commune Council Sessions, 1953–1954), 49, Referat Ogólno-Administracyjny, 1–117, Wojewódzki Archiwum Państwowy w Koszalinie: Słupsk.

13. Applebaum, *Iron Curtain*, 276; Korbonski, *Politics of Socialist Agriculture*, 163n9; Paczkowski, "Poland," 382.

14. Jędrychowski, *Recovered Territories*, 8.

15. Korbonski, *Politics of Socialist Agriculture*, 177–79.

16. Ibid., 178.

17. Jędrychowski, *Recovered Territories*, 8.

18. Korbonski, *Politics of Socialist Agriculture*, 177.

19. Numer 13, 1953–1954, Protokoły z sesji Gminnej Rady Narodowej, 1953–1954r. (Minutes of the National Commune Council Sessions, 1953–1954), 49, Referat Ogólno-Administracyjny, 1–117, Wojewódzki Archiwum Państwowy w Koszalinie: Słupsk.

20. Ibid., 52.

21. Ibid., 51–52.

22. Numer 3, 1948–1950, Protokoły zarządzenia Zarządu Gminnego, 1948–1950 (Minutes of the Commune Board, 1948–1950), 3, Gminna Rada Narodowo-Zarząd Gminnej w [Bursztyn], Oddział Ogólno-Organizacyjny, 1–46, Wojewódzki Archiwum Państwowy w Koszalinie: Słupsk.

23. Korbonski, *Politics of Socialist Agriculture*, 144.

24. Numer 13, 1953–1954, Protokoły z sesji Gminnej Rady Narodowej, 1953–1954r., 51–55.

25. Ibid., 56–57.

26. Ibid., 59.

27. Dziennik Ustaw z 1950, Numer 51, Pozycja 475, Rozporządzenie Ministra Rolnictwa i Reform Rolnych z dnia 19 października 1950r. w sprawie norm wynagrodzenia za świadczenia z tytułu pomocy sąsiedzkiej w rolnictwie oraz uiszczaną w gotówce równowartości opłat, oznaczonych w zbożu (Regulation of the minister of agriculture and agrarian reform of October 19, 1950, on the standards of remuneration for tribute in the name of neighborly help in agriculture and the compensation in cash in the form of grain), 708–9, Dziennik Ustaw Rzeczypospolitej Polskiej, http://www.dziennikustaw.gov.pl/DU/1950/475/1.

28. Dziennik Ustaw z 1959, Numer 48, Pozycja 294, Rozporządzenie Ministerstwa Rolnictwa z dnia 3 sierpnia 1959r. w sprawie norm wynagradzania za świadczenia z tytułu pomocy sąsiedzkiej w rolnictwie (Regulation of the Ministry of Agriculture dated August 3, 1959, on standards of remuneration for the benefit of neighborly help in agriculture), 562, Dziennik Ustaw Rzeczypospolitej Polskiej, http://www.dziennikustaw.gov.pl/DU/1959/294/1.

29. Dziennik Ustaw z 1949, Numer 63, Pozycja 494, Ustawa z dnia 20 grudnia 1949r. o państwowym gospodarstwie leśnym (Act of December 20, 1949, on the state forest economy), 1199–1203, Internetowy System Aktów Prawnych, http://isap.sejm.gov.pl/DetailsServlet?id=WDU19490630494; Numer 18, 1952–1953, Budżet na rok 1953 (Budget for the year 1953), Prezydium Gminny Rady Narodowej w [Bursztyn], 3, Referat Budżetowo-Finansowy, 1–70, Wojewódzki Archiwum Państwowy w Koszalinie: Słupsk.

30. Numer 13, 1953–1954, Protokoły z sesji Gminnej Rady Narodowej, 1953–1954r., 24.

31. Ibid., 13.

32. Gibney, *Frozen Revolution*, 239.

33. Śmigielska, "There's the Beef," 111.

34. Numer 13, 1953–1954, Protokoły z sesji Gminnej Rady Narodowej, 1953–1954r., 9.
35. Another report stated it began in 1951 (Żurawski, Zarys Dziejów, 51).
36. Ibid., 5.
37. Ibid., 4.
38. Ibid., 7.
39. Ibid., 4.
40. Ibid., 7.
41. Korbonski, *Politics of Socialist Agriculture*, 173.
42. Dziennik Ustaw z 1952, Numer 29, Pozycja 195, Ustawa z dnia 9 czerwca 1952r. o zmianie ustawy o obowiązkowych dostawach zwierząt rzeźnych (Act of June 9, 1952, on amending the law on the mandatory supply of animals for slaughter), 294, Dziennik Ustaw Rzeczypospolitej Polskiej, http://www.dziennikustaw.gov.pl/DU/1952/195/1.
43. Scott, *Domination*, 38.
44. Kornonski, *Politics of Socialist Agriculture*, 175.
45. Numer 13, 1953–1954, Protokoły z sesji Gminnej Rady Narodowej, 1953–1954r., 3.
46. Ibid.
47. Numer 14, 1953–1954, Protokoły z posiedzenia Prezydium Gminnej Rady Narodowej r. 1953–1954 (Minutes of the meeting of the Presidium of the Commune National Council, 1953–1954), 15, Prezydium Gminnej Rady Narodowej w [Bursztyn], Referat Ogólno-Administracyjny, 1–217, Wojewódzki Archiwum Państwowy w Koszalinie: Słupsk.
48. Ibid., 59.
49. Numer 13, 1953–1954, Protokoły z sesji Gminnej Rady Narodowej, 1953–1954r., 57.
50. Numer 14, 1953–1954, Protokoły z posiedzenia Prezydium Gminnej Rady Narodowej r. 1953–1954, 6, 91.
51. Ibid., 80, 156; Dziennik Ustaw z 1959, Numer 48, Pozycja 294, Rozporządzenie Ministerstwa Rolnictwa z dnia 3 sierpnia 1959r. w sprawie norm wynagradzania za świadczenia z tytułu pomocy sąsiedzkiej w rolnictwie (Regulation of the Ministry of Agriculture dated August 3, 1959, on standards of remuneration for the benefit of neighborly help in agriculture), 562, Dziennik Ustaw Rzeczypospolitej Polskiej, http://www.dziennikustaw.gov.pl/DU/1959/294/1; Dziennik Ustaw z 1950, Numer 51, Pozycja 475, Rozporządzenie Ministra Rolnictwa i Reform Rolnych z dnia 19 października 1950r. w sprawie norm wynagrodzenia za świadzenia z tytułu pomocy sąsiedzkiej w rolnictwie oraz uiszczanią w gotówce równowartości opłat, oznaczonych w zbożu (Regulation of the minister of agriculture and agrarian reform of October 19, 1950, on the standards of remuneration for tribute in the name of neighborly help in agriculture and the compensation in cash in the form of grain), 708–9, Dziennik Ustaw Rzeczypospolitej Polskiej, http://www.dziennikustaw.gov.pl/DU/1950/475/1.
52. Korbonski, *Politics of Socialist Agriculture*, 175.
53. Numer 13, 1953–1954, Protokoły z sesji Gminnej Rady Narodowej, 1953–1954r., 31.
54. Numer 14, 1953–1954, Protokoły z posiedzenia Prezydium Gminnej Rady Narodowej r. 1953–1954, 61.
55. Numer 13, 1953–1954, Protokoły z sesji Gminnej Rady Narodowej, 1953–1954r., 90.
56. Ibid., 31. He was referring to collective farm workers, not uncollectivized peasants.
57. Numer 14, 1953–1954, Protokoły z posiedzenia Prezydium Gminnej Rady Narodowej r. 1953–1954, 101.
58. Numer 13, 1953–1954, Protokoły z sesji Gminnej Rady Narodowej, 1953–1954r., 71
59. Humphrey, *Marx Went Away*, 9.
60. Numer 13, 1953–1954, Protokoły z sesji Gminnej Rady Narodowej, 1953–1954r., 31.
61. Kligman and Verdery, *Peasants under Siege*, 143.
62. LaPierre, *Hooligans in Khrushchev's Russia*, 10.

5   Proletarian Memories

IN JUNE 1956, one hundred thousand workers poured onto the streets of Poznań demanding bread and higher wages. The Polish-Soviet general Marshal Rokossovskii, under the military authority of Nikita Khrushchev, crushed the demonstrators with ten thousand soldiers and four hundred tanks, killing several dozen protesters and injuring hundreds.[1] The carnage in Poznań, as well as the outbreak of the Hungarian Revolution of 1956, emboldened calls for the end of Stalinism and precipitated the return of Gomułka to power. At the Eighth Plenum in October 1956, the newly reappointed First Secretary of the Polish United Workers' Party (Polska Zjednoczona Partia Robotnicza) vowed the return to a "Polish road to socialism." Collective farms had become abysmal scenes of peasants abandoning work in the fields, reclaiming equipment, and stealing food to feed their families and livestock. Poland was importing 1.5 million tons of grain to cover the losses, but that was not enough; workers were still spending 90 percent of their wages on food.[2] If the peasants were not happy, then no one was happy.

New "Polish October" reforms called for the decollectivization of agriculture.[3] Only those who took back more than two hectares of land would still be legally obligated to produce food quotas for the state. Gomułka had to find a way to supply those peasants with quick and easy access to fertilizers, seeds, credits, and machinery in order to bolster their quota production while also giving them control over the process. In 1956 he announced the return of an agricultural cooperative called the Agricultural Circle (Kółko Rolnicze). This was a beloved form of peasant self-government founded by nationalistic peasants as a form of resistance in nineteenth-century partitioned Poland, but it had been banned by communists after the war. Their return symbolized the rebirth of a Polish state, a state that would move away from Soviet agriculture and validate peasant methods of organizing resistance against an occupying foreign power.

The outpouring of peasant support for the circles was overwhelming. Membership swelled to 327,000 in just two months. But Gomułka was not called the "rebellious compromiser" for nothing. He was still a communist at heart and strongly believed the role of peasants was to produce quotas to feed the proletarian revolution.[4] These socialist cooperatives would not be like capitalist ones, where peasants had free reign over their own production and would use the cooperative centers to sell their produce. Rather, peasant members would be transformed into a state-controlled worker-peasant class (*robotnik-chłop*) who would split their time between producing quotas on their own farms and earning wages in the circles by providing sowing, plowing, and harvesting services on peasant farms.[5] Self-governance would be allowed only within those parameters.

Once peasants realized that the socialist circles were just another round-about way for the state to force them to produce quotas, membership stalled and confidence plummeted. At the First National Conference of Agricultural Circles in September 1959, a defensive Gomułka claimed: "Some may say: we do not want such circles, which will develop in the socialist direction. Let them go and some will quit. . . They will be back because there is no other way. The great socialist truth [is] that only through collective work . . . can productivity be raised and peasants' needs be satisfied."[6] But peasants were tired of being cogs in the great socialist experiment. By 1961, only 873,000 of 13.5 million eligible peasants had signed up.[7] Funds were limited, too.[8] In 1961, 11,000 of 25,563 circles had no tractors; by 1969, 34,814 circles shared 12,165 tractors. Chairmen used circle credits on their own large farms and distributed usage rights for state machinery and circle building materials to their patronage networks.[9] Instead of fixing problems, the state blamed the kułaks.[10] Self-government resembled backdoor collectivization.

In Bursztyn kombinacja became a key method peasants used to shift the balance of power into peasant hands and reclaim self-governance in the circle and in the village. In the spirit of Gomułka's thaw, in 1957 Bursztyn officials disbanded collective farms and gave peasants the option of taking back their land grants. Jadzia and Zofia, along with their collective farm coworkers, chose to take back only five hectares of land to protect themselves from any future enrichment taxes and high quotas. The peasants "embraced" the state's broader revolutionary strategy to "proletarianize" the peasantry. However, this created a logistical problem for the commune: what was it to do with all of that unwanted collective farm land? The solution: rather than fully decollectivizing, the commune would partially decollectivize by downsizing the farm and relocating its base to a colony of small Ukrainian peasants on the village outskirts who would work its 314 hectares (about 3 percent of commune land), which they did until 1989.[11] Whether the Ukrainian peasants agreed or were forced was unclear. One Ukrainian villager explained that the state maintained the collective farm in their colony as a means to retain control over the highest quality land in the commune. The Ukrainian peasants could not reclaim their original land grants. The end result was that decollectivization created new ethnic castes of land ownership: more Polish and Belarusian peasants received land than did Ukrainian peasants.

During this period of partial decollectivization, quota production was abysmal on peasant farms and the collective farms because of "poor soil and low culture in agricultural production," a local historian wrote.[12] The peasants who had survived Stalinism and *szarwark* (corvées) were exhausted. It is unclear both in peasant memories and from the archival material what happened with quota production in those post-Stalinist years, but it was not until 1961, six years after Gomułka's speech, that peasants finally "organized" a circle in Bursztyn. Zofia and her peasant neighbors, who had already been pioneers, peasant farmers, kułaks, collective farm workers, and peasant farmers again, had proletarianized into worker-peasants.

The advent of the circle marked a golden age for the worker-peasantry in Bursztyn. Unlike in the collective farm, where membership was based on pooling land, machines, and livestock into a communal warehouse and working on collective land, circle membership meant simply that one was willing to work and perform mechanized plowing and sowing services on peasant farms for wages. The circle headquarters located one street over from Zofia had a director, vice-director, head accountant, worker accountant, warehouse accountant, and brigadiers. The circle provided machines and mechanical training programs. There was even a tractor, and Zofia's husband, Konrad, became the village's first certified tractor operator, and later combine harvester driver. Konrad's worker-peasant life consisted of waking up in the morning and walking over to the circle headquarters to pick up scheduled jobs for the day, driving to the peasant farms that requested the service, and returning at midday to his own farm, where he worked with Zofia to meet the farm quota that they were obligated to sell to the "Peasants' Self-Help" Commune Cooperative (Gminna Spółdzielnia "Samopomoc Chłopska") at low prices fixed by the state, just as before in the *kołchoz*. But now, they received two sources of income: circle wages and quota earnings.

The introduction of the paper contract (*umowa*) as the standard procedure of procuring peasant services for the state was the most revolutionary change ushered in by circles. The szarwark system and the feudal tax system that imposed harsh burdens on the kułaks was phased out in a series of Polish October laws between 1957 to 1958.[13] According to a new 1959 law, any service the state wanted from peasants had to be written out on paper, and paid for.[14] Whereas under the szarwark system the peasants signed some paper that they would never see again once it was taken into the commune, under the new law the worker-peasants would have their own copy of the services. Circles therefore represented the democratization of the paper trail. This new system, Zofia said, allowed worker-peasants to keep receipts of their services, to see and verify exactly which services they had completed and which circle services they paid for on their farms, "for there to be no kombinacja!" as she put it. Life was better in the circle, but it was not free. Quotas provided wages and job security, but ultimately, circles were just another way for the state to extract labor from worker-peasants. Worker-peasants in the circle were locked into their class: they produced agricultural quotas as "peasants" and earned wages as "workers." They could not just sell their farm and find manufacturing jobs in the city. Their state-defined function was to produce for the workers, and that was it. Worker-peasants had to be in two places at once: on their farm and in the circle.

However, the traditional importance of circles as a form of self-government captured the worker-peasants' imagination: they could use kombinacja to carve out territories of control in the circle. "There was state work, but also private work. If one wanted to use kombinacja, then he found a way to do it," Zofia recalled. One benefit of circle members' locked class status is that it allowed them the daily mobility to cross the agro-industrial crevices of the command economy and perform jobs without the direct supervision of a brigadier patrolling from a watchtower. The objective of the circle was to devise new ways of extracting labor from the worker-peasants, but the worker-peasants found new ways of extracting resources from the circle and forcing the state to subsidize their quota production. Three activities in particular involved kombinacja: siphoning circle resources during the autumn grain harvests on the circle fields, moonlighting with state machinery on peasant farms for private pay, and erasing (or reducing) outstanding balances in the circle's accounts.

In the 1960s the circle acquired commune land and began to produce quotas for the "Peasants' Self-Help" Commune Cooperative just like the collective farm. Matylda, the former circle treasurer, recalled that the circle hired day laborers who picked potatoes, threshed the grain, or picked wheat stalks on that land during harvests. Many of the laborers were local tannery workers who wanted to earn extra wages. Most of the kombinacja in the circle occurred during autumn harvests. "In the circles there was a lot of kombinacja near the threshers, near the digging up of the potatoes. There were many of those who used kombinacja so that there would be some for oneself. One did not look to the state," Zofia recalled. With winter approaching, the laborers pilfered potatoes and grain before bagging, before the circle transported bags to the GS and weighed them. Of course, many of the day laborers were the worker-peasants' own children, so pilfered grain and potatoes made it back to their farms.

These tactics could be adapted to new conditions. When the circle bought a combine that mechanically threshed the grain and separated the husk from the stalk, "we had to keep watch, what is going on, where is everything. They only waited around for him not to notice. When the combine came, everyone just kept a look out," Matylda recalled. My mother, a circle day laborer in her twenties, recalled that when Konrad, who operated the first combine harvester in the circle, dispensed the grain from the circle's fields onto the wagons, "a lot of kombinacja occurred because not always did the circle authorities there control where that wagon went with the grain, whether it was to the GS or to someone else's pockets and it was this kind of kombinacja because everyone wanted to have something free for oneself. This was only about kombinacja of grain in the circle, because peasant farmers that ordered the combine on their farms closely monitored their wagons." Family members with different work relationships to the circle all played a role taking advantage of the blind spots of the administration and pilfering the harvest.

Pilfered harvests traveled across an underground network of local barns at night. Worker-peasants wanted the circle's lower-quality grain harvest as a substitute for the higher-quality harvest they produced on their own farms toward the state quota. So, instead of sending their harvest to sell to the GS to meet their farm quota to the state, they filled up their wagons with the pilfered circle harvest to sell back to the state. This way, they retained their high-quality food for themselves or sold it at a higher value on the black market. Another key thing they could do with the circle harvest was to feed it to the livestock that they were obliged to sell to the GS; in effect, they systematically fed their "state livestock" lower-quality feed "subsidized" by the circle. The third major option was to sell the circle harvest on the black market to peasants who had suffered a failed harvest and would not be able to meet their state quotas that season. Zofia recounted to Matylda her run-in with a worker-peasant named Jurek who showed up at night with a "runaway" wagon in her own barn located in the rear of her farm. He hid the wagon in her barn the first night, then proceeded to sell off the harvest at night to buyers who needed it to sell to the GS as "their" individual quota. When Zofia told Konrad, he supposedly reported Jurek to Bartek, the circle director. An irritated Matylda replied that such marketeering defeated the cooperative model: "There were mottos: that 'we need to work,' that 'this is ours,' and that 'it is a cooperative.' Everyone knew that he had to work honestly, one could not steal because 'that is our clean money,' no? From the profits, there were various bonuses, and if they did not labor, did not work, did not guard it, then they got nothing!" Without independent unionizing rights, decision-making power over quotas, or access to class mobility, worker-peasants pilfered harvests to negotiate quota conditions, increase profits, and provide aid to peasants in need.

The kombinacja involved in moonlighting with state machinery on peasant farms had less to do with the practice itself and more to do with its politics, that is, who allowed it. To Matylda, spontaneous kombinacja disrupted the system of informal perks already in place in the circle. The director, she said, would not penalize members who used the state tractor to work their own farms as long as they owned up to it, and as long as they did it on their own farms rather than moonlighting to obtain supplemental income: "He could plow his own land, but he just had to say it because if he went to plow someone else's land but said that he went to plow his own . . ." she trailed off. But no one liked confessing their poverty to the director and waiting for him to absolve them. Zofia fired back: "Supervisors, oh, the brigadiers, and the director and he cared about it, and looked at it, and inspected it, but they kombinowali anyway." Bartek himself had ordered the state machinery services to plow his own farm without paying his due balance, and worker-peasants followed his lead, rather than subverting the spirit of the cooperative. For example, when Konrad wrote down the number of hectares he plowed on his farm using the state machines in the circle records, my father, Czesław, who tallied the circle invoices, decreased Konrad's balance or erased it so that his wages would not have to go back into paying the circle for mechanical services that Konrad himself had performed. My father's colleague in the circle administration also sold off mechanical parts from the circle warehouse on the black market to peasants who needed them to fix their wagons and machines. Bartek knew about this, but since he was paid off, he allowed it. Worker-peasants and the administrators both benefited from a broken circle, but who got to practice kombinacja freely and who was punished for it played out along patronage networks. Not all kombinacja was created equal, and some kombinators were more equal than others.

If these kombinacja tactics sound trivial and mundane, that is exactly the point. No one in Bursztyn's circle was trying to overthrow the circle per se; they were trying to reform it. By pushing the boundary of kombinacja, worker-peasants forced small concessions (e.g., free machine perks) out of local authorities (sometimes without trying too hard), and in effect, they gently rocked the boat, gradually taking control over key territories in the circle, and shifting the trajectory of local agricultural production in a way that focused on keeping high-quality food circulating in the village rather than allowing it to be exported en masse by the GS. It was not Gomułka's ideal of the circle that ushered in the golden age for the worker-peasants, but their success in reworking those circles to fit their own interests. Stopping the state's encroachment into everyday life was a victory villagers nostalgically recall today.

What was happening in Bursztyn had parallels elsewhere during the same period. In fact, ethnographer Douglas Holmes reported a similar phenomenon in northern Italy, where the rise of a welfare state that directed programs at the worker-peasantry effectively halted their proletarianization. Italian worker-peasants adopted strategies coincidentally called *combinazione* to combine wage earning and agriculture to negotiate the economic boundaries of their class status. *Combinazione* referred to a cultivator's improvisation in combining multiple sources of sustenance, which included renting and sharecropping land with temporary wage-labor pursuits. An individual who used combinazione was called a *figura mista* (transient actor) because of the liminality she achieved by traversing the agro-industrial divide.[15] Germans called the worker-peasantry *Pendler* because of their pendular swings across the divide: they "react[ed] partly like peasants (e.g., in questions of land ownership or farm prices), partly like workers (e.g., about wages and strikes)."[16] I am not making an essentialist association between all worker-peasantries and kombinacja, but in Bursztyn, the historical meaning of the circles, the locked-in class identity of worker-peasants, and the particular bifurcated identity of the worker-peasant as a class all created a perfect storm for adapting kombinacja as a means to reclaim the village after 1956. Informality bred in the spatial interstices of the state command economy.

Demographic shifts beginning in the late 1960s dramatically escalated this trend. A second generation of pioneers was entering the workforce and starting new families. Although worker-peasants could divvy up their land among their children, the lack of access to state housing and the lack of a private housing market transformed the first-generation settlers' farms into extended-family households. Zofia and Konrad were locked in their worker-peasant class, but their children became factory workers, teachers, mechanical enterprise workers, and forestry workers who secured wages during their work shifts, then returned to the farm to continue producing agricultural quotas. My mother, Bogusława, had helped on the farm since she was six years old, but she was old enough to work as an accountant in the state tannery. Her sister became a biology teacher and joined the party; her brothers worked in the mechanical enterprise and state forestry. As worker-peasant farms became more integrated, with proletarians and party members living together under one roof, the worker-peasant class interests began to spread and co-opt the proletarian and nomenklatura classes as the new generation adapted kombinacja to increase wages and informal perks to bring back to the farm. The goal, as villagers saw it, was to ensure the state subsidized production so they would not have to toil in the fields to produce quotas. Intermarriage created more ethnically integrated (Polish-Kashubian, Ukrainian-Belarusian, German-Polish) farms that became more resilient against any state tactics that played on wartime ethnic tensions to further the state's goals. Integration also expanded the reach of family and acquaintance (*znajomość*) networks. These demographic shifts, coupled with the ongoing food and housing crisis, contributed to the social reproduction of kombinacja as a survival strategy, further streamlining all kombinacja networks across generational, ethnic, class, and agro-industrial divides. Demographics established kombinacja as a key process in the formation of the "collective" in Bursztyn.

Gomułka's reforms could not solve pervasive food shortages that were compounded by the peasantry's diversion of food from the state supply chains linking villages and cities. In December 1970 widespread food shortages and skyrocketing food prices sparked worker demonstrations across the Pomeranian cities of Gdańsk, Szczecin, Elbląg, and Gdynia. Workers demanded wage increases to offset rising food costs. When the military fired on the workers, killing dozens and injuring hundreds (and then fired away again at women textile workers on strike in Łódź in 1971), Poles began to question Gomułka's priorities. Despite having risen to power with the goal of de-Stalinizing Poland, he often borrowed Stalinist tactics: "We shall combat ruthlessly provocateurs . . . who disturb public order," he warned.[17] In 1965 when Stanisław Wawrzecki, the director of a state meat trade in Warsaw, admitted to accepting more than three million złoty as bribes from directors of meat shops to hide black marketeering from the warehouse, he received the death penalty, and Gomułka did not spare his life.[18] In 1968 Ryszard Kowalski, a Polish Jewish black marketeer, who had operated various schemes since the 1940s, such as owning several dozen hundred-hectare apple orchards under different names and state contracts, was caught and prosecuted for selling water, not wine, to the state on a contract worth twenty-six million złoty.[19] Gomułka's political "solutions" to economic problems transformed these kombinators into martyrs. In his 1966 novel *Kamienne tablice* (Stone tablets), Wojciech Żukrowski reflected this growing public perception of kombinacja as a new type of freedom of expression when he connected con-artistry with individualism: "Kombinator, he wanted to persuade me into buying a ticket to Paris. He spoke so persuasively, that he would share his fame with me, until I ordered him to show me how he paints. . . . But it was clumsy, simply—nothing. But he did not lie, it is important to add. He is not a copyist, or photographer, he wants to be himself."[20] The con artist symbolized an honest portrayal of self-expression.

In 1970 Edward Gierek rose to first secretary of the Polish United Workers' Party, replaced Gomułka, and rushed through new emergency measures to rapidly modernize agricultural production by infusing it with high-capital investments loaned by the West. In 1972 the state introduced flexible contracts that, while still requiring peasants to produce quotas, allowed them to choose what they wanted to produce and how much of it they wanted to sell to the GS.[21] Gierek increased prices on agricultural goods bought from the peasants by the GS, provided easier access to credits to purchase machinery, and improved social security provisions.[22] Worker-peasants welcomed the relief but still felt repressed by the abhorrent quota system. Gierek also offset liberalization with new centralization measures to streamline circle, state farm, collective farm, and factory supply chains. Until then, circles existed as their own administrative and economic entity in each village, but after 1973, they would be centralized under a single administration in Bursztyn called the Agricultural Circles Cooperative (Spółdzielnia Kółek Rolniczych). Bursztyn's SKR-controlled circles spread across ten villages, cultivated a total of five hundred hectares of land, and employed fifty-nine worker-peasants. Neighborly help offset the shock of restructuring: during one particularly rainy season, an SKR from Wrocław sent its workers 450 kilometers north to Bursztyn to "help" with the grain harvest so that locals would not pilfer it.[23] Centralization did not stop kombinacja, which had become deeply embedded in local power relations between the worker-peasants and the state. A small administration spread across a broader terrain made it much easier for worker-peasants (and brigadiers) to moonlight without getting caught. By 1974, after more political solutions were thrown at economic problems, the price of virtually everything was still increasing faster than the real income of the population.[24] It was déjà vu all over again.

Dystopian Utopias

In the 1980s kombinacja infiltrated every niche of the command economy. The rise of the first independent trade union called Solidarity (Solidarność) in Gdańsk, the eruption of nationwide hunger demonstrations, and the state's declaration of martial law in 1981 all signaled that the apocalypse was nigh. Food was scarce. Poland borrowed twenty billion dollars on credit from the West, yet state stores still sold only vinegar. Ration cards for meat, sugar, butter, vodka, flour, milk, candy, lard, and grain did not guarantee a ration, just the possibility of one. Sales clerks at the state stores fixed the scales so that the meat weighed more, and they saved special rations for their families and acquaintances (*znajomych*). Kombinacja bred kombinacja. Instead of waiting in queues for the possibility of a slab of pork at the state store, people spent their wages buying piglets, which peasants sold out of the trunks of their Trabants. Everyone found creative solutions to survive. In Łódź, a pensioner and trout fisherman who lived across the street from a state manufacturer of nylon thread cast a line with a hook through the factory window and onto a giant bobbin, allowing him to draw a single thread across the street from the state bobbin to his private bobbin. He became the country's largest supplier of black market nylon thread. In Warsaw two bus drivers cleaned up an old bus and hooked it into the tram system, operating it as a "free enterprise bus," which denied access to party members. (This was how they got caught).[25] All Poles adapted kombinacja to carve out state territories for themselves, each with its own distinct rules of access. Even a "professional speculator" complained to a reporter in 1981 about this "flood of thousands of laymen, thousands of amateurs, who try to kombinować, grandmothers, pensioners, cashiers, drivers, various marginals and other bunglers who have made a mess of a decent economic activity."[26]

As the world turned its gaze to the drama of the Solidarity movement in Gdańsk, the Pomeranian countryside began to undergo a quiet but critical agrarian transformation. The first generation of peasant villagers who had originally settled in the province after the war was growing too old and tired to continue producing agricultural quotas even with the help of the agricultural circle. An aging worker-peasantry was problematic for several reasons. Because there was no robust and legal private housing and land market, the original peasant pioneers, like Zofia and Konrad, still held most of the land and housing titles that they had been granted by the state when they settled in the village after the war and again after decollectivization in 1957. The only way they could relinquish land was by signing it over to their children, who would then be legally required to produce quotas just as their parents had. Although they still lived with their parents because of the housing crisis, the second generation of settlers had become more proletarianized. They held jobs in factories, schools, enterprises, and offices. During the 1980s crisis, no one wanted to take over the burden of producing cheap food for the state when produce could be cultivated in lower quantities and sold at higher prices on the black market. The second generation began putting an end to the quota system by refusing to take over the quota production roles from the first generation. But this came at a cost. Peasants could not receive retirement and sell their farms at the same time; so, if their children refused to accept their land, the peasants had to "return" their land and livestock to the state in exchange for their retirement. It was as if they had never owned the land in the first place. This is what happened to Zofia and Konrad in 1983. Retirement finally freed them of the quota system, but it also stripped them of the very land that had defined their identity as peasants since they had settled on the farm in the postwar period.

This "proletarianization" of the worker-peasantry was a political victory for a state that had spent decades directing repressive campaigns against the "capitalist elements" of the very producers it had created and depended upon to produce quotas. It was equally an economic catastrophe that sent shock waves across the quota system in the village and in the province. Less quota production meant less food to go around. Quotas were not only a key lifeline for nonagricultural producers in Pomeranian villages like Bursztyn, but also for the working classes in Pomeranian cities such as Gdańsk who were already rioting for food and higher wages. As more worker-peasants exchanged their land for retirement, communes became increasingly burdened with surplus land and labor deficits. In Bursztyn the commune leased that land to state farms, which in turn leased it to workers from the village and city who needed the land to produce for their families. Lessees produced for their own subsistence needs on the condition that they sold a portion of their harvest as a quota to the state farm. In this way, agricultural quota production shifted away from the first generation of peasants and toward the second generation of proletarians in the state farms. This nationalization of peasant land stood in stark contrast to the dominant narrative of privatization in the 1980s. The peasant-state relationship drastically changed. Retired worker-peasants, unburdened from quota production, directed their labor and retirement income into producing food on a smaller scale on their half hectare of agricultural land near their house. They fortified relationships with those neighbors who still produced quotas. One of my favorite things to do as a little girl was to walk with Zofia to Mychajlo's farm, which still produced quotas, to pick up fresh milk still warm from the cow. However, this transition also placed more pressure on second-generation pioneers like my mother who lived on their parents' farm: the second generation needed to secure wages and other perks in the workplace to help support the entire family.

Agrarian change transformed kombinacja as a practice and discourse in Bursztyn. When worker-peasants retired from quotas and the circle, they were no longer on the daily front lines of resource struggles with the state. Instead, it was their children who had to adapt kombinacja techniques to offset the shortage crisis. Consequently, first-generation kombinacja memories that took place on the collective farm or within the agricultural circle began to fade and be replaced with second-generation memories that positioned kombinacja at the site of state factories, enterprises, state farms, offices, and schools—sites that the first generation usually did not have access to on a daily basis. The strategy also changed. Worker-peasants' kombinacja had focused on withholding harvests or finding a means of extracting state harvests to subsidize their own quota production. Workers, however, focused more on forging networks to extract nonagricultural resources from the workplace, moonlighting to increase wages, and withholding labor to reduce working hours. This is not to say that kombinacja did not continue on peasant farms, or that it was not already present in industrial workplaces, but this intergenerational and proletarian break in the narrative that I heard from villagers had become more pronounced. Inheritance of kombinacja replaced the inheritance of land. Proletarian memories of kombinacja among those who were born and raised under socialism, the only system and world that they had ever known, were different in texture and scope. They were not situated in personal experiences of evading authorities during the Nazi occupation or decades-long vendettas between warring families over village power. In fact, proletarian memories of kombinacja were just as much about forgetting the kombinacja of the past where the peasants and worker-peasants were at odds with the state. "What kołchoz? There was no kołchoz in Bursztyn." These were memories without a history, vague, suspended in time and space, machinelike, repetitive. There were no faces, just "one" or "the human" or "they," and there were no motives, just the idea that all kombinacja fed back into what the collective was doing at that time. Everyone was doing it, no matter how brutal or exploitative the kombinacja may have been. While first-generation settlers justified kombinacja using historical experience; second-generation settlers justified kombinacja by situating themselves in the collective. A new kombinator voice speaks and takes on a new struggle.

Uncle Roman was a bachelor; he had lost several fingers in various brutal accidents working on Zofia's farm and in the former State Agricultural Machine Enterprise (Zakład Naprawczy Mechanizacji Rolnej). He had a scruffy face, few teeth, and permanently glazed eyes. He wore a nondescript blue cap on his head and a plaid shirt, like many of the working-class men in the village his age. Roman had been born and raised in Bursztyn, but by the time I arrived to begin my research he had suffered decades of alcoholism and was one of the unemployed men who did not have the will to sign up for welfare or unemployment benefits.

He lived off the land (fungi, tubers, vegetables, fruit, poultry) and Zofia's retirement checks, as he had done for decades. In the 1970s and 1980s, though, life was different: he had a job, lived on Zofia's farm with the family, and was a valued villager. When I spoke to him in Zofia's dining room, I was very nervous because we did not have a rapport and he never really spoke to anyone. But we found common ground on the subject of kombinacja. His definition of kombinacja—"take from the state and the state, the PGR, pays for it"—was synonymous with the three state farms (państwowe gospodarstwo rolne) that buffered Bursztyn and Słupsk. He proudly recalled how those farms were bastions of socialist modernity. Hundreds of hectares of cultivated fields stretched over the horizon. There were even cargo planes that landed to transport machinery and harvests. The state farms represented everything he did not have in the village. They operated on a much grander scale, with modern machinery and had a seemingly endless supply of resources from the Council for Mutual Economic Assistance (Rada Wzajemnej Pomocy Gospodarczej). His eyes lit up with pride when he spoke about them, even though he was always on the periphery of that modernity.

As a mechanical enterprise worker, his job was to fix state farm wagons in the warehouse in Bursztyn. When workers received the wagons for repair, Roman recalled, they "would put the old part into the wagon, and the new one, to the Jew, as one would say, no? And it was [a] type of, like I say, kombinacja" ("to the Jew" was an anti-Semitic reference to the association of kombinacja and entrepreneurialism with Jewishness). When repairing the wagon, they disassembled it and substituted state screws with peasants' old screws from their wagons at home. A state and a peasant wagon would be repaired simultaneously. "If he [the director] knew about these matters then he would fire that worker . . . for such 'antics.' But so what? The wagon was working—after fixing, it is working," Roman explained. A fixed peasant wagon helped his family deliver their state quota to the GS. Kombinacja in some sites of the command economy helped actualize citizen duties and bolster production for the state in other sites of the command economy. When the enterprise sent Roman and other enterprise workers to the state farms to set up thirty-two-ton silos to store grain harvests, they too "scratched" (*skubali*) paint by dilution and painting fewer layers on the silos: "Always, a couple of liters of that paint one would scratch, no? Ha, ha." Roman loved talking about his kombinacja days in the enterprise. He revealed no pro-capitalist inclinations, nor did he express any desire to sabotage the state farm or enterprise. Rather, he saw himself on the outskirts of modernity, and when he scratched paint or replaced screws, he connected with modernization. His kombinator identity was the most evolved version of his socialist self, the competent version of who he had become in the 1980s. He and his coworkers knew the nuts and bolts of the system so well—every blind spot and loophole—that they could siphon state resources for their own private needs without suffering the consequences in their jobs. The "high" of this addiction to scratching a piece of utopia never wore off. He laughed and lit up when telling the kombinacja story and then trailed off, as if becoming conscious of reality.

Kombinacja stories equipped proletarians with the tools to mythologize their socialist selves. I heard similar stories from former state farm workers. Apolonia's story, like Roman's story, revealed the most brilliant version of her socialist self, a woman who could simultaneously pilfer resources she felt entitled to and outmaneuver the director:

> But they [the PGR administration] did not say anything. There was theft but no one was punished for it. I put my fingers into the soil and took a couple of potatoes. And the director is driving by from the PGR. He comes, and says this, "Hello, what are you doing?" And I said, "Mr. Director, I do not have potatoes, I do not have a husband. I do have my own field, but it is very far. And here, I have them so close [to the PGR] and I did no harm." And he said "Apolonia" because he knew me well because my in-laws lived in that PGR. So he says, "Apolonia," he says, 'You know it is not allowed.' And I said, "I know it is not allowed, but I did it quickly!"

What I find fascinating about these stories is how they expose the psyche of the proletarian mind. In Polish, the phrase "not allowed" (*nie wolno*) also means "not slow," so Apolonia played on his words to get him to laugh. Her joke also hinted at the bodily aesthetics of kombinacja. Because she performed the maneuver quickly, she achieved a speed of liminality that "blurred" the pilfering from the gaze of the state. It is as if she had performed the gesture in the blind spot of the state allowed by the collective, as if the speed of the kombinacja, or the fact that it was not visible, made it justifiable. Several other farm workers also said something along the lines of "no one even saw" and "what they stole was not visible" to justify the action of kombinacja. Apolonia's joke played on the same idea Roman was getting at: if the kombinacja was liminal, invisible, then it was justified because it reflected a worker's skill in performing it. The individual body blurred into the collective. You can see in these kombinacja narratives how much more intimately connected the proletarians felt to the machine of socialist production. To perform kombinacja, they had to become ghostlike, manipulating their bodies in particular spaces and at particular speeds to perform a kombinacja that would render the action invisible and therefore "justifiable."

Rather than seeing these practices as pro-capitalist resistance against socialist production, many state farm workers saw themselves as proletarians who were entitled to resources because they owned the means of production. Taking state farm resources was not stealing them: "They did not steal over there. When they dug out the potatoes, one took some potatoes in one's pocket or in a bag for dinner. I did not consider that stealing." They justified their kombinacja within a socialist worldview. I heard similar variations of this rationale elsewhere. Fidelis, who was a commune administrator in Bursztyn at the time, solved his coffee shortages one Christmas holiday through his daughter, who worked in the clothing section of a state department store in the city. She acquired a packet from an acquaintance (*znajoma*) who worked in the food section of the store. Fidelis said that his daughter's "kombinacja was not stealing. It was normal. If I could not purchase it, I had to kombinować." He added, "To steal it, it would have been that she would have put it in her pocket and would not put the money in the cash register. That is stealing. But, she [her acquaintance] took it and sold it to normal people. It has to be someone who has a right to it." If someone accessed state goods through a worker with official access to those goods, then it was not stealing; if someone had barged in and extracted state resources outside of a patronage network, then it was stealing. It was impossible to tell whether the workers truly believed they were performing their socialist roles as proletarian revolutionaries, but it was a clever discourse that pushed back against any state official who denied them the right to pilfer: to deny them would be to expose the state as the true owner of socialist property.

The ability to pull oneself out of poverty through kombinacja, and the state's allowance of it or inability to control it, contributed to the very socialist ideal of the state farm. State farm workers, bound by the collective experience of poverty, adapted kombinacja to negotiate wages, hours, and entitlements, like a loosely formed shadow labor union, without overtly rising up against the state farm administration. They pilfered state harvests and dairy to feed their families and private livestock to offset the cost of food on the black market, sold state farm harvests to city workers at night to earn extra wages, used state farm horses and equipment on their allocated gardens. Irena, a former state farm worker, explained to me that conditions of collective poverty bred conditions of collective kombinacja, but it was the very free reign of kombinacja on her state farm that attracted workers and became a part of the proletarian culture:

> A lot of people went into the PGR because in the PGR, one had a home and guaranteed work. Because in the PGR, one did not earn a lot—one could steal a lot because one was raising a cow and pig and everything to that, right? It was the state's. Everyone somehow made it through. Everyone received their own ration, but if one wanted more, one stole it, right? Brought it and fed it and no one was interested with that because the earnings were small and the work was difficult in the PGRs, but many people made ends meet in the PGRs. The mind has to work! Use kombinacja! Without kombinacja, no one will make money, because one would only make pennies! Yes!

Utopia was achieved not by following the rules and being the perfect worker but by reworking the rules for one's own benefit without punishment. It was a new kind of labor power by which the sheer masses of workers overpowered state officials. Kombinacja memories of the proletarians portray these dystopian utopias. However, it was in the state directors' best interest to allow kombinacja so that workers could find solutions to pervasive poverty, feel in control of the farm, maintain high confidence in socialist production, and feel no need to unionize. Whether kombinacja was a form of passive resistance or a way for pacified workers to rationalize their world is unclear. Either way, kombinacja kept the peace. State farm workers began to see themselves as a new collective that could manipulate state discourses and blur the boundary between resistance and accommodation.

Kombinacja became the process whereby villagers worked up to and helped actualize the state's vision of socialist modernity. While Gierek's reforms allowed people to build structures on their farms, basic building materials and hardware were not available in state stores or allocations. The only available materials existed in state workplaces. "If one wanted to renovate something, then one had to kombinować everything! There was no possibility of [state] allocation, so one had to simply use some type of kombinacja," Fidelis recalled. An informal services sector exploded onto the village scene. When Bursztyn planned to build four apartment blocks, only three were built because the materials for an entire building had vanished. Workers like Roman in various state enterprises who had daily access to the state's wrenches, screws, pipes, fixtures, paint, metal, glass, and glue moonlighted and installed state property in clients' homes. Residents like Apolonia, the retired postal worker who joked with the state farm director, received free home renovations from a state farm construction crew. My mother, Bogusława, recalled how metal fences on people's properties had the same paint color as state machines. Officials allowed it: "They were looking through their fingers, the directors!" claimed Gosia, a retired tannery worker. Her partner Kacper, the unpopular Soviet official, added that directors too were villagers and needed services: "It happened often. If someone needed to renovate the home, but how? You looked for someone who worked in the enterprise who 'had' parts and there, if they [the clients] wanted, simply stole it. And they said, 'He *kombinuje*,' yes."

Collective silence about proletarian kombinacja contributed to this new process of identity formation. A new currency fueled this practice: half liters of vodka. "When one put the half liter [on the table] it [was] meant for there to be silence," Zofia recalled. Vodka did not leave a monetary trail and was consumed on the spot, shared by worker and client to erase the transaction, reinforce fraternal bonds, establish mutual interests, and pave the way for future business dealings.[27] A new shadow services sector fed off of porous state enterprises, but in ways, such as vodka rituals, that reinforced the imaginary of a classless and collective village identity. (People are nostalgic for that feeling of the collective, but not for the economic conditions that required people to work together to secure resources.)

As a new village collective took form, one heavily saturated in proletarian identity but disconnected from the "gaze" of the state, new underground spaces opened up to contain this more experimental identity formation. Women who received vodka rations on their cards but did not drink themselves opened illegal pubs in their homes called *meliny* where factory and enterprise workers could congregate after work to drink fifty-milliliter shots of vodka, listen to Radio Europe, watch the news on the developments in the Solidarity movement, and make deals. Grażyna, a retired tannery worker, expressed the sense of camaraderie she felt when people visited her *melina*: "We had the television in the window in the other room. We put it out in the window. The men would come, we put down half a liter, they drank some, they talked, they did not get drunk but they drank a half liter, sat, talked, and somehow it was good." Meliny also sold illegal moonshine (*bimber*) that became increasingly popular as workers began to dabble in makeshift home distilleries created out of tubes, bottles, and sugar acquired from state factories and enterprises through kombinacja. This was a big deal. When the Polish Committee of National Liberation (Polskiej Komitet Wyzwolenia Narodowego) came to power in 1944, one of the first laws it passed was the nationalization of alcohol, and the state cracked down on illegal alcohol production that competed with its vodka revenues. Reclaiming vodka and meliny became bundled up with reclaiming value, capital flows, redistribution, production, spaces of consumption, and new identities. Nonetheless, meliny were still risky. They were operated by a trusted network of friends, family, and neighbors who would deny an operation's existence if the police burst in. Alcohol would be held in the neighbors' basement or in the trunk of someone's car.[28] Alcohol allowed villagers to escape into a new liminal state. In the meliny, everyone drank to transition, and everyone was in transition also.

Mixed forms of production emerged. A shadow tannery opened alongside the state tannery in Bursztyn. This shadow project produced leather and fur goods using locally sourced foxes and mink but used chemicals and processing equipment systematically siphoned from the adjacent state tannery. My mother, who worked in the state tannery for fifteen years as an accountant, recalled that the director knew about it, but that it was part of the broader culture of kombinacja in the state tannery that ranged from pilfering screws and fixtures from the factory floor to purposefully sewing defective hats, gloves, shoes, and jackets to keep for personal use. The state factory even organized trips to flea markets in Budapest, where the factory workers could earn extra income by selling defective leather goods at the open-air markets.[29] When the director of the state factory was interviewed for a small book that was published for the village's fortieth anniversary in 1985, he claimed, "It does not matter to us, obviously, to work up to large profits. [Meeting quota] is enough."[30] As long as the factories met the quotas, they could do whatever they wanted with the rest of production.

Villagers loved the shadow tannery because it catered to them rather than sending all leather goods down the factory supply chain to other consumers. And it came to good use. During hyperinflation in the late 1980s, villagers like my mother invested their złoty into mink hats, scarves, and gloves produced by that tannery. In the larger scheme of things, the private tannery represented locals' reclaiming of local production, rerouting its supply chains, and reinvesting capital into their own village. It required a coordinated kombinacja and culture of silence on all levels, from the workers to the directors, to ensure that the factory would not be shut down by county authorities. Shadow enterprises like these were not the "private" sector, however, because they were far too dependent on the state supply chains, and so they went down with the mother ship.

In the 1980s Bursztynians were living out the most evolved version of their socialist selves. They recall kombinacja during the late socialist period most vividly not only because it was practiced openly and without legal consequence but also because it marked the apex of village unity and collective consciousness. The informal economy of kombinacja could not have co-opted the redistributive function of the state were it not for villagers' collaborative spirit and ability to coordinate resource flows across the very ethnic and class divisions that had plagued the village since its genesis in the postwar era. Back then, villagers still did not have access to Western media that portrayed the inevitability of communism's end or that linked the Solidarity movement to Poles' collective desire for capitalism. Most villagers had been born under socialism; it was the only world they had ever known. They grasped the crisis with a socialist worldview. To them, kombinacja was "taking" rather than "stealing," because as the proletariat, they rightfully owned state property and were entitled to redistribute it. They also did not believe in the inevitable collapse of socialism. When the Solidarity union representatives arrived in Bursztyn to sign people up, villagers were skeptical because they believed it was a foreign, capitalist takeover—just another authority with power. Through kombinacja, they were achieving a different brand of "solidarity," a mixed economic model that they had collectively established on the grassroots level, not by following a plan. In Marxist-Leninist theory, when citizens reach the most advanced stages of socialism, they no longer need an organizing state apparatus to suppress the enrichment elements from co-opting society; instead, they take over the reins of the state and devise self-policing mechanisms that begin the process of "withering away of the state."[31] Was this how Bursztynians saw the end of their world? Did they see an alternate noncapitalist future?

The state's dystopia had become their utopia. By carving out their kombinacja niches in the state "territory" and redistributing state resources outside of the state "plan," villagers achieved a taste of liberty. One had to "use kombinacja! Think! One's own method! To somehow escape from the poverty or from this imposed structure," Fidelis recalled. "If it was not included [in the state alloca-tion], then it was kombinacja," Zofia added. Progress for them was not based on how many people signed a petition but on reworking the entire state apparatus, rejecting form and structure, and finding freedom in transience and temporality. A lot of outsiders did not feel comfortable with these liminal states. Describing a 1980s Wisłok village in southeastern Poland, Chris Hann wrote that kombinować "refers to the whole undignified, frequently underhand and devious, maneuvers persons must make to accomplish anything." To an outsider, that is probably what it looked like. But I have attempted to take into account the broader his-tory of kombinacja in the making of Bursztyn since 1945, not as a practice that exploded in the 1970s and 1980s when scholars and Westerners started to pay at-tention to it, but as a progression of adaptations to the changing system to keep ideas and spaces of freedom alive. Intergenerational stories of kombinacja cap-ture a much longer struggle against the claustrophobia of state repression. And in the 1980s, claiming freedom did not mean accepting a new capitalist doctrine. It meant maximizing one's control over local state "territories" or resource pools, denying the state its form, keeping power away from the oppressors, and creating one's own utopian reformulations of supply chains. The achievement villagers remembered most fondly was taking hold of the state and rerouting all supply chains to their homes and for their own domestic use. Instead of the state order-ing their lives, villagers could use the state to reorder their own lives.

Villagers' memories from the late socialist period reflect these private uto-pias: stories about the best versions of themselves, siphoning state resources with-out penalty, living in united families and communities in which people talked to one another. They reveal a life in which one's value was based not on economic capital but on social capital accumulated through ingenuity and creativity, one in which the classes were unified and officials suffered from the same scarcity of resources as the rest of the villagers. Everyone was a victim but still worked to create solutions and secure state resources. While this idea of the unified collec-tive was prevalent in their memories, and often a justification for kombinacja in and of itself, the stories revealed a heightened form of individuality expressed through the formation of creative and imaginative solutions. In her ethnography on peasants in Łódź and Podhale, Frances Pine found that peasants' usage of the phrase "Trzeba umieć kombinować" ("One must know how to kombinować") symbolized "the most basic way in which villagers make themselves social per-sons and craft their social world."[32] Even making a substitution to a recipe was kombinacja because it represented creativity. Like organic work in the nineteenth century that allowed ordinary people to resist the foreign occupier in their own way, the practice of kombinacja became much more democratized in the late so-cialist period, when everyone could engage in collective individualism in their ev-eryday lives. People were not thinking about change on a large scale, but through strategic substitutions and deviations, they created new material landscapes that reflected their individuality outside of the "state plan." Proletarian memories of collective individualism are curious: although kombinacja was perceived to be a mass phenomenon nestled in the socialist ideology of the state, these memories were also atomized, as if drifting away on millions of thawing ice floes.

This intense period of identity transformation from peasant to proletarian within the village is often summarized by one word: *miracle*. "Cudy się działy!" (Miracles happened!) was a common phrase. "Everyone knew! Those were miracles! Miracles occurred here," Motylek recalled. The word *miracles* brings to mind the image of Jesus in the New Testament, using his divine powers to create something out of nothing, change water into wine, feed crowds with fish and loaves, do the impossible. But in this case, miracles (*cudy*) were a bad omen of change that comes through shifts imperceptible to the naked eye. Fidelis recalled that local officials, struggling for power, even further exploited forced volunteer labor projects for workers called *czyny społeczne* (the Polish form of Soviet *subbotniks*) to extract labor from them: "So they would buy all of these rakes, and shovels, and miracles. Then they distributed them during the *czyn* because one had to work somehow! But then, it was like this: one person walked off somewhere from the *czyn*—because no one patrolled it!" The workers no longer wanted to participate in state miracles. Miracles represented the new, out-of-this world, dystopian extremes with no moral backing that took hold of the state and people. They reflected the psychological domain of class struggles between the villagers and the officials, struggles based not on what was visible or formal but on the terrain of the invisible. Miracles' dystopianism and invisibility stood as a curious subtext to the ubiquity and openness of kombinacja that everyone professed existed in the 1980s. The subtext exposed their understanding of the world being split apart by new and powerful forces. The state searched for miracles to stay in power; villagers countered with new miracles to distance themselves from the state.

Solidarity Lost

The Pomeranian province, where Bursztyn is located, was one of the more nationalized and proletarianized provinces in the Recovered Territories and Poland, but it suffered decades of failed policies and implementations at the local level. The failures began as early as the postwar period, when the agrarian reform created a middle peasant class that it later attempted to destroy with dekulakization campaigns while simultaneously forcing peasants to produce agricultural quotas to feed workers in Pomeranian cities like Słupsk and Gdańsk. This effort to turn peasants into both second-class citizens and socialist experiments caught up with the state. When the peasants decided they'd had enough and began using kombinacja to withhold quotas or to ensure that the state subsidized the agricultural production forced on them, this further emptied the shelves of the state stores in the cities and shifted the circulation of food in the province into the black market, where prices were much higher. Rural and urban kombinacja responded to a broken system and further broke it down. Decades of fighting against Soviet occupation had been waged in the blind spots of the state where workers, peasants, collective farm workers, and worker-peasants negotiated higher wages, agricultural subsidies, and better working hours without the representation of an independent trade union. The state's strategy of denying workers and peasants their rights and instead throwing political solutions at economic problems only fanned the resistance. The explosion of hunger and wage demonstrations across Pomeranian cities starting in the 1970s and the Soviet military crackdown on the demonstrators further fueled the sentiment that Poles were under occupation both by the Soviet Union and by local elites. And so, the Pomeranian province became the cradle of the world famous Solidarity movement that tore down the communist system in Poland and contributed to the collapse of the Soviet Union.

It is tempting to conflate the late kombinacja mentality described in the previous section with the rise of the Solidarity movement in the 1980s because both express a kind of labor power, but they are not the same. When the Solidarity trade union activists came to Bursztyn's factories, workers were wary of any "persuasion" (*namawianie*) by outsiders promising yet another utopian vision of modernity. That is not to say that kombinacja and Solidarity do not have the same roots. In fact, the independent trade union formed in 1980 not because workers wanted foreign-bred capitalism but because Anna Walentynowicz, a Stakhanovite crane operator in the Lenin Shipyards in Gdańsk spoke out against her supervisors' stealing of shipyard money to buy lottery tickets and was fired for defending the socialist discipline of work. Workers were fed up with elite corruption; they wanted changes, like a five-day, forty-hour workweek, wage hikes, and less hazardous working conditions. This call for reform was, in many respects, an extension of workers' strategies that had sought fair wages and working hours through informal kombinacja tactics. Did Walentynowicz really see the solution in foreign and elite-driven "capitalism" when she spoke out against elite corruption and in favor of workers' rights? Or was she calling out for a third way, an experimental mixed system, similar to that in late socialist Bursztyn?

The Solidarity movement and the concept of freedom itself were quickly co-opted and defined by people who had never worked a day in a factory or on a field. David Ost argues that Warsaw and Western elites' co-optation of the Solidarity movement, during the years from 1981 to 1983, when General Jaruzelski instated martial law and imprisoned the original organizers like Walentynowicz and Wałęsa, radically transformed Solidarity from a labor to an anti-labor movement. The infiltration of the movement by elites was its demise. Warsaw intellectuals like Adam Michnik, whose attempts at resistance against the state had been largely unsuccessful, were drawn to the magnetic victories of the worker demonstrations. They began to visit the factories and sign up with the trade union themselves, but they became increasingly vocal against Solidarity's working class. Angry and brutish unionists were viewed as a threat to an intellectual and more refined "democracy." Famous Polish economists like Leszek Balcerowicz, who had initially supported early Solidarity's self-management, pushed for shock-doctrine policies that were encouraged by Harvard economists like Jeffrey Sachs and that reflected the worldviews of Ronald Reagan and Margaret Thatcher. "Little by little, a new intellectual consensus began to emerge: that democracy was grounded not in an active citizenry, as had been argued from the mid-1970s through 1981, but in private property and a free market," Ost writes.[33]

By 1987 Solidarity's program included major cuts to wages and social programs, and those workers who had formed the movement were pacified and isolated, paying dues and pitifully distributing *samizdat* press.[34] Shana Penn writes that this purge also masculinized the movement. Helena Łuczywo, Barbara Labuda, Ewa Kulik, and many others who kept the movement alive by community organizing, operating underground newspapers like *Tygodnik Mazowsze*, and working out of "floating offices," were pushed away from the bargaining table as Nobel Peace Prize winner Lech Wałęsa sold out and became the leader of this pro-capitalist movement. By 1989 the famous Round Table Talks that took place in Warsaw between the government and opposition were male dominated and elite driven, without the participation of labor or women.[35] When miners spoke of occupational diseases and advocated for labor code changes, they were called "utopian" and schooled on "marketization."[36] Solidarity "solutions" included privatization, liquidation of jobs, and the shutting down of entitlement programs. What could be more anti-labor? Furthermore, the speed of the transformation and the readiness of the Solidarity elites to usher in the shock-doctrine liberalization reforms further empowered the communist-era elites. There was no time to hold them accountable for their crimes under communism. Rather, the new authorities promising freedom and waving the banner of capitalism needed these same communist elites—the only "trained" government personnel in the villages—to usher in privatization. There was no justice for the peasants and the villagers who saw flag-waving communists "rehabilitate" themselves into capitalists and carry out privatization on their terms. The more elites hijacked the Solidarity movement, the more workers' confidence in the movement failed.[37] By 1990 membership was a fifth of what it had been in 1981, with few women and even fewer youth.[38]

My family was desperately straddling the subsistence chasms caused by these tectonic shifts. In Bursztyn, the very communist elites who had misused power and against whom the entire idea of Solidarity had originally been organized took charge of the privatization process. They were the most competent, supposedly, to be capitalism's representatives and redraw the very world they had created and policed. When the officials commenced the privatization of a local state restaurant, my parents, who waited tables there part-time, decided to buy it and become Bursztyn's first private restaurateurs. But my mother recalled in horror how the old ways of nomenklatura privilege infected the restaurant:

> It was 1987. In those years communism was no longer around, but people lived under the communist ghost. One of the bigger problems was people's dishonesty. Often people did not have money but they came to the restaurant, ordered meals and alcohol and after eating or drinking said that today everything was *na kreche*. That term means, "Today, I do not have money and when I get paid then I will pay the bill." Often, this *krecha* visited our restaurant. We set up a notebook of debtors but all for nothing because they were in talks with the tricksters and hooligans who played pranks and vandalized the restaurant. The police did not react to our complaints. The police were afraid [of authorities] or they were waiting for extra money.

When the Berlin Wall fell in 1989, my parents had already declared bankruptcy on the private restaurant and were back to what they knew: producing quotas for the state. Thanks to Solidarity reforms, when all economic safety nets and state workplaces were "liquidated" by the same state officials who had controlled the village for decades, we struggled to survive. We found normalcy only in the diminishing pools of what was once our Soviet world. After the agricultural circle was abruptly shut down and liquidated—by the circle director himself, of course—my father, jobless, found work in the still-nationalized transportation administration in Słupsk. We briefly moved to the city, where we lived in a 1970s apartment block for workers and leased land from a dying state farm outside of Słupsk. To make ends meet, we cultivated strawberries on that land by hand and sold a portion of the crop to the state farm so it could meet its quota. We sold the rest along the side of the road to people driving between Słupsk and the Baltic port town of Ustka. When we won the immigration lottery and left for America in 1992, it was probably the only way we could have truly freed ourselves from the corruption spilling over from the old to the new regime. Those who stayed behind were not as lucky. Communism's ghosts and their conjurers continued to haunt and torment those villagers throughout the transformation.

Thus, when villagers talk about the age of Solidarity in the 1980s, they do not refer to the same moments that Westerners talk about, like Lech Wałęsa's Nobel Peace Prize in 1983, Ronald Reagan's "Tear Down This Wall" speech in 1987, the fall of the Berlin Wall in 1989, or the end of the Cold War. In fact, communism's end came at different moments for them. Some will say it ended in 1983; others will say it ended in 1996. There are even those who will say that not much changed for them because they were, remain, and will be poor for the rest of their lives, regardless of the economic and political system. Villagers narrate transformation not through grand international events but through their memories of when they personally became disconnected from the umbilical cord of collective kombinacja. As the quote above shows, for my mother, communism was over by 1987, well before the fall of the Berlin Wall, because it was when she transformed into a private entrepreneur. The transformation was not about "winning." Proletarian memories of kombinacja may be filled with stories of pilfering resources from the state, but they are equally about what the workers lost in the 1980s. Many people in Pomerania were not ready to leave the socialist system; rather, they wanted to reform it, make it their own world. Kombinacja stories are memories of loss: loss of labor power, loss of human dignity, loss of employment, loss of access to the fields, loss of property, loss of capital, loss of family. The memories themselves reveal the moment before the storm, a moment in time when there was a true collective sense of labor power in the village among women and men, workers and peasants, elites and nonelites. It was a brief moment of experimentation and self-determination in which the power to pilfer resources from the state, albeit grim, was still a means of taking control of one's condition of poverty and making something out of it. It was self-determination even if it was set in the bowels of socialist dystopia. And we, the third generation in the Recovered Territories, have inherited their proletarian memories of Solidarity lost.

Notes

1. Applebaum, *Iron Curtain*, 456.
2. "Rebellious Compromiser," *Time*, 30.
3. Dziennik Ustaw z 1957, Numer 39, Pozycja 172, Ustawa z dnia 13 lipca 1957r. o obrocie nieruchomościami rolnymi (Act of July 13, 1957, on the trade of agricultural property), 458–59, Dziennik Ustaw Rzeczypospolitej Polskiej; Dziennik Ustaw z 1958, Numer 17, Pozycja 71, Ustawa z dnia 12 marca 1958r. o sprzedaży państwowych nieruchomości rolnych oraz uporządkowania niektórych spraw, związanych z przeprowadzeniem reformy rolnej i osadnictwa rolnego (Act of March 12, 1958, on the sale of state-owned agricultural property, and ordering certain matters related to the carrying out of land reform and agricultural settlement), 299–301, Dziennik Ustaw Rzeczypospolitej Polskiej, http://www.dziennikustaw.gov.pl/DU/1958/71/1.
4. "Rebellious Compromiser," 30.
5. Davies, *God's Playground*, 2:596; Korbonski, *Politics of Socialist Agriculture*, 284–91; Kruszewski, *Oder-Neisse Boundary*, 124; Lewis, "Peasantry," 48.
6. Korbonski, *Politics of Socialist Agriculture*, 296.
7. Hann, *Village without Solidarity*, 42.
8. Ibid.
9. Lewis, "Peasantry," 77.
10. Ibid., 61.

11. Żurawski, *Zarys Dziejów*, 53.

12. Ibid., 52.

13. Dziennik Ustaw z 1957, Numer 39, Pozycja 172, Ustawa z dnia 13 lipca 1957r. o obrocie nieruchomościami rolnymi (Act of July 13, 1957, on the trade of agricultural property), 458–59, Dziennik Ustaw Rzeczypospolitej Polskiej, http://www.dziennikustaw.gov.pl/DU/1957/172/1; Dziennik Ustaw z 1958, Numer 3, Pozycja 7, Ustawa z dnia 28 grudnia 1957r. o dostawach, robotach i usługach na rzecz jednostek państwowych (Act of December 28, 1957, on supplies, work, and services for state entities), 33–34, Dziennik Ustaw Rzeczypospolitej Polskiej, http://www.dziennikustaw.gov.pl/DU/1958/7/1; Dziennik Ustaw z 1958, Numer 6, Pozycja 17, Rozporządzenie Rady Ministrów z dnia 13 stycznia 1958r. w sprawie dostaw, robót i usług na rzecz jednostek państwowych (Council of Ministers of January 13, 1958, on supplies, works, and services for state entities), 50–52, Dziennik Ustaw Rzeczypospolitej Polskiej, http://www.dziennikustaw.gov.pl/DU/1958/17/1; Dziennik Ustaw z 1958, Numer 17, Pozycja 71, Ustawa z dnia 12 marca 1958r. o sprzedaży państwowych nieruchomości rolnych oraz uporządkowania niektórych spraw, związanych z przeprowadzeniem reformy rolnej i osadnictwa rolnego (Act of March 12, 1958, on the sale of state-owned agricultural property, and ordering certain matters related to the carrying out of land reform and agricultural settlement), 299–301, Dziennik Ustaw Rzeczypospolitej Polskiej, http://www.dziennikustaw.gov.pl/DU/1958/71/1; Dziennik Ustaw z 1958, Numer 17, Pozycja 72, Ustawa z dnia 12 marca 1958r. o umorzeniu niektórych długów i ciężarów (Act of March 12, 1958, on the redemption of certain debt and burdens), 301, Dziennik Ustaw Rzeczypospolitej Polskiej, http://www.dziennikustaw.gov.pl/DU/1958/72/1; Dziennik Ustaw z 1958, Numer 31, Pozycja 136, Ustawa z dnia 22 maja 1958r. o popieraniu melioracji wodnych dla potrzeb rolnictwa (Act of May 22, 1958, supporting land reclamation for agriculture), 445–48, Dziennik Ustaw Rzeczypospolitej Polskiej, http://www.dziennikustaw.gov.pl/DU/1958/136/1.

14. Dziennik Ustaw z 1959, Numer 48, Pozycja 294, Rozporządzenie Ministerstwa Rolnictwa z dnia 3 sierpnia 1959r. w sprawie norm wynagradzania za świadczenia z tytułu pomocy sąsiedzkiej w rolnictwie (Regulation Ministry of Agriculture dated August 3, 1959, on standards of remuneration for the benefit of neighborly help in agriculture), 562, Dziennik Ustaw Rzeczypospolitej Polskiej, http://www.dziennikustaw.gov.pl/DU/1959/294/1.

15. Holmes, "Peasant-Worker Model," 736.

16. Bergmann, "Change Processes," 87; Holmes, "Peasant-Worker Model," 742.

17. "Rebellious Compromiser," 34.

18. "Syn Warzeckiego dostanie 200 tyś. zł za śmierć ojca" (Warzecki's son will receive 200,000 złoty for his father's death), *Newsweek.pl*, February 4, 2010, http://polska.newsweek.pl/syn-wawrzeckiego-dostanie-200-tys--zl-za-smiercojca,53160,1,1.html.

19. Sampson, "Second Economy," 54–55.

20. Żukrowski, *Kamienne tablice*, 43.

21. Dziennik Ustaw z 1971, Numer 27, Pozycja 253, Ustawa z dnia 26 października 1971r. o zniesieniu obowiązkowych dostaw zbóż, ziemniaków i zwierząt rzeźnych (Act of October 26, 1971, on the abolition of compulsory deliveries of grain, potatoes and slaughter animals), 265, Dziennik Ustaw Rzeczypospolitej Polskiej, http://www.dziennikustaw.gov.pl/DU/1971/253/1.

22. Kubik, *Power of Symbols*, 22–24.

23. Żurawski, *Zarys Dziejów*, 52.

24. Kubik, *Power of Symbols*, 22–24; Kurczewski, *Resurrection of Rights*, 143; Mazurek, "Keeping It Close," 298; Wedel, *Private Poland*, 80.

25. Steven, *Poles*, 56.

26. Kochanowski, *Tylnymi dzwiami*, 93.

27. Hann, *Village without Solidarity*, 89; Firlit and Chłopecki, "When Theft Is Not Theft," 103; Wedel, *Private Poland*, 29; Łoś, "Dynamics of the Second Economy," 37; Pawlik, "Intimate Commerce," 81.

28. Kochanowski, *Tylnymi dzwiami*, 223–24.

29. When my mother read this passage in 2017, she said that it was not true. She claimed that the state tannery only produced hides and sold them farther down the supply chain to other state entities. The Budapest trips were organized informally through the GS, and everyone who signed up sold their own private goods on an individual basis at those markets. They were not, as I suggest, selling defective leather goods from the state tannery. Since her earlier and later recollections clash, I have chosen to keep both of them.

30. Żurawski, *Zarys Dziejów*, 81.

31. See Lenin, *State and Revolution*, 15.

32. Pine, "Dangerous Modernities?," 193.

33. Ost, *Defeat of Solidarity*, 41.

34. Ibid., 42–43.

35. Penn, *Solidarity's Secret*, 181.

36. Ost, *Defeat of Solidarity*, 46–47.

37. Ibid., 46.

38. Ibid., 54.

6   Kombinacja's Ghosts

Reunification street, running through the heart of Bursztyn, is booming with liquor shops and convenience stores heavily stocked with walls of alcohol. The bus stop benches alongside the commune headquarters are occupied not by passengers but by middle-aged men with red faces, toothless grins, and missing fingers. They wear trucker hats, plaid shirts, and dusty, blue worker jackets they were once allocated by the state. Some are prostrate, in and out of consciousness, others are already passed out on or underneath the benches; some are sitting on the benches with elbows propped on their knees and engaged in slurred conversations. Then, one of them spots a patron—a former coworker—and quickly jumps up from the bench to ask this acquaintance for spare change. The men pool their złoty and walk across the street to the store to purchase the 190-proof ethanol called *spirytus* they share back on the benches. They drink it all day, until they pass out on the street or in ditches. At night, they are dragged home by the police, sober up, and restart the cycle. These are the former peasants, enterprise workers, factory workers, and state farm workers who represent Bursztyn's broken dreams. They rely on socialist-era fraternal bonds to create resource niches around the village. By coercing money out of people and pooling their resources, they reproduce the collective. They only look like they are "in transit"; they never actually make it onto the bus of capitalist modernity.

Uncle Roman was a regular on the benches during my fieldwork. He got there through a series of unfortunate events. After returning from the Polish People's Army (Ludowe Wojsko Polskie) in the 1970s, he suffered from alcoholism and in the 1980s was forced through multiple state-sanctioned detoxification programs. Whenever he came back to the village, the alcoholism returned as soon as he met up with his drinking fraternity. After the state mechanical enterprise shut down in 1990, many of the former workers, like Roman, never found employment again. Many of them were too young for retirement benefits, so during that period, they spiraled into alcoholism they never crawled out of. Although villagers see them as a cancer in the village because of the violence they bring to their families and to the public sphere—women's faces are bruised canvasses of their violence—the villagers are also fascinated by how these men are still alive after decades of alcoholism. This is all that these men have left: proof of their superhuman strength.

After Konrad's death from colon cancer in 1997, Roman assumed the traditional role of the peasant patriarch (*gospodarz*) of Zofia's privatized farm. While in theory his role required him to work on the farm, secure it from poachers, produce profits, reinvest in production and so forth, the widespread collapse of peasant agriculture in the village left him with only the title. The only land Roman and Zofia had left was the garden behind the farmhouse, where they produced cabbage, potatoes, carrots, cucumbers, garlic, tomatoes, and various herbs. Zofia's thousand-złoty monthly retirement checks paid for everything from property taxes to seeds. With rising prices, this fixed budget plunged them further and further into poverty. Without funds, access to adequate rehabilitation programs, or widespread community action, Roman and other middle-aged men like him who do not qualify for retirement and who are too stricken with alcoholism to register for unemployment or welfare benefits, are left stranded. When Zofia gave Roman money to secure welfare in Słupsk, he never got farther than the alcohol benches. The benches are a perfect metaphor for the purgatory these men face on a daily basis.

Uncle Kuba, Zofia's younger son, claims that Roman is a kombinator, a master of disguises who can manipulate faces and events all to end up with money for alcohol. At home, Roman neoliberalized his domestic duties. He collected fees for chores he was expected to fulfill as the patriarchal head of the farm. Every morning Roman would perform a small "job": he might, for example, pick up the newspaper or fill the coal oven to "earn" money. Then after breakfast, Roman would ask Zofia for "cigarette money" (*pieniądze na papierosy*), meaning alcohol money. Often, though, he did not even have to ask her. When I was in the kitchen, the two skirted around me, working together as a team to evade my eye and to make sure the five złoty passed unnoticed. This went for larger projects too. Instead of hiring a private-sector construction crew to take down an agricultural barn that resulted in high property taxes, Zofia "hired" Roman, who spent more than a year taking it apart while she continued to pay taxes on it. His regime of terror and abuse forced Zofia into submission. She was afraid to cut Roman off.

This was not just a problem with Roman; it is what many of the first-generation villagers face with the second generation of fallen workers who continue to work for alcohol like they did under communism. Village women complain that the men are taking over every niche of even the smallest "services." On Sundays, they have begun to push out the children who hold the church doors for the congregation after mass in exchange for a piece of candy. Władysława, a retired machine operator who lost her son to alcoholism on the benches, explained how they "work":

> When they get together in the morning, they are so deprived! Every one of them searches, searches, and meets a known face and "Lend me [złoty], sir, lend me." And so they pool [złoty] together, come to the store, and in the store, they are short two to three *groszy* and the woman at the store waves her hand because they are regular customers. Or the store clerk is sweeping outside of

the store, so then he grabs the broom from her and "helps" out. Then she gives a *grosz* or two and they beg like that. He will stand and will see a female acquaintance coming, "Can you please lend me [złoty]?" So for holy peace, one gives it to them, and that is how they help one another. Some will find bottles and cans, yes, yes. Sometimes, that Szymon—when there is some place to cut some wood, or to hold even the piece of wood, then he is there. When here Janina was cutting wood, here [points], the neighbor Władek was doing it [for her]. So, Szymon—no one called him over here. He came and looked, and then they were holding something up and he immediately came and helped them carry it. They finished cutting the wood, she gives Władek the money and [Szymon] says, "And me? Five złoty?" And she says, "For what? I did not ask you!" And he says, "But I helped." And she said, "And did I ask you?" So, they force it out like that.

Men like Roman make deals from the benches for alcohol money. One day during my fieldwork, a city couple drove into the yard and told Zofia that they wanted to pick up the horseradish they had already paid Roman for. Zofia was upset because while Roman made the deal, she had to do the labor of hacking away at the horseradish plant for the strangers. On another occasion, a man entered Zofia's farm without asking her permission and hacked away at another horseradish bush. Property relations between trusted neighbors are quite lax. Once, Roman and Zofia walked across the street to a neighbor's house to take, without permission, several bundles of hay that had come in on a wagon; however, it is different when strangers trespass on the farm. In the 1990s and 2000s, during Christmas Roman sold rabbits he bred in the barn to urban patrons for alcohol money. When the family put an end to his rabbit scheme in 2010, he adapted by selling off a family gotyk. Uncle Kuba had to ask around to find out who had bought it and then buy it back from that villager. While under socialism Roman used his kombinacja to extract resources from the state and exchange them for liters of vodka, today Roman adapts his kombinacja techniques to liquidate the farm in exchange for money, which he pools with his friends to buy alcohol.

A key terrain of struggle between Roman and Zofia was whether to continue agricultural production on the farm. It was cheaper to buy supermarket food than to produce it on the farm. But Roman refused to eat supermarket food. Zofia would get very upset when the sowing season came in the fall and Roman decided to start yet another cycle of production. One autumn afternoon, Roman opened up the front gate to the yard. Leonid, an elderly Ukrainian man, rode in on a half-mechanical, half-wooden wagon on rubber wheels, pulled by Basia, an old brown horse. Leonid unharnessed Basia and accompanied Roman to the back, where he began to plow the field (see figure 6.1). The precision and expertise in Leonid's work was awe inspiring, and Basia needed little direction. Leonid split the field down the middle and perfectly plowed each half without pause. He

Figure 6.1. Leonid plows Zofia's field while Roman waits to pick up loose potatoes. Photo by author.

plowed into the fallow land (*odłogi*)—something Zofia had told Roman not to do because it forced her to put more labor into the farm. Roman, however, wanted extra vegetables to exchange for alcohol money. Instead of paying Leonid for the job, Roman boarded Leonid's wagon, and Zofia informed me that the two were off to drink. Looking out the window, I could see the two men jovially talking as Basia pulled them toward their libations. Roman's work was done, and the rest of the cultivation and digging of the potatoes would be Zofia's burden. Then, he would sell them from the benches to his customers. So much for decades of state attempts to modernize the peasantry.

Roman believes that the entire world works according to the laws of kombinacja. "Where is there no kombinacja? It appears to me that it exists in every country. Someone always does something 'on the left [*na lewo*],'" he says. He depicts a world in which he was oppressed by others using kombinacja against him and alienating him from resources, and in which he in turn had to devise kombinacja to access those resources. Leonid, the Ukrainian peasant who plowed Roman's farm, expresses a similar sentiment. He owns one of the two remaining horses in Bursztyn and is what villagers call the last "real" gospodarz. He belonged to the agricultural circle until all of the workers were laid off and the entire cooperative liquidated in the late 1980s. But it was the corruption that angered him.

Nomenklatura elites did not lose power during the 1990s. The current mayor is the son of the former mayor under communism, so the same families still hold power in the village. Additionally, the current mayor's brother, the "vice mayor," had purchased the agricultural circle headquarters, its machinery, and the base with the warehouses around it. The lands that had belonged to the cooperative remained unprivatized and under commune control. Recently, Leonid claimed, the vice mayor used commune lands to secure European Union funds, which he used to produce a harvest for his own private profit. Leonid explained to me that although he himself was the rare recipient of a ten-thousand-złoty ($2,300) grant from the European Union to work his own farm, he was frustrated that the vice mayor could access much larger grant amounts to buy expensive agricultural machinery, which he stored in his private circle warehouse surrounded by wire fencing and patrolled by German shepherds. Leonid, who paid property taxes on his land, could afford only to feed his horse and fix his wagon. He was perplexed by the European Union's grant process. How could some people get so much more money than others? With special access to European Union funds, the officials have become a shadow class of farmers who do not pay taxes on unprivatized commune lands but use them as their private property and pocket the profits from the harvest.

Leonid is not the only one who feels shut out by the nomenklatura control of these funds. Villagers have complained on internet forums. An anonymous entry from December 2012 states: "Clearly, [the mayor] is not the only one, look at what villa his vice mayor built . . . and do you know how much he paid for the Agricultural Circle with machines??? For a laughable forty thousand złoty!!! That is how one uses kombinacja" (*tak się kombinuje*). As one villager eloquently summarized, "The people are sowing taxes and [the vice mayor] is gathering the harvest, a true peasant of the people." They called him "Expert of Nothing" and recommended cutting his job first in order to balance the budget from debts incurred through his corrupt practices.[1] The internet forums also suggest that this corruption has many more tentacles. They accuse the mayor of corruption (*korupcja*), cronyism (*układy kolesiostwo*), and of having a "super appetite"; the "commune and people do not interest him." One villager wrote, "He does not think, he just does it, and to add, corruption is unraveling beautifully but as always there is silence, etc." At one point, a villager in favor of the mayor wrote that the mayor had hardly finished high school but managed to lead a business and be elected. Another villager sarcastically responded, "He must have used kombinacja well" (*musiał dobrze kombinować*). Supposedly, the mayor is now misusing European Union commune funds to buy private forest land for himself, buying allotment gardens and a new car with taxpayer money, raising taxes for his staff to use more petrol and travel greater distances to conduct their informal business relations, promising renovations only before elections, and so forth. Villagers have been calling for a referendum for two years, but officials have not listened to them.

Villagers have shifted their kombinacja discourse to attack corruption in the village among the nomenklatura. "Authority *kombinóje* now. People, no. Authority. Now, they call it 'corruption,'" said Gosia, the retired tannery worker.[2] The gossip on the street is that the mayor employs only Belarusian secretaries and administrators from his home village who keep silent because they are benefiting from the perks. No one knows for sure what is going on because the commune headquarters are a Kafkaesque labyrinth of closed offices and papers flying—no faces and no transparency. The thing about European Union funds is that they require a level of bureaucratic skill that many Westerners may take for granted. The process of seeking out funds online or through government offices, gauging one's eligibility, and applying for them seems like an alien process. Many expect the local government to give them access to these funds rather than seeking out avenues to secure the funds themselves. At least in the communist period, villagers said, one could travel to Słupsk and complain about nomenklatura kombinacja to the county-level authorities, and they would investigate and handle the situation. Today, villagers feel atomized from the higher state powers that could check local corruption. During my fieldwork, a scandal erupted when European Union funds were acquired for roadwork in the nomenklatura-dominated neighborhood of Bursztyn. Most villagers had never heard of such road funds; only elites have access to that information. The mayor refused to be interviewed about postsocialist transformation, telling me to "look for history among the elderly," but the more the elderly talked, the more it brought me back to the mayor. Just as he withheld information from me, his office withholds information about European Union funds and secures them for its own private and class interests.

Nomenklatura privatization in the 1990s was based on the premise that only socialist-era elites had the bureaucratic and administrative know-how to carry out a privatization process using shock doctrine tactics. As a result, not only did they retain power, like the mayor's family in Bursztyn, but they continue to have privileged access to information that benefits their private interests. Their lack of concern for the public well-being contributes to the pervasive problems of unemployment, alcoholism, and the failure of agriculture among the peasants. For example, to crack down on alcoholism in Bursztyn, the commune removed the benches in 2014. But that solved nothing; the men started congregating on the supermarket steps. To combat alcoholism, the elderly women would have to stop giving cigarette money at home, former coworkers would have to stop lending money on the streets, and store owners would have to stop selling alcohol. But this is what a free society looks like in the liberated and capitalist Recovered Territories. The collective has dissolved, and it is the dystopian features of the communist past that offer some sense of normalcy to villagers lost in the wilderness of Western-style capitalism.

In the absence of any real solutions, families continue to fall apart. Roman suffered a massive stroke in 2014 and was in rehabilitation for several years. He lost the ability to move his body and the ability to speak, and we thought that this would finally be the end of his regime of terror. Zofia broke her hip and passed away from complications on Christmas Eve 2016. But just recently Roman was released from the rehabilitation center and was back at the farm. He is getting stronger day by day and is walking. Moreover, his friends from the benches are coming to visit him. On the outside, Zofia's farm is in shambles. It looks like it has been bombed: the roof of the barn is imploding, old rusty machinery and tubing are spread around haphazardly, wasteland expands across the fields in the rear of the farm, and the largest barn Konrad once built is in various stages of disassembly. It reflects the state of our family. We are broken apart, living in different corners of the globe, and constantly engaging in petty arguments. This is what capitalism has done to us: alienated us all and destroyed the farm. We are a microcosm of Bursztyn. The king of the farm is now Roman, who has won control. Likewise, in public, the men on the benches operate an unhinged regime of terror while the nomenklatura in the commune headquarters cleverly use their position in state power to secure European Union funds. Both are geographically at the heart of the village, and both centers of power are right next to each other: on the benches and in the commune headquarters. Both are also at the heart of villagers' complaints about what is "wrong" with neoliberal capitalism. The kombinators are, again, at the very center of village life.

Bird's Milk

DAMA is a small, private candy factory hidden along Reunification Street in Bursztyn. It blends in with the dilapidated warehouses and factories that are surrendering to nature after the state's retreat from production in the village. In 2009 there was no sign in front of the rectangular, one-story building with peeling pastel-blue paint, large dirty windows, and a metal fence; there were no cars, trucks, or people outside. It is owned by Mażena, a Polish woman who kept in close contact with the German family who owned the factory before the German expulsion in the late 1940s. In the 1980s the German family invited Mażena to West Germany, where she received investment funds and training to restart the candy factory under her private ownership. DAMA is a prime example of how the continuing transnational networks between German families expelled from the territories and the Polish families who settled on their properties have continued to reap rewards for both parties. Mażena got ahead of the entrepreneurial game with funding, the Germans could secure their property by having someone they knew involved, and they could continue to influence the factory.

DAMA produces its own recipes of Polish candy such as bird's milk (*ptasie mleczko*), a rectangular, vanilla-flavored "milk" sponge covered on all sides with a thin layer of hardened chocolate; sugarcoated and chocolate-covered fruit jellies; and chocolate-covered gingerbread cookies (*pierniki*). The bird's-milk candy was neatly stocked in signature yellow boxes in the town's small convenience stores. It was priced at eleven złoty and competed on the same shelves against the global candy manufacturer E. Wedel, which produced bird's milk that sold for thirteen złoty. E. Wedel's candy underwent a much more streamlined manufacturing process with taste experts, more rigorous inspections, more advanced machines. It was seamless and smooth throughout. DAMA's production process was less advanced and the candy had a "Soviet" texture. Its bird's milk was larger, darker, and grittier, with less sweet and crisp chocolate coating, and a more watered-down vanilla interior than that of its competitor.

One night in late fall, when the usual thick smoke from coal fires filled the already-wintry village streets, two DAMA workers, Leona and Ola, knocked on Zofia's front door. They were Zofia's neighbors who also lived with men like Roman. They came to see my mother, who was visiting me during fieldwork. Leona and Ola looked like my mother and like most middle-aged women in the village: they had thick hands and unmanicured nails, coarsely cut hair they dyed themselves, and they wore secondhand industrial shirts and boxy jeans. No one dared wear a hat unless they wanted to be accused of displaying bourgeois inclinations and called a "Lady" (Pani). Hats were very taboo and nearly forbidden in the village. Still, Aunt Magdalena, who sat in the kitchen, was noticeably different. A Kashubian and a migrant worker in Norway, she had polished nails, mascara, and fashionably styled hair. I was somewhere in between with soft hands and unmanicured nails. Hands were the most conspicuous expression of class status. Rough and thick fingers were proof of hard labor, whereas gentle, soft skin represented higher class status (or that one did not work too hard). Zofia's hands were the most contorted.

With the exception of myself and Zofia, all four women were second-generation villagers who had once worked in the now-defunct state tannery. In 1982 the state factory signed up with the Solidarity trade union during martial law, but that stronghold of labor over the administration was short lived. In 1991 the tannery was privatized and laid off five hundred of the six hundred workers. In 1995 further layoffs and unpaid wages led to workers' strikes and the collapse of the tannery. The local trade union chapter collapsed. In 1996 a German businessman bought the factory and has since been producing small fox and mink furs in the tannery, employing a handful of seasonal, temporary workers from the village. Like DAMA, it does not even look from the outside like an operating factory. The graffiti, the dilapidated buildings, and the high crooked fencing throughout are not inviting. Nor are the people who work there willing to talk about the factory, let alone help secure a tour. The gossip was that it was "on the black" (*na czarno*), or black-market work, and no one wanted to talk because they did not want to lose a key source of income. Those who could not secure their job in the German-owned tannery had to look for work elsewhere. Leona and Ola stayed in the village and found jobs working part-time in Mażena's candy factory for a measly seven złoty per hour. Magdalena became a migrant worker on Norwegian farms, and my mother had already been long gone cleaning homes in the United States. Nearly two decades after the collapse of village industry and being scattered into various working-class jobs around the globe, the women were back around the kitchen table at Zofia's.

That evening, we all sat around the table drinking fifty-milliliter shots of Magdalena's homemade cherry-plum brandy (*śliwowica*). From the pantry, my mother brought out a thick chunk of cured bacon that she placed on a wooden cutting board and cut into thick slices. Thick slices, like thick hands, were significant because they aesthetically symbolized the robustness of working-class identity. No one wanted to eat delicately cut, thin and flimsy pieces of bacon. She kept the pieces warm atop the iron furnace that she left slightly ajar, with wood and coal crackling inside. The smell of bacon filled the kitchen, and after several shots of brandy, everyone was enjoying themselves. Then Leona reached into her bag and pulled out a plastic bag filled with DAMA bird's milk and placed it on the table for dessert. When I inquired about which candy took the longest to produce, she said that machines did all the work, but the candy types and quantities depended on the production cycles. Leona casually mentioned that in late October, the factory was making its final push for candy production for the Christmas season. The stores received only the boxed version of the candy, but the workers could purchase loose candy at ten złoty per kilogram. Zofia then asked Leona to bring her a kilogram of the bird's milk for Christmas and to bring some for me, for which she would pay Leona. The women who stayed in the village rely on one another for food and services they cannot afford to buy in the formal economy. In a way, they operate much like the men on the alcohol benches, relying on their socialist-era networks to make deals with one another, like an informal guild, but in private. The friendly chat quickly transformed into a business meeting of women using their decades-old socialist-era networks to get candy for free or for a lower price than at the local supermarket.

After the kombinacja deal, Leona and Ola complained about Mażena in a way that made clear the workers and their employer did not share similar economic goals. Mażena was once a tannery worker who worked alongside these middle-aged women, but in the 1990s, she chose the entrepreneurial route while most of her coworkers became her employees. Whenever Mażena needs temporary labor, she telephones the middle-aged women in the village and asks them to come "help out" (*pomóc*)—without individual or group contracts—for twelve-hour shifts in the factory for two or three consecutive days. She exploits socialist-era networks to access cheap local labor. DAMA produces its products in batches and puts workers on the workshop floor only during production bursts. The middle-aged women she hires on a temporary basis were particularly desirable because they had enough years of work to secure retirement but had yet to reach the proper age; thus, Mażena did not need to hire them full-time and take on the responsibility of paying workers' benefits to the Social Insurance Institution (Zakład Ubezpieczeń Społecznych) for their retirement. To stay competitive, in addition to relying on cheap labor organized through socialist-era networks, DAMA depends on the locally ingrained practice of neighborly help (*pomoc sąsiedzka*) to complete the production quota just like the early socialist state once did to secure peasant labor in the state forestry or on state farms. Socialist-era practices provide a kind of safety net for both Mażena and her workers in the wilderness of capitalism. Failed by formal privatization and trade unions, these women are working *na czarno* (in the black market). While Mażena uses socialist-era networks to secure local labor, her non-union workers are relying on socialist-era methods of self-compensation by extracting surplus candy and selling it on the side to earn extra money.

While the non-unionized women workers despise the arrangement and want full-time employment, most grudgingly consent because they have no other employment opportunities. Leona complained that when Mażena calls each worker, she expects her to drop everything and rearrange her plans for the production period and to exert herself in long shifts. If anyone tries to negotiate, Mażena threatens to call other willing women. Some workers, however, have begun to reject Mażena's requests for help because the work is temporary, earnings cover only a single supermarket trip, and there is no guarantee of a callback during the next production cycle or any other job security. They describe these arrangements as moving "from work to labor" (*od pracy do roboty*), meaning descending down the slippery slope of full employment under socialism into the temporary, hard labor under postsocialism. (The phrase is versatile and can also refer to the everyday shifting between informal labor obligations at home or in the field and formal work obligations in the factory or someplace else.) Without formal employment, union representation, or pay negotiation, when the factory women gather, they communicate their dissent in social terms. Gossip was an important means of airing these grievances about factory conditions and also discursively legitimizing the practices of extracting bird's milk from the production floor. Conjuring images of Chełmoński's *Woman's Summer* painting, Leona complained that Mażena is paralyzed by internal thoughts and does not communicate properly with workers. The women compared their struggling livelihoods to Mażena's opulent lifestyle: for example, they note she is building a brand-new house in the village and that her daughter brags about purchasing from the top shelves at the supermarket—an attitude of bourgeois tendencies. Still, these women workers in the province of Pomerania, the cradle of the Solidarity Movement that brought down communism a quarter-century ago, would not join a trade union chapter in Słupsk. Exposing black market employment and poor conditions would jeopardize their only source of income. Trade unions are for those employed in visible, formal, and legal work.

Socialist-era alliances and practices keep Mażena competitive and her workers employed. The use of neighborly help to mobilize and organize workers to meet production goals without proper compensation under socialism continues as a management strategy that coincides with the increasing flexibility and more frequent temporary contracts in the capitalist workplace. Women workers, who once helped the state economy meet quotas, are mobilized by their old coworkers to help private factories stay competitive. In both cases the women are not independently union-ized and are organized on the basis of this management principle. Consequently, they use kombinacja as compensation for this labor that they consent to perform out of necessity rather than generosity. This exemplifies another way that neighborly help and kombinacja jar against each other: postsocialist neighborly help is bad kombinacja, a top-down extraction of labor from the workers, whereas good kom-binacja is a bottom-up extraction of commodities. If Mażena were a good employer, she might even use bird's milk as an incentive for workers to take on the labor so they could sell or exchange the surplus candy to supplement their earnings. This is where socialist-era networks and socialist-era strategies can help everyone win. They provide imperfect but workable models for securing informal labor, operating informal guilds, and keeping a bulk of the production process off the books.

That night in Zofia's kitchen, after they made candy deals and gossiped about their jobs, the women asked me not to bring their boss into any sort of trouble (*kłopotów*). In its most exploitative form, DAMA, even in spurts of production, is one of the few employers in the village, especially for female pensioners. Mażena's kombinacja was well known, as was the factory workers' kombinacja—however, their strategies were a negotiation tactic to make both the owner and the workers agree on labor conditions. Outside scrutiny of Mażena's exploitative economic practices would put both her factory and their temporary employment at risk, as well as their access to whatever kombinacja activity they were carrying out with the bird's milk to supplement those temporary wages by making deals within their networks. While the labor conditions disenfranchise these women workers, some work is evidently better than no work, especially when there is the possibil-ity of kombinacja. The women factory workers still exchange commodities from the workplace with their produce, to supplement their sporadic wages and so-cially reproduce their domestic roles as mothers who secure candy for Christmas.

Right before my departure from Bursztyn, Leona again came by with several boxes of bird's milk that would have been an overwhelming cost for either her or Zofia. They were gifts for me to take back to London. She completed the deal. It was a success. Regardless of the details, the deal showed that DAMA workers used fac-tory candy to carry on other economic activity in the village by selling, exchanging, or distributing to their networks. The selling of loose bird's milk at below-market prices—lower than the DAMA boxes in the local supermarket—lowers DAMA's competitive edge alongside the E. Wedel boxes. How could the owner allow this? I was reminded of my conversation with Motylek, the ex-commune official, who claimed the activities that would have constituted kombinacja under socialism be-gan to qualify as theft because the workplace structures and capital flows became more closely monitored. Yet at DAMA, it appeared that workers were comfortably making deals involving "surplus" candy among their female acquaintances (*zna-jome*) in the village, like Zofia. Was this stealing, "scratching," kombinowanie, a local form of women's postsocialist agency, or all of the above?

The Gleaners

On a cold and rainy October afternoon, I rode the bus back to Bursztyn after completing archival research in Słupsk. Across the thirteen-kilometer stretch of privatized land that had once belonged to the Krynica, Kaszubska, and Lipowa state farms, I would usually see large-scale monocropping of rapeseed or potatoes that would be harvested by a few combines and tractors and prepared for export to supermarkets in Western Europe and fast-food chains like McDonald's. The German and Danish owners of these "private" farms do not live in the German Junker estates, nor do they seem to care about the former state farm workers who have become the rural poor, stranded in former state worker colonies, now "villages," surrounded by these vast stretches of privatized land. Their invisible hands mold the landscape around them, picking and choosing which crops to produce and sell, which tractor operators to hire. They are faceless rulers on these farms who play with people's lives, moving pawns across the fields like in a game of chess. It is difficult for the rural poor to "see" the benefits of capitalism. In Soviet times, the harvests were exported to the Council for Mutual Economic Assistance (Rada Wzajemnej Pomocy Gospodarczej), but the state farms directors and staff on site employed hundreds of workers, and cultivated dozens of crops. Now, production is sent to the West, but none of the material stuff of production is there. Emptiness has replaced the workers in the fields, and that is all one usually sees from the window.

This day was different. As I squinted through the fog and rain on the bus windows, a scene I had never witnessed before unfolded in the fields. Dozens of cars were haphazardly parked; men, women, and children holding buckets and bags were on their knees in the soil or walking around, searching, picking things up, and putting them in their buckets and bags. Others were hauling full, lumpy bags to the open trunks of their cars. Far off in the distance, small groups congregated around the tractors parked by the pine forest (see figure 6.2). When the bus arrived in Bursztyn, I rushed back to Zofia's house to call Marek to drive me to the fields. On my way, I encountered a very jolly Mychajlo, the Ukrainian peasant who lived across the street from Zofia, walking his bicycle almost bent over by three bulky pillowcases hanging from the steering handles. Mychajlo looked alive: his eyes were bright, and he excitedly informed me that villagers and city folk were gleaning (*zbierają*) leftover potatoes that the harvesters had left on the fields. The light in the eyes was the same I saw when villagers foraged mushrooms and berries in the forest. When Marek arrived, we sped toward the fields.

Gleaning is a public declaration of poverty. Most people do not have the money to buy food in supermarkets year-round and have to subsist off the land. When we parked the car on the side of the road, Marek would not go out with me to interview and photograph people. The optics were not right. People recognized him, but not everyone knew who I was. Maybe I was a German or Danish

Figure 6.2. The gleaners. Photo by author.

observer with a camera in hand, conducting surveillance. When a woman kneeling on the ground saw my camera, she said something to her child, who huddled in closer to her. They both turned their faces down to the ground. No one wanted to be photographed. I could have introduced myself and explained my interest, but something else kept me back from the fields. I saw myself in those children in rural poverty wearing thick hats over their ears and secondhand jackets, reaching their fingers into the ground to help out their mothers. Back in the 1990s, when we cultivated strawberries on the dying state farm, I was not so different from them. I just happened to be lucky enough to have left the economic transition at an opportune moment. Some of these children might get lucky and go to school, but most will become migrant workers on Norwegian and German farms starting in their teenage years. They reminded me what I likely would have become. This not-too-distant past still haunted me at the time. I was too scared to step onto those fields. Asking people why they are poor felt very inappropriate. There was an invisible wall blocking my path. So we both stayed and watched on the sidelines.

Marek explained to me that foreign owners are oblivious to the gleaning on their lands. Like Uncle Kuba, who claimed that Norwegian farmers cannot detect kombinacja, Marek imagined gleaning as a local form of working under the bourgeois capitalist's nose without him having any clue about it. He added that gleaning actually helped the capitalist save labor costs in the production process. It was a service. During the potato harvest, the tractor drivers and combine operators leave behind patches of potatoes around electrical poles and between each row on the fields. Once the harvest is complete, former state farm workers, villagers, and even city folk who had the "will to work" (*chęć do pracy*) could come to glean leftover potatoes in the fields. It also made economic sense; rather than picking the potatoes for sixty cents (*grosze*) an hour and then buying those potatoes from the farmer, they cleared the fields of leftover potatoes themselves. In effect, no food was wasted and no potatoes rotted; moreover, they helped prepare the fields for the next sowing season and reduced labor and machine costs for the owner. The gleaners were not doing anything illegal, Marek defensively explained. If they thought that they were doing something wrong, they would not have picked in broad daylight. It was not like in the socialist era when they gleaned nocturnally. Any outsider from a capitalist country would have called their actions "poaching" or "stealing" on "private property," but that is not how villagers see it.

My mother recalled that socialist-era gleaning was widespread but also illegal (*nielegalnie*) on the state farms. I could not find laws in Poland against gleaning, but a 1932 "law on gleaning" in Soviet Russia considered gleaning a physical manifestation of kulak greed and led to hundreds of peasant incarcerations during dekulakization campaigns before the collectivization of agriculture.[3] My mother recalled that since the state farms were late in harvesting the potatoes in the late fall, "it was already a profit loss for the PGR but people knew that and they dug for themselves, because in this way they saved their money, because for the entire winter they had reserves. Kombinacja." It was predominantly a proletarian activity of tannery workers and administrators who did not have access to land but who needed to prepare for the winter. Individuals gleaned in the peripheries or in hidden places, and then kept on coming every day until they had enough reserves. "At times, acquaintances [*znajomi*] met up there, but usually everyone dug for himself for it not to be seen, because it was illegal, but I also never heard of anyone actually having a problem." The authorities kept silent because they also benefited. She added, "That is how people used kombinacja to not buy and not spend their money. They said that the state farm will not become poorer, while they can buy themselves shoes or a jacket for themselves or their children for winter." By clearing potatoes off the land after the harvest, gleaners prepared the fields for the sowing of rye in late fall.

Gleaning is a common practice in agrarian societies. The Old Testament book of Leviticus allows for gleaning rights as a form of aid to the poor: "When you reap the harvest of your land, you shall not reap your field right up to its edge, neither shall you gather the gleanings after your harvest. You shall leave them for the poor and for the sojourner." Gleaning was portrayed in the nineteenth-century painting *Des glaneuses* (The gleaners) by Jean-François Millet (1857), showing French peasant women picking wheat grains in the fields after the harvest, and Pierre Heouin's *Glaneuses à Chambaudoin* (1857), where female gleaners flee a storm. Agnès Varda's documentary *The Gleaners and I* (2000) explores this practice today in the French provinces, where the rural poor rely on food they could not afford to buy in a supermarket. Thus, when gleaners encroach on the former state farms, they are operating under a much broader system of agrarian customs and religious laws that has existed in other countries, and well before the most recent transition from socialism to capitalism. Capitalism has not propelled them into modernity; it has forced them to retreat to old agrarian safety nets. They abide not by the laws of capitalism but by the laws of their stomachs.

Besides, a private property marker will not stop them from accessing subsistence territories they have depended on for decades. Many state farm workers were born on these farms and had worked in the socialist model of production all of their adult lives. Then in January 1990, the Balcerowicz Plan launched Poland's neoliberalism project via "shock doctrine." The plan's reforms sought to privatize state property, slow down inflation, eliminate shortages, increase market-based mechanisms for the economic system, devise a framework for divesting state ownership, begin the sale of state assets, break up monopolies, and eliminate central planning.[4] Jeffrey Sachs, an architect of the shock doctrine, was so confident of Poland's "jump to the market economy" that he wrote, "The hardest part of the transformation, in fact, will not be the economics at all, but the politics."[5] He believed that Polish society was bound to flourish under capitalism. The Recovered Territories, the Sovietized region of Poland, emerged with the highest percentage of privatized state and collective farms. However, today, it has the highest concentration of poverty in Poland.[6] Privatization was pauperization for the rural poor, peasant and proletarian alike, who depended on access to state land and state workplaces to eke out a living during crisis. Gleaning became a method of reinvading land.

It also represented a rejection of capitalist elites. One of the significant failures of the privatization process was the speed at which it was to be carried out, via shock doctrine, without replacing old local governments with newly trained authorities. This empowered the communist nomenklatura, who were the only "trained" governing officials in the villages, to "rehabilitate" (*zrehabilitować*) themselves by publicly admitting their ideological mistakes, then proceeding to take the reins of privatization as capitalism's new believers. Villagers who had been punished and repressed for decades by nomenklatura families who represented the socialist state were ushered into capitalism by those same people. Just as General Wojciech Jaruzelski would never face the consequences of murdering hundreds of protesters during hunger demonstrations before and during martial law, nor would local officials, who would continue to shop at the same stores, walk the same streets, and even attend church with those whom they had forced into labor, interrogated, and spied on. Villagers viewed the nomenklatura's evasion of consequences as one of the greatest injustices of the privatization process, and that immediately turned them into cynics about capitalism. Capitalism prioritized profit margins over justice.

The nomenklatura emerged as the capitalist elite in Bursztyn and in Pomerania. Starting in the 1980s, state directors of the agricultural circles, mechanical enterprises, and state farms who had touted the ideology of collective ownership laid off workers and privatized workplaces. This began gradually in 1986, when the State Enterprise Law permitted directors of state-owned enterprises "to enter into associations with private partners and contribute a part of the physical assets as a share." As a result, they undervalued state physical assets to generate higher profits for the private enterprises. They collaborated with those enterprises when setting up new businesses like the shadow tannery in Bursztyn. With one foot in state enterprise and the other in private enterprise, the nomenklatura channeled state enterprise assets into their private ventures, and in doing so, they transformed themselves into the new capitalist entrepreneurial class.[7] Communist elites' seizure of state assets during privatization is commonly referred to as "nomenklatura privatization."[8] The most prevalent form was "liquidation privatization" or the sale of state assets.[9] If the director decided to liquidate the enterprise or state farm, anything of potential value was to be stripped away and passed on to the Ministry of Privatization to be sold piece by piece. Or a new company would be created that would then lease the assets from the ministry.[10] From what I understand, in Bursztyn privatization was mostly an informal process led by directors who sold state assets on the black market and pocketed the profits.

All privatization roads led to the nomenklatura's pockets. A dramatic example of this was the privatization of state farms. In January 1992 the state created the State Treasury Agricultural Property Agency (Agencja Własności Rolnej Skarbu Państwa) to lead the privatization of the 1,576 state farms—nine hundred thousand hectares of state farmland—which had an amassed bank debt of 7.5 billion złoty. While privatization policies gave state farm workers the right to form joint-stock companies out of the state farms, that is not what happened. Privatization excluded former state farm workers from contending for those assets and afforded a preference for state, nomenklatura, or bourgeoisie ownership of the farms. Laid-off workers complained to researchers that they had not been properly informed about their eligibility to participate in the privatization process. Farm administrators responded that the workers had displayed no interest in the matter. Former employees who were well informed faced financial barriers to forming joint-stock companies. Even employee-formed joint-stock companies leased state property to a narrow managerial and administrative group that had governed under socialism. The nomenklatura recruited only just enough employees to meet the "employee" quota for the joint-stock company, but in reality they secured profits and benefits within their nomenklatura networks.[11] AWRSP had another problem. Six months after its founding, it received sixteen thousand ownership petitions from former German owners who wanted their Junker mansions and land back. Rather than welcoming German investors who were willing to pour millions into the revitalization of these gigantic mansions and estates, it denied their property claims on the premise that German "revanchism" would scare away Polish investors.[12] Fearing a German return and lackluster investment interest for redeveloping entire state farm colonies that still housed former state farm workers, the state retained or "restatized" the farms into nomenklatura hands.[13] Reforms aimed at fixing historical injustices, restoring rights, and avoiding the specter of a German return only empowered those who had symbolized Soviet domination.[14]

Most Bursztynians are still upset by the injustices of privatization to this day. "When they took apart the PGRs, it was kombinacja . . . because they were liquidating the PGRs and people were pushed to the side. And those who liquidated them, benefitted from that. It was their kombinacja!" Zofia recalled in anguish. It was the ultimate kombinacja; the nomenklatura found loopholes that let them privatize everything for themselves (so the story goes). The failures of privatization have given old Stalinist elites, who crushed the peasants, a new political pedestal as self-proclaimed protectors of the village. Motylek, the former highest-ranking Stalinist-era official in the village, railed to me against the widespread injustices of privatization on the state farms:

> I would hang [Lech] Wałęsa by his legs and [Leszek] Balcerowicz by something else. Those sons of bitches! What have they done with the PGRs? They argued that socialist farms could not exist but what did they do with those people? Did they take care of those people? They destroyed everything! Those who were close to power stole and sold the machines, the inventory and abandoned everything. There were wooden barns left, the authorities took them down and burned the wood. They took apart the grain ethanol plant and sold it at the scrap metal yard. They destroyed everything! And yet they left such a massive amount of people out in the cold! They should have merged the enterprises together, freed the people from taxes for three to four years, and let the PGRs be managed by the workers.

Privatization tore apart lives and families. Tens of thousands of state farm workers, jobless, had to find new ways survive. This was before the Schengen Agreement in 1997 that opened up borders for Poles to work in places like Germany and Norway. This was before Poland's entrance into the European Union. My cousins, who were not lucky enough to win an immigration lottery like my family did, became illegal migrant workers on horse farms in Norway, where they worked and lived in squalor, but life was better than it was in the village. Norway was the rich and successful socialist country Poland never became. During one border crossing, my cousins were caught and incarcerated for days, then received red stamps on their passports indicating that they had a history of unauthorized crossings. But they were trying to survive. Those who did not become migrant workers became gleaners, living off the land and welfare checks and any part-time employment they could find for seven złoty an hour in a shadowy factory. Others spiraled into depression and alcoholism; they became the invisible people who did not bother to sign up for welfare. They subsist on their parents' retirement checks and live on food they grow in their gardens, forage in the forests, or glean in the fields. Former state farm colonies have become humanitarian disasters, with former farm workers suffering from alcohol addiction, poverty, low education, violence, and insecure property rights. Even on the state farms that have been privatized many inhabitants subsist on welfare and retirement checks, still pay rent directly to the state, and need to grow their own food.

Nomenklatura privatization has ghettoized the state farm worker settlements. Take, for example, Lipowa, one of the former state farms bordering Bursztyn where Marek and I watched the gleaners. Marek was born in Lipowa in the 1950s and worked there as a mechanical worker in his youth. Today, Lipowa looks like a bomb site. All the windows, metal, and bricks have been stripped from the former state barns. When we visited, spotted pigs roamed the street. There were no stores, schools, or supermarkets. No sign of life. Marek, despite having ties to the place, suggested that we stay in the car as we drove through the rural ghettos of stranded former state farm workers and their families. I sensed people watching us from behind the curtains in the kitchen windows. Some men were processing grain in a large warehouse that stood in the middle of the village, but there was no sign or indication that this was a registered operation.

A German investor bought out a portion of the former state farmland and cultivates rapeseed. He employs some of the former state farm workers to work the land using private machinery. However, the German Junker mansion is still state owned and is used as public housing occupied by "squatters," many of whom are the children of former state farm workers. When we entered the estate to visit Marek's family friend, a young man in a leather jacket appeared in the lobby with one of his hands noticeably hidden in his breast pocket. He asked what we were doing there. When Marek responded that we were visiting his family member, the young man forcefully claimed the woman was not there and told us to leave. Believing the man had a knife, Marek escorted me back to the car, and we left. There are also several 1970s-style apartment blocks that house the former state farm workers, many of them retired. Many never privatized their apartments and still pay monthly rent to the state. They produce land on their former worker allotments and when their neighbor dies, they take over that person's land for their private cultivation. Residents get by on state welfare, part of which they use to pay rent to the state, and they use state land to grow food. This is how people get by, living in a state-owned ghetto surrounded by private, German-owned fields.

Across the street from Lipowa is the gigantic Krynica farm. There, a Danish businessman owns both the German Junker estate and the fields. In the 1990s the vice mayor of Bursztyn commune took over the managerial ownership of the Krynica state farm as a joint-stock company with a German investor. However, the vice mayor tricked the German investor and sold the entire estate to the current Danish owner, without sharing the profits (so the story goes). The Danish owner uses the farm for large-scale, mechanized potato production and employs a handful of machine operators from the former state farm to harvest the potatoes. He does not live on the Junker estate, which is hidden deep in the forest and accessible only by a tree-lined, cobblestone road. The estate is managed by the son of the former state farm director (another example of nomenklatura privilege) who lives in a house at the gate of the eighteenth-century neoclassical mansion. The warden uses the facilities for his own small projects (e.g., *bimber* production, cooking potatoes, fixing machines). When Marek and I arrived at the gate of the estate, the warden stepped out and said with a sigh of relief that he had thought we were Germans coming to look at our "so-called Heimat." He let us right in and we walked into a devastatingly beautiful mansion in equally devastating condition. The aristocratic past was still there: gigantic hand-painted ceramic furnaces, a massive ballroom with frescoes of angels peeling from the ceiling, beautiful old carpets that were placed on top of shattered stained-glass skylights—like booby traps for trespassers—on each floor of the mansion, German-built wooden credenzas scattered throughout. One section of the mansion was outfitted in 1970s diplomatic decor from the old Soviet administration. It looked like the communists had just left for a lunch break. Other parts of the house looked like they were used for whatever purpose the warden felt like; beds and other belongings of squatters were arranged around the house, bottles of alcohol on tables or floors. In the back of the house were vast wastelands and a destroyed gazebo, still with the bullet marks from when the Red Army murdered the Junker estate owner, before soldiers helped transform the feudal estate into a state farm in 1945. Estates like this one are beautiful, but they are also symbols of German and Soviet domination that few Poles feel inclined to revitalize.

Not far from Krynica is the village of Raj, a former state farm, where a completely different scenario plays out. The new owner of the German Junker estate, whom villagers have nicknamed "Black Mamba," after the venomous snake, lives part-time in this beautifully renovated estate farm as the "new" bourgeois. I spent an evening with Black Mamba (Polish) and his wife Ewa (of mixed German-Polish ethnicity) discussing property transformation. They were the most "Western" individuals I had encountered throughout my fieldwork, and I liked both of them a lot because I felt I had more in common with them. They knew life on the "outside," in the West. After saving up money from working construction jobs in the 1990s and 2000s in the United Kingdom, where he learned English and met Ewa, Black Mamba came back to Poland to buy a German Junker estate and become a large-scale private property owner (*prywaciarz*). They owned the former state farm land and had taken advantage of the European Union's agricultural subsidies. They also receive the European Union funds to provide summer school lessons for Romanian orphans throughout the summer on their estate. Their attractively renovated house has been the subject of German documentaries about the Heimat, but Black Mamba is not too excited about the attention that this has brought the estate. German tourists trespass, urinate on his property, and try to fight him. Black Mamba and Ewa live for most of the year in Gdańsk, where their children go to school, but they come to the estate regularly because they employ former state farm workers to produce grain subsidized by the European Union. Black Mamba's relationship with the workers can be described as antagonistic at best, and has resulted in altercations that on one occasion led to a group of workers holding a knife to his neck. In our discussion, Black Mamba complained that his farm workers, whom he pejoratively calls *Homo PGRicus* do not respect "private ownership" (*własność*). Instead of pressuring the commune to build better roads, they drive over his fields. They steal from the farm because during the socialist period the authorities allowed them to do so. Black Mamba has to deal with the ghosts of kombinacja. The actions of the former state farm workers affect him in the same way they once damaged the state farm and affected the state. Black Mamba picks up the bill for kombinacja and for their destruction and mismanagement of the farm capital. The former state farm workers, who were told for decades that they "co-owned" the state farm and enjoyed much leeway in calibrating its resource flows and labor arrangements, are struggling with Black Mamba's private regime over their lands. Yet no one calls the police or gets the state involved.

Kombinacja flows through the government offices, alcohol benches, factories, homes, and across the fields of everyday life in postsocialist Bursztyn. Back in 1992, the sociologist Piotr Gliński asked, "Will the kombinator, Capitalist, Committed Craftsman, or the Enfranchised Nomenklatural Man model prevail?"[15] He was skeptical, explaining that kombinacja taught Poles to do business informally rather than act within a competitive market. However, kombinacja has flourished in the failures, interstices, and injustices of privatization. In Bursztyn, villagers adapt it to embed themselves into the market economy. Entrepreneurs rely on socialist-era networks to secure cheap labor pools, workers rely on socialist-era extraction methods to bolster their low incomes, the fallen worker-peasant men rely on old fraternal guilds to engage in entrepreneurial activity, the nomenklatura adapt new ways to use their position of power to secure European Union funds for private production on their farms, and gleaners perform an unpaid service for the foreign entrepreneurs on former state farm lands to cut down agricultural production costs. All of these kombinacja practices are designed to retain capital and keep it circulating in the village. The kombinator is indeed thriving, always adapting, always overcoming obstacles, and winning. The men on the alcohol benches, the women factory workers, gleaners, entrepreneurs, and the nomenklatura all perform a daily balancing act between survival and corruption. Postsocialist informality is a game that all that the villagers know how to play to secure something for themselves and to navigate the uncertainty of postsocialism.[16] Stripped of work, health care, free education, and access to land, many seek refuge in kombinacja. Others, bloated with power, exploit it without consequence. However, all villagers know that to end bad or corrupt kombinacja also means to put an end to the field of kombinacja that they too need to dabble in to survive. That is why the factory workers do not want any trouble for their boss and why the gleaners are allowed to operate in broad daylight without any local police or village officials around. By protecting each other, the villagers are also protecting their access to those local practices they need to deploy to survive. Thus, survival and corruption have become helplessly intertwined in the dystopia of postsocialism. One kombinator's form of survival has become another kombinator's expression of corruption. Yet, no one is ready to give up the practice of kombinacja altogether.

Notes

1. "Gmina [Bursztyn], w innych gminach ok a u nas bagno dlaczego?" Online forum, http://forum.gp24.pl/gmina-[Bursztyn]-w-innych-gminach-ok-a-u-nas-bagno-dlaczego-t78813/.
2. This association of kombinacja with elites has also been reported in the media. See "Zaczyna się kombinowanie przy okręgach wyborczych?" (Is kombinacja beginning around the district elections?), *W Polityce*, February 6, 2014, http://wpolityce.pl/polityka/185010-zaczynasie-kombinowanie-przy-okregach-wyborczych-mac-zapowiada-nowe-granice-przed-wyboramisamorzadowymi-oficjalnie-chodzi-o-prawa-mniejszosci.
3. Polian, *Against Their Will*, 87.
4. Telgarsky and Struyk, *Toward a Market-Oriented Housing Sector*, 107–11.
5. Sachs, *Poland's Jump*, 3.
6. Stenning et al., *Domesticating Neo-Liberalism*, 8.
7. Hardy and Rainnie, *Restructuring Krakow*, 124.
8. Zbierski-Salameh, *Bitter Harvest*, 222; Myant, *Transforming Socialist Economies*, 238; Hardy and Rainnie, *Restructuring Krakow*, 124.
9. Hardy and Rainnie, *Restructuring Krakow*, 127.
10. Zbierski-Salameh, *Bitter Harvest*, 235–36n45.
11. Ibid., 226.
12. Ibid., 222–23.
13. Ibid., 209.
14. Verdery, *Vanishing Hectare*, 162.
15. Gliński, "Acapulco Near Konstancin," 151.
16. Kubik, "From Transitology," 59.

7 Border Memories

ONE DAY IN JULY 2015, I was standing on a small bridge linking the German town of Görlitz and the Polish town of Zgorzelec. To the left of me was the beautifully preserved city of Görlitz that had been untouched by Allied bombing. Gothic, Renaissance, baroque, and art nouveau buildings with red roofs towered over a labyrinth of cobblestone streets. Black paint peeled from old Gothic-font signs from pre-1945 storefronts. It was a glimpse of what German towns had looked like in the Recovered Territories. In Görlitz lived the Germans and a Germanized West Slavic group called the Sorbs, who had been expelled from newly renamed Zgorzelec after the war. To the right of me was the Polish city of Zgorzelec, a mirror image of Görlitz, but grayer and more Sovietized, with 1970s apartment blocks. Its residents were Poles and the descendants of ten thousand Greek communist partisans whom the state resettled after World War II.

The two towns were separated by the dark and metallic Lusatian Neisse, the river's stillness reflecting and distorting the buildings from each country. Life around the border looked almost as still as the river. At the height of summer, there was no activity on the water or people alongside it to admire its nature. I imagined the river as haunted—by too many memories of people crossing, fleeing, and perishing from war. "Hate Nazis" and "Anarchy" signs were stuck on the railing in the middle of the bridge. The German side of the border was almost comically cluttered with European Union and German road signs, reminders to the easterners that "Europe" began here. At the border, German police were searching a Polish service van. On the Polish side I recognized the red-and-white border block marking the border that I had seen in so many photographs from the postwar period that was the signpost for where the German border began and the Polish border ended. Next to it was a Pope John Paul II memorial—a religious talisman to ward off German revanchism perhaps? Although the border treaties had been signed and both countries belonged to the European Union, I sensed a tense and fragile peace along this bridge.

Border treaties are a kind of fiction. In 1950, the Treaty of Zgorzelec signed between the Soviet puppet governments of the German Democratic Republic and the Polish People's Republic approved the demarcated Polish-German border. Still, a Soviet treaty was hardly enough to quell German claims to their lost eastern territories. In 1950 expelled Germans (*Heimatvertriebene*) who had struggled to integrate into West Germany and understandably longed to return home, where their ancestors had lived for centuries, formed the League of Expellees and Deprived of Rights (Bund der Heimatvertriebenen und Entrechteten).[1] West German history textbooks from the 1950s and 1960s still featured Germany with prewar borders.[2] Although the 1970 Treaty of Warsaw between Chancellor Willy Brandt of Western Germany and Prime Minister Józef Cyrankiewicz of the Polish People's Republic accepted the Oder-Neisse line, the question of reclaiming Germany's lost east became an incubator for conservative-driven territorial claims. A 1974 report in West German archives that revealed the number of expellees from the former Recovered Territories who died during the expulsion to be at around four hundred thousand was suppressed because the numbers were too low to serve as political justification in comparison to Nazi atrocities that numbered in the millions.[3] Memories of atrocities against the Germans paled in comparison to memories of German atrocities. Until the German-Polish Border Treaty of 1990, the Federal Republic of Germany and the North Atlantic Treaty Organization (NATO) never formally recognized the Treaty of Zgorzelec. A European border treaty also has not translated into reconciliation. The idea for an expellee museum advocated by the powerful nonprofit Federation of Expellees (Bund der Vertriebenen) since 2008 has been criticized by the Polish government and the public as a vehicle for German historical revisionism and revanchism.

The expellee figure symbolizes German victimhood in the last stages of the war, which is warranted to a large degree, but it has not always been clear who was an expellee and who had been a Nazi colonizer. Per Hitler's wartime foreign policy of *Heim ins Reich* (Homeward to the Empire) that sought to create a "Greater Germany" from the North Sea to the Ural Mountains, German colonists settled in Nazi-annexed Polish territory in the Generalgouvernement. Although they had no claim to Polish land at all, some counted themselves as "victims" and "expellees" of the German expulsion. Erika Steinbach, a conservative German politician who became the leader of the Federation of Expellees, was the daughter of a German corporal from Hesse who was stationed as a *Luftwaffenhelfer* in the Nazi-occupied Polish port of Rumia in Pomerania. After Germany lost the war, her family returned to Germany. Steinbach, who was born in Rumia in 1943, has made a career as an "expellee" leader and Christian Democratic Union politician even though her father was a part of the Nazi occupation of Polish lands.[4] Distorting the expellee or colonizer identity does an injustice to the expellees with deep historical roots in the east and dangerously reproduces the imaginary of a greater Germany. The Piast myth served a similar function.

Treaties are not enough to silence claims to land. I was on the border when Chancellor Angela Merkel opened Germany's borders to Syrian refugees, an opening that many Germans welcomed, but one that also sparked right-wing protests and attacks against refugee shelters like the one in Tröglitz in eastern Germany. Germany's president Joachim Gauck called this anti-refugee sentiment the "dark Germany."[5] In a BBC report from Saxony in eastern Germany in October 2015, Gabriel Gatehouse reported, "The refugee crisis, and the sense of injustice among some Germans, presents an opportunity to the far-right to reopen older wounds, to revisit the past, including the issue of Germany's postwar borders and territory that is now in Poland." He interviewed René Dick, a far-right German activist who claimed: "All of us are afraid that there will be a civil war, that people will come together to form an armed resistance. I, personally, am from the peaceful faction. But I know people who have armed themselves. And they are preparing for civil war." Then he added, "For example, Silesia is occupied, East Prussia is occupied. Step by step, plans have to be made to right this wrong . . . in a peaceful and civilized manner."[6] Merkel, whose own family came from Danzig and Elblag, has vested her political legacy in creating a home for refugees, but right-wing reactionaries point to the fact that neither treaties nor open borders easily solve deeply rooted territorialism. One has to wonder how revanchism is transferred to successive generations and reemerges in key historical moments. How did debates about the Syrian refugee crisis turn into a discussion about Poland's occupation of former German lands? If right-wing reactionaries knew the plight of the refugee from their ancestors' experience with expulsion from the east, why would they attack new refugee shelters?

This brings me to why I was on the border that July afternoon. I was en route from Berlin to Wrocław with Anke, an eighty-year-old expellee I had met in New York. Just like Frau Agathe visited Zofia in the 1970s, Anke was embarking on her first trip back to her Heimat in Śląsk (Silesia), the southeastern region of the Recovered Territories from which her family had been expelled by the Poles in 1945. My role was to ensure that we located her home village near the city of Nysa (Neisse). Henrick, a retired burly truck driver, was waiting for us to embark on the first leg of our trip to Wrocław, or, as Germans still insist on calling it, Breslau. Neither Anke nor Henrick had ever stepped foot in Poland. And I would lead them there based on Anke's memories from her childhood. Just as I had spent years recovering territories in the Polish imagination, I was about to recover territories in the German imagination.

I liked Anke because she reminded me of the strong-willed women in my family. When the Poles arrived in 1945, they threw her family in a "concentration camp"—as she put it—in Nysa and then they were resettled to a former Jewish home in Hamburg. She "always moved westward" and ended up in New York. When we first talked on the phone, she asked me to tell her about myself. I described to her how my grandmother's history starts off where hers left off, and how I too lived a life of exile away from the village. When Anke interjected with the question of whether I was born in the United States, I said no, born and raised on the farm. She gasped. She said, "But your English is perfect! Harvard-educated English!" She wanted me to go back with her to her Heimat, and I accepted.

"How would we portray ourselves to the villagers?" she nervously asked. "We tell the truth," I replied. There was no reason not to, I thought. I cherished the idea of us two women going to these overlapping homelands to engage in recovering territories together. The process is not something that happened in the postwar period but something that border people like myself and Anke could do now to "recover" the land's various identities, and in the process, connect with one another. Recovery could replace revanchism. I was equally excited that Anke and I, two women whose lives were shaped by that border, were undertaking this journey, for much of the border decision making was done by men, while women had to suffer the horrendous consequences.

In preparation for the trip, I brought her books and my own manuscript. She read at lightning speed and said, "I see what you are up to." She showed me a linen cloth from former Germany made by her grandmother with the red initials "M.S." written on it. It was one of the only gotyks that she had left from the expulsion to Germany. "History is all around me in my house," Anke said when she took out her old black-and-white photographs of her and her mother taken during World War II. The images on the photographs were very clear, unlike the blurry and faded photographs I had seen in the 1970s in family albums in Poland. Little Anke and her mother had perfectly sculpted hair, clean and elegant dresses; they were standing in the yard of their home with a large oak tree in the background and a high wooden fence behind them. I was struck by the photograph's utopianism. There were no markings of hardship or worry on their faces that would be impossible to hide even with a smile. In another photograph, her two uncles, who looked like statues, stood tall and smiling with their horses outside of the house. In yet another photograph, her aunt and her uncle, in a Wehrmacht uniform, dined together with a bottle of schnapps on the table, a Christmas tree against the wall, and to the right of it, a portrait of Adolf Hitler staring straight at the camera. Everyone except Hitler was laughing in these photographs, as if there was not a care in the world, giving no indication that the war going on the other side of the fence had scarred, worried, or troubled them in any way. This was some kind of a golden age.

Borders change people. When we landed in Berlin, I discovered that the American Anke I knew in New York had stayed home. I would be traveling with the German Anke. In America, I was the Harvard postdoctoral fellow; in Germany, I was the *Untermensch*. All of a sudden, I was instructed to "watch" when I was entering her nephew Johann's "expensive" Audi. Johann, who was around my age, coolly and factually stated that he refused to accompany us to Poland because "Eastern Europeans want to steal German cars." His wife Sandra forbade her daughter from coming along with us. Over dinner with her German family, I was dumbfounded when I heard Anke make comments like "Poles did not come there [Recovered Territories] to work, they came there to loot," and "Typical Poles:

they deny everything." I received a barrage of questions such as whether there was an "Autobahn" or even "chocolate" in Poland, and patronizing comments such as "This is the Germany way: classy." Then there were the "Poles did not know how to" comments. Anke recalled that when the Polish settlers had first arrived at her family's house in Neisse (now Nysa), they "did not know how to feed horses," so they fed them potatoes and killed them. Sandra also complained that when she went to Moscow, the Russians "did not know how to make salad dressing" because they put mayonnaise in it. I came from the land of kombinators who could find an innovative solution to any problem, but in Berlin, these innovative practices were recast as symptoms of backwardness and ignorance of the proper way.

In the imaginary of these cosmopolitan Berliners, Poland was a dangerous and backward agrarian society; not their common ally, trade partner, or a four-hour drive away for an enjoyable weekend trip. Their exchanges brought to mind Christian Democratic Union of Germany (Christlich Demokratische Union Deutschlands) propaganda posters I had once seen from the 1949 elections in the Federal Republic of Germany. The CDU that year ran on a platform that denied the border change and its posters portrayed the map of prewar Germany still intact. One CDU poster, "No: Vote CDU," displayed a map and a dark-red, Mongolian-featured behemoth reaching toward West Germany with his large, red hand. (German colonial literature before and during the war had portrayed the Poles as "black" and Germans as "white."[7]) Poles and Russians alike were still those Mongolian thieves from the CDU propaganda posters. When Anke and her family laughed at Slavs, I felt uneasy. Germany paid dearly for the Holocaust but never for racism against the Slavs. As someone who had benefited from the privilege of being white living in the United States, this was my first taste of casual racism, the feeling that everything you are is predetermined by some imaginary paradigm that cannot be altered, shattered, or escaped.

In fact, I had heard this "did not know how to" narrative before, but refused to listen to it. It was back in New York during one of our interview sessions. Anke recalled that during the war, when she spent her summers with her grandparents in a village called "Dorf" outside of Neisse, there was a house right across the street from them reserved for Polish, Ukrainian, and Russian forced laborers who worked on their farms. Anke lightheartedly recalled that their Ukrainian laborer Olga "did not know how" to take care of her menstruation, so when she was picking apples from the trees in a white dress, she had stuffed her underwear with newspaper, which did not stop the menstrual blood from bleeding all over her white skirt. Anke found this funny. Perhaps most perplexing was Anke's confusion about why it was that after the Red Army came through in 1945, Olga just "took off"! Olga remained a wild easterner who "did not know how" to take care of herself, whom they had treated well, and who rudely "took off." Anke did not feel the same level of empathy for Olga as she did with Ingrid, a twenty-one-year-old medical student whom her family hid from the encroaching Red Army. Anke proudly recalled how Ingrid ingeniously used her training to paint a "Typhus" sign outside of the house to scare away Russian rapists. When the Russian front arrived, Anke's family hid Ingrid behind the sewing machine. Why was Ingrid's sign innovative but Olga's creative use of newspaper to catch menstrual blood backward? Why was it that Olga's misfortune was funny, but Ingrid's was retold with horror?

In *House of Day, House of Night* (2003), set in the Silesian village of Nowa Ruda, along the border of Germany, Poland, and the Czech Republic, the novelist Olga Tokarczuk writes about the German Heimat trips and the uncomfortable recasting of Polish innovation as backwardness:

> Every year the Germans come pouring out of coaches that park timidly on the hard shoulder, as if trying to be inconspicuous. . . . They take photos of empty spaces, which many people find puzzling. Why don't they take pictures of the new bus stop or the new church roof, instead of empty spaces overgrown with grass? We have often treated them to tea and cakes. They never sit down or ask for more. They just finish their tea and are off. We feel embarrassed if they try to press a few marks into our hands. We're afraid we must look like savages, living as we do among eternal repairs, with flaking plaster on the walls and the rotten steps on the terrace stairs. . . . One year an old couple turned up on our land and showed us where houses that no longer existed had stood. Afterwards we sent each other Christmas cards. They reassured us that the Frost family was no longer interested in our home. "Why should anyone be interested in our house?" I asked Marta resentfully. "Because they built it," she replied. One evening, as we were clearing the empty teacups and plates from the terrace, Marta said that the most important human duty is to save things that are falling into decay, rather than create new ones.[8]

While saving and recycling old structures around the village are symbols of ingenuity and resourcefulness to many Poles, to an outsider German, they represent the Polish desecration of the lost Germany. They symbolize the unjust degradation and backwardness of the once pristine and developed German village that lives in their imagination of the Heimat and in the golden age photographs. I had heard similar complaints about Heimat trips in Bursztyn: the Germans would drive around in their cars and take out their cameras to photograph "barefoot" and "hungry" Polish children in the village to confirm their viewpoints about Poland rather than just realizing that most kids in the villages play barefoot and that all children like candy. The Heimat trips help preserve and reproduce the discourses, memories, and imaginaries of wild, reptilian easterners.

These double standards were just the tip of the iceberg of racism. When we crossed the border from Görlitz to Zgorzelec, Anke and Henrick were too afraid to step out and waited for me on the Polish side of the border. Although she wanted to pay for the entire trip, Anke distrusted me with handling her money and made me immediately report all expenses to her, even for one postage stamp, in front of Henrick who had free rein. When I began to reject her requests out of a sense of self-dignity, she claimed: "What, do I have to force-feed you the money like the Poles force-feed food?" At one point, Henrick claimed that he had left two hundred euros on the dashboard and that it had been "stolen." Anke yelled, "You don't leave money out like that! You know *they* will take it!" While I was always suspected of theft, the only loss of money that occurred on Henrick's watch was blamed on the Poles. Everything was oriented around the "loss" of German capital to the Poles. As we drove toward the modern highway system in Silesia, they were "shocked" that the bathrooms in the restrooms were clean, there was suburban development, large Tesco supermarkets, Western brands, fast-food chains like KFC and McDonald's, Polish people driving their own BMWs, and that Poland more or less thrived in this region. When Anke saw a girl with a cell phone, she grabbed Henrick in shock—"Did you see that [Polish] girl with a cell phone? She had a cell phone!" This was the year 2015.

All of these everyday conversations and slanting of memories and contexts revealed to me the careful, and almost intuitive, crafting of the German historical narrative that positively spins German settlement of the east and victimizes their postwar expulsion. Even in the midst of all this modernization, of the ways that Poles have transformed these lands, Anke and Henrick "saw" Germany. There was a sense of denial that this, in fact, was currently Poland. When Henrick spoke about his family origins in the east, he proudly recalled that his German mother was from "Köningsberg" in former East Prussia and his German father was from Weißrussland (White Russia, meaning Belarus), where their families had lived since Tsarina Catherine the Great. The empress of German descent had signed a decree in 1763 encouraging Germans to legally set up colonies in Russia. Even though he and Anke shared family stories of the postwar German expulsion from Eastern Europe, they navigated the east using wartime geography. Henrick referred to Kaliningrad as "Köningsberg" even though the name change has been in effect and internationally recognized since 1946. I had heard this back in Berlin too. When the forty-something-year-old manager of a Berlin hotel was handing Anke the bill, he said, "My brother was born in Silesia—not Poland— *Silesia*." They would not try Polish food, only German or Western dishes that had the potatoes and meat arranged the other way around than the identical dishes with Polish names. This is not the kind of border reconciliation that I had hoped for, but a way of tailoring memories that perpetuate the myths of the Heimat. It reminded me of the fantastical rhetoric Bursztynians used to prove to themselves that the Recovered Territories had always belonged to the Polish nation.

The farther east we drove toward Anke's Heimat, the more she demanded subservience. When we stayed in a beautifully restored German Junker estate nestled in the Silesian countryside owned by a Polish-Italian couple, Anke introduced me to fellow German travelers on their own Heimat trips not as a researcher, but as "my little Polish girl." She portrayed me as "her" personal Slav. The memories between past and present blurred. I was her Olga. At that moment, something stirred inside me. I had never felt nationalistic really, and I already had a far more sympathetic view of the German expulsion than most Poles (some of whom called me a traitor), but I felt compelled to rebel against Anke. The spirit of the kombinator possessed me. I found refuge in the realm of kombinacja, which, in my case, was simply about finding ways to unhinge myself from Anke's regime. At first, I tried to secure transportation to the airport to leave the country, but we were too isolated for a taxi to drive me anywhere. Rather than orienting my mind totally to Anke's trip, I began to forge emotional alliances with the Poles we met. I spoke to them in Polish and told them about my situation with Anke. They understood completely, and in fact, it was that "hidden transcript" between us that made me feel a stronger emotional connection to these people. I also began to retreat mentally from Anke's Heimat search and started focusing on writing my notes, communicating with my mother, drinking vodka with the hosts, and shopping or visiting the archives. I began to think of the trip in terms of my own research and how I could add to it. Anke hated what I was doing, but I felt freed from the sense of suffocation. I finally understood what kombinacja felt like as a liberation strategy in the mind. It was a form of carving out some space in everyday life, whether in a physical environment or in one's head, to form a double persona, one that is other than that imposed on you by a regime or oppressor. It is the space of anarchy within the few cubic centimeters inside our skulls, a space where we can escape, get away, and break the rules, when the living conditions during personal or systemic crises become too much to bear. Like Olga, I needed an escape, and I found that refuge in kombinacja. I had transformed into a kombinatorka. And it was intoxicating.

Conjuring Ghosts

The past, present, and future seemed more alive in Silesia than in Pomerania. The southern region of the Recovered Territories was more economically robust than the north where Bursztyn was located, with seas of corn, rapeseed, and wheat fields stretching over the horizon. Unlike in Pomerania where many of the peasant and former state farmlands lay fallow, in Silesia, peasants lease their private fields to corporations that process the corn they grow for corn oil production in large silos. The former state farm fields, too, were privately owned and lush with corn crops. The green and golden fields were split by a modern highway system filled with cargo trucks and exits for rest stops with BP gas stations and American fast-food restaurants. It was a capitalism I was more familiar with back in the United States, unlike in Bursztyn, where capitalism had been a soft form of German revanchism, of reclaiming agricultural and industrial property in the former Recovered Territories and imposing poor working conditions on the Polish workers; or freezing development for "security reasons" to make room for the American construction of the antimissile shield in Rędzikowo; or destroying private property rights to allow American shale-gas exploration on farmland without owners' consent. Glowing Silesia showcased the promises of capitalism; shadowy Pomerania showcased its lies.

As we drove across Silesia, I was astonished by how much of the past had not been erased by human will or negligence or both. While Pomerania was defined by emptiness, Silesia was defined by pluralism. Different layers of history seemed to have their own place and were allowed to coexist. Like in Görlitz, I spotted remnants of a German-era sign "Eisenwaren Georg Nigawe Kolonialwaren" (Georg Nigawe's Ironworks and Imports) that had once been painted on a building in Tułowice village. In another village, I found an EU-supported, socialist-era Agricultural Production Cooperative (*Rolnicza Spółdzielnia Produkcyjna*) that still specialized in fisheries. Such fragments of the past were very difficult to find back in the north.

Take, for example, the round, German-era, family coat-of-arms (*herb*) plates that once adorned the front of each family home when Bursztyn was still Bernstein. They were built into German homes and were usually located behind the top of the front door and the roof of the house. They included scenes from everyday life, like a girl with a dog, or a dinner party. In the postwar period, denazification policies resulted in settlers taking down or shooting down the plates to eliminate the former German family's connection to that property. There was only one that I had seen still intact in Bursztyn, whereas most of the other ones were simply empty holes in the buildings. In Silesia, however, the *herbs* were still intact in nearly every village we drove through. This may have been due to the large Silesian (*Ślązacy*) minority—a Germanized Slavic ethnic group—who had remained in their homes after the war and pushed back against denazification policies. Whereas in the north the "holes" in missing plates were left empty, in Silesia, they were replaced most often with religious statues of Mary. I thought about the Pope John Paul II monument on the Zgorzelec side of the Polish-German border and wondered whether the insertion of religious statues in the former coat-of-arms plates in the homes was also a kind of protection. In one village, I even saw a house where the plate had been replaced by a communist sickle, which had been left intact ever since. Silesia was a place of hyphenated spaces and identities. It looked far more welcoming than the north.

With so much history all around us, searching for the Heimat was a kind of mystical experience. During Anke's search for one her former family homes in the countryside, we came across a house in a village, "Bajka," where she spotted a garden and structure that aligned with her memories of once having played there as a child. We entered the home, and we met a woman, Sylwia, whose deceased German father had been in the Wehrmacht. There was some frantic exchanging of family-tree information, and then Anke went into the family photo album. It felt like a ghost-conjuring ceremony, where she badly wanted to "connect" with their dead, touching the gotyks lying around, looking around the house structure. Nothing. No memories. They were not "hers." But strangely, the garden outside was. She was sure of it. I became interested in Sylwia's history when she brought out a portrait of her father, Werner, wearing a Wehrmacht military uniform, a cap with a swastika on it, and a Hitler mustache. He had written a series of diaries for different members of the family, and she had been one of the recipients. I wanted to know what life was like for a Wehrmacht German who remained in these Recovered Territories. She handed me the diary, written in Polish in a thin, lined notebook. There is little in there about Werner himself; he focuses on the lives of his sister Ulrike and her husband, Otto, who, like Werner, had also served in the Wehrmacht. The story in the diary goes like this: After the Red Army passed through Silesia and took over the government in 1945, a German communist sympathizer in the village told the newly formed Polish-Soviet Ministry of Public Security (Urząd Bezpieczeństwa) that Otto had been in the Waffen-SS, which had been responsible for many Nazi war crimes. The UB arrested Otto and tortured him, even though Otto denied the accusation and said that he had only been the private driver of a director general whom he had driven around to "hunt" (*polować*) in another county. What this means is unclear. It could have referred to a feudal labor obligation like a Scharwerk. However, in Polish *polowanie* refers to the act of chasing Poles to force them into labor in Germany. It could have been both: Otto may have been conscripted into providing transport for a general to catch Polish laborers. Whatever the circumstances, as a driver, he had remained close to home and not "off" at war.

The UB took him for six weeks under "investigative arrest." There he was interrogated and tortured in secrecy. Otto's wife, Ulrike, had long been looking for witnesses to testify that he was innocent. Someone helped her in this, and the UB stopped torturing (*katować*) him, but they did not release him, because they said he had worked for the Wehrmacht and for that would have to pay the price and work for them. They treated him like they owned him. He was forced to repair old cars left over in ditches from the war, so that the UB could sell them. Although Otto was innocent, he stayed with the UB and there found out that the Polish state would be resettling the Germans. He begged the UB to let him go, but the UB had different plans. Werner writes that Silesians who knew the Polish language could become Polish citizens. This was temporary citizenship. Germans and Silesians did not care too much about accepting Polish citizenship because they did not believe that German lands would be incorporated into Poland. Almost everyone took advantage of it so that they could stay on their farms. When one went to the commune headquarters, the Poles checked only the date of birth.

But it turned out that anyone who did not take on Polish citizenship at that critical point in time was soon expelled west of the Oder-Neisse line into Germany.

Life in Poland was not easy. Werner, Otto, and Ulrike were spied on and persecuted in the village and in the commune offices. They were forbidden to speak German. People spied on them even under their own windows. Toward the end of 1948, the Poles began to force the Germans to change their last names and began to threaten that if they did not, they would send them for several weeks to forced labor camps (*lagry*). When they returned, their homes would be nothing, with no doors or windows, and they would not be allowed to go to Germany. This, Werner noted, was what happened to Frieda, a German widow who played the church organ and whose husband had been killed in the war. They had a nice house and nice furniture. One night she was coming home from the neighbors' house when the Polish mayor (*sołtys*) took her key and locked her in her own house. By the doors he put two guards who patrolled the village. She already knew what they were going to do to her. She hid and looked out the window through a peephole, and when she saw that they had fallen asleep, she jumped out the window and ran through the night to the train station and took the first train to Kedzierzyna to her parents. Her eight-year-old son was with her parents, who spoke Polish.

Meanwhile, the UB drove to Frieda's house and took all of her clothes and down covers and plates. Werner wrote that the mayor was a serious looter and was even taken to court for his widespread looting but never brought to justice. Later, a drunk UB officer claimed that Frieda was supposed to have been murdered by the UB. In 1957 she left for West Germany with her parents. However, that too proved problematic because they had temporary Polish citizenship and wanted to leave for Germany. If the state allowed everyone with passports to leave, then everyone would want to leave for the West. Otto eventually took retirement and in exchange gave his property to the state (like Zofia in 1983) before he died. Ulrike left for Germany. Werner writes that those Germans who stayed in Poland continue to feel German. In the last entry from November 1977, he writes in scribbled handwriting:

> It is 33 years after the war in Poland and instead of it being better, it is worse and worse. Sugar and coal are rationed. Coal rations are only 1,400 kilograms, so one can only burn 4.4 kilograms daily. But this is Poland—the backward nation. In Poland, it was never, continues not to be, and never will be, good. The German Republic bore the brunt of losing the war and now there is an economic miracle [*cud gospodarczy*]. This miracle the wealthy Poles know about this. There everything is accessible. RFN [West Germany] is the wealthiest nation in Europe. There one can buy a Volkswagen for 4,000 marks while in Poland one has to work for a Fiat 126P. In NRD [East Germany] it is a socialist country just like Poland. In Poland it is not good but in the Soviet Union it is

even worse because communism has been around for more than 50 years. Will there ever be freedom and prosperity [in Poland]?

What fascinated me about this history was how it blended Silesian, German, and Polish identities all into several pages. It exposes the German and Silesian past and a struggle to survive through a total transformation not only of a person's physical homeland but also of a man's emotional and psychological transformation from German Wehrmacht soldier to Polish citizen. The Germans who stayed in Silesia during the transformation under Polish communism also suffered through the economic crisis, also were looted and forced into labor by officials, also had to give up their agricultural land "in exchange" for retirement, and also had to work hard to survive. At times Werner's story was Zofia's story. Werner wrote this for his own children, and nowhere does he write about revanchism. His Heimat and history show that what constituted the Heimat in the pre-1945 period had transformed and evolved through the decades of communism.

This is life on the Polish-German borderlands: no one wins and there is no singular national or ethnic identity. Everything is hyphenated. Both the Polish Piast myth and the German Heimat myth create a border imaginary of a pristine past utopia, one that never existed and never will exist. Thus, I found Werner's memoir to be in stark contrast to the Heimat lands that Anke was trying to recover. A lot of the Heimat experience was about making multiple circles around a single block, waiting for Anke to recall a small path or a rock or some semblance of the past, a redbrick chimney, for instance, still peeking out from under the reconstructed homes that could lead us to her family homes. Driving around was like playing a Ouija board game, waiting for the ghosts to speak to us. In addition to Bajka, Anke wanted to visit the village "Dorf," where she spent her childhood visiting her grandparents during the summers, and Nysa (formerly Neisse), the city where she lived with her parents. The former was a rural settlement of twenty homes lining a single street. We had to find only the house and its owners, but this was difficult because all the homes were nearly identical and had been covered over with cement during renovation. We parked by the cemetery at the edge of the forest, where we found German tombstones intermingled with Polish ones. As we looked for Anke's family, an elderly couple named Augustyn and Stanisława, wearing neon vests, were cleaning up the gravestones. They looked at us curiously. When we introduced ourselves and showed them the photographs; it turned out that they were the current neighbors of the woman who lives in Anke's grandparents' former house. They took us to her house and initiated the contact with Marysia, the original settler, who invited us in. Marysia had a son named Radek who looked like Zofia's Roman—one of the fallen village men on the alcohol benches. Radek had glassy eyes, few teeth, and several missing fingers. Marysia had coarsely cut gray hair, a wrinkled face, and a skinny frame, and she spoke in a raspy voice. In contrast, Anke sported a large sun hat, white pants, a white Oxford shirt, colorful bangles, large sunglasses, and a stylish bob. The women came from different worlds, and yet when Marysia opened the door and agreed to let Anke in, the two cried in each other's arms as if they were family members who had not seen each other since 1945. It was a powerful connection.

When Anke walked into her grandparents' house, and saw with her own eyes the home from her memories, she broke out into a wailing cry and immediately showed us into the living room, and into the corner where she was born in her grandmother's bed, where the large furnace used to be along with the Singer sewing machine. She held on to her utopian images of her youth, the life that the Poles had destroyed. As she walked toward the kitchen, she pointed out the little German-era gotyks still hanging on the walls (but did not seem to notice the small painting with a rabbi and Torah in the foyer). It was an incredible experience seeing Anke unlock the past with her memories by walking around the house. Anke had an excellent memory, and she knew the spaces before she opened the doors. Marysia stood awkwardly to the side like a visitor who did not know where to sit down in someone else's house. As Anke went up to the attic and walked toward an old wooden armoire, she opened up immediately and started taking out the "very old porcelain," as she put it, and asking Marysia if these pieces were from the German era. Marysia was a bit dumbstruck by this stranger rummaging through her personal belongings and said they were just old plates. Anke remembered that her family had hidden porcelain and planted an apple tree on top of the burial site. When we visited the tree in the back of the barn, Anke said that they had likely dug it up, even though Marysia said her family had not known about it. Anke did not want to dig for it. The meeting was cordial, and we shared coffee and chocolates outdoors. It was quite incredible patching together their pasts, which they had experienced in the same location but in different "countries." Marysia, who arrived at the house with her parents when she was Anke's age, also remembered Ingrid, the young medical student Anke's family hid from the Red Army. The Heimat encounter, in some ways, can help unearth the stories and people lost in the interstices of border changes, which offer a fascinating historical text for scholars interested in writing about the borderlands. Those stories can also be a source of healing for the expellees and the settlers.

However, that balance is difficult to achieve. When we said our final goodbyes, Marysia kissed Anke's hand—a common gesture of friendship in Poland among the older generation. Anke beamed with superiority and pride because, I assumed, to her it represented Marysia's subservience. After our Heimat meeting, we walked over to Augustyn's house next door. Augustyn was born in 1947 in the village after his parents had been repatriated from the eastern borderlands, now in western Ukraine. He loved to give speeches about history, and I listened with interest, but Anke was after something else. I am not sure what exactly. She pressed me to ask him if he was Jewish, because he was "so well spoken and different from the Poles" and he reminded her of her husband. Augustyn, taken aback, politely responded that he was not Jewish. Then he continued on with his life story. He recalled from his parents' recollections that the Slavic forced laborers had been kept in the German barracks right across the street from Anke's home. After Anke's family had left, Olga had returned with a Red Army officer looking for Anke's family and had threatened to shoot them all. However, because most of the Germans were already gone, Olga left, never to be seen again. I never found out what really happened to Olga and why she wanted revenge, because that would require Anke to open up about the dark past. Perhaps Olga's blood was not always menstruation but the effects of rape or other violent crimes against her. To my surprise, Anke was unfazed by the Olga story. Perhaps because it was outside of the snippets of her memory about the Heimat as a sacred German space that had been desecrated by the Poles.

Augustyn went on to tell the story that when his parents arrived, they found two thousand German reichsmark—the official currency used in Nazi Germany until it was replaced by the deutsche mark in 1948—in the attic of the barn. Remarkably, he had kept the entire stash of money should the German owners return to claim it. He brought it out, an old and rolled-up pile of cash and set it on the table. It was the moment I was waiting for: there in front of Anke and Henrick was proof that not all "Poles" were thieves. I saw no reaction on their faces. Augustyn and Stanisława gave me a ten and a fifty reichsmark note as a gotyk to remember this piece of history with the border. They offered one to Anke and Henrick, who politely declined it. They then left the house out of "boredom" and waited for me in the car while I talked to Augustyn. We were venturing into historical territory that they did not feel comfortable with, territory that cast a shadow over the utopian photographs in Anke's grasp. And herein lies the danger of the Heimat: it is too easy to walk away from the other side of the story or anything that threatens the ideal.

After Anke left his house, Augustyn whispered to me that just twelve kilometers south of Dorf was a notorious prisoner-of-war camp, Stalag VIIIB/344 Lamsdorf, where from 1939 to 1945 the German army held one hundred thousand Western prisoners of war from Australia, New Zealand, the United States, France, and other countries. Nearby, a separate camp, Stalag VIIIF, essentially became an extermination camp for forty thousand Soviet prisoners of war. When his parents arrived and were cleaning out the German barn, they found a dog tag and clothes of a prisoner whom they assumed had escaped from Lamsdorf. This also was the overflowing camp from which Olga and the other Ukrainian prisoners were distributed to the German villagers nearby to work as slaves on their farms and fields. Lamsdorf was not too far from the other side of the fence in Anke's black-and-white photograph. When I mentioned this to Anke, she responded quite nonchalantly, "Oh, yes, we called it a 'catch-all' camp." When we left Dorf, I insisted that we visit Lamsdorf. Henrick did not go in at all and sat in the car. Anke spent only a minute on the wartime section and went straight for the exhibit on the postwar German expulsion. One image from the exhibition that burned into my mind was a photograph of German women digging up mass graves with the Red Army soldiers watching over them. So when the Soviets found the camp, they wanted justice, and one way to accomplish that was to force the Germans to see the graves with their own eyes and to inhale the typhoid from the decaying Soviet bodies. How curious that Anke's Heimat photographs and the museum photographs were snapped almost in the same moment of history and in the same region but exposed two different worlds. When I stepped out of the camp, Anke and Henrick were gone. They had pretended to leave me. Five minutes later, when they finally drove by and opened the door, they laughed at their prank.

Finding Anke's family home in Nysa was more difficult because the city had spread well beyond its original borders. We located a region of the city, and slowly drove around in circles while Anke tried to match fragments of the landscape with those she had recalled in her dreams. We finally stopped at the monastery— the "concentration camp," as Anke called it—where she was looking for an old shortcut through the fields that linked it to her family's neighborhood. We had by chance parked next to it—it was used but still unpaved—and when we drove through it, Anke remembered that there should be an old watchtower on the corner, and indeed, there it was. The landscape then began to unlock. We made a right turn, as she had when she was a little girl, and finally located the street. Then we drove up and down the street, over and over again, with little luck. Anke said Poles were "camouflaging" homes, as if they were purposely trying to hide their true identities (rather than renovating old German houses). Finally, she spotted the remnants of an old chimney next to an oak tree—the tree from her black-and-white photograph. The house was painted an eye-jarring neon green color and surrounded with a very tall fence. We rang the bell and a huge dog jumped out and began lunging at us through a hole in the fence. Finally, the owner, a young man in his late thirties, came and let us onto his property. When he and his wife invited us into their home, Anke pointed out that there were dead Germans her father had buried by the lamppost in front of the house after the war. Their jaws slightly dropped in horror. Just like in Dorf, Anke ran into the house and began to open doors, even into their teenage daughter's room, who was still sleeping and confused about the ruckus. This couple had actually purchased the house, so they were not the original settlers, but they said that they had some sort of plaque in the attic that stated the year of the house. Anke disagreed about the year and insisted that they had it wrong. The woman said that she could show Anke the proof, but her husband told her in Polish to drop the subject. They became concerned about Anke's motives. Not everyone was prepared for the Heimat experience, yet Anke held them liable for that history.

Anke remembered that when the Poles took over the city, the Germans were rounded up and relocated to the brick-walled monastery that the Poles and Soviets had converted into what she called a "concentration camp." Her brother was born on the very first night her family spent in that camp. Anke and her mother lived in the camp while the Soviet Red Army took Anke's father, an architect, to help reconstruct the bridges leading into the city, which had been bombed by Allied powers. When we arrived at the monastery, Anke sought out the middle-aged priest and demanded to speak with him. When he came out from his office, he asked what we needed. Anke proceeded to state confrontationally that she "knew" there was a concentration camp here for Germans. He denied that there had ever been a camp there but said there might have been one in another Franciscan monastery in Nysa. Anke refused to believe him and continued the confrontation. When I asked if there were any archives in the building perhaps, the priest sharply asked, "And what purpose would these archives serve?" He sounded defensive, but then provided the name of the archival office. Anke wanted none of that, no archives or anything: she wanted him to confess that he had known all along and was hiding the truth. She also wanted to tour the monastery, but he said that it was a school grounds and we would have to get permission from the school to do so. He resisted giving Anke the satisfaction. The next day, Anke, Henrick, and I went to the outer walls of the monastery and sat down on the grass while she told us the story of the "concentration camp" and pointed to every single window. She remembered where the communal kitchen was, the theater, where her mother gave birth, and so forth. I completely believed her and later felt guilty about not pressing the priest enough to get the confession Anke wanted. She had just been a little girl at the time and wanted justice for her family's suffering. I told her that not everyone knew about that history, but those words felt cowardly coming out of my mouth. I felt almost complicit with the person who had covered over the German tombstone road in Bursztyn.

There were positive moments with Anke, especially those times where she helped fill in small mysteries about the landscape in the Recovered Territories. I learned that the trees that line the road—a giveaway of the German-era landscape—were there because they used to give the horses shade as they pulled carriages. When I showed her my work on the potato foragers, Anke recalled that this was a German agrarian labor institution called *Nachlese*, very common on German lands. I was amazed at how the everyday realities of harvesting and sowing crops for consumption that constituted agrarian livelihoods cut across notions of nationhood, nationalities, ethnicity, and linguistic boundaries. Speaking about the postwar period, Anke also recalled that when the first Polish families arrived to settle Dorf, they were very "bewildered" because there was nothing around, scarcity. They too had been forced to settle the land, so they were very confused as to what had happened. Anke's mother traded a Singer sewing machine for a pound of butter with the Poles. She said that the Germans would say that the Polish farmers had carpeted stables because they had taken so much through barter. Anke had undoubtedly lived through hard times as a little girl. At some point, Anke remembered that during the war, she and the children hunted swallows—the most magnificent little birds whose pirouettes through the air symbolize freedom and life—and then gave them to the woman of the Junker estate who cooked them into sparrow soup for them. It is a story that I cannot get out of my head, because I cannot decide if the memory reveals an innovative quest for survival even among children, or if it represents the murder of innocent life that even children committed. And then there was the mysticism of the landscape, when Anke spoke about the giant that once lived on the Schneekoppe (Snow-Top Mountain) in the dark blue Sudeten mountain range, which one could see in the distance from the Silesian lands.

Everyone has the right to take a trip and revisit their homeland, but Heimat trips are generally more about confirming the fragmented memories of the German tourists rather than filling them in with the new realities of their old homes. They are more about what has been lost than what has been gained. They bring out the way we pick and choose narratives to decode certain layers of landscapes but not others. Anke, for example, reordered the Polish landscape to confirm her prejudices and experiences. She was pleased to find that in the Silesian communities many of the redbrick homes were intact. And then there was the fantasy reconstruction of the Heimat based on evidence that was not there: when we visited Sylwia's house in Bajka, Anke did not care about the lack of real connection between the family histories; rather, she "knew" that it was the place because of the gardens and structures of the house, even though the actual story of the family did not add up. Anke was not looking for the truth, but rather reassembling the landscape and people to conform to her own vision of a long-lost German empire. When I showed the videos and photographs from the trip to Anke's nephew later on in Berlin, he angrily replied that he would "go back for it and take it all back." Now that she knew the route, Anke said that she would return each year to show her family their Heimat. No treaties have helped bring closure or a sense of belonging to these lands.

Four Gotyks

A gotyk is a farewell as well as a token of remembering a common past. Gotyks must be "earned," like the gotyk cross Frau Agathe gave Zofia as she was leaving Bursztyn. At the end of the trip with Anke, it was also time to leave the borderlands. For me, this was a final farewell—final for a while at least—as a native ethnographer. I would never see Anke again after Berlin. But what made this Heimat trip significant is that I formed some sense of emotional and personal connection with the settlers of the Recovered Territories. I received several departing gotyks on this trip, and to me they represent the different ways people reached out to me in dire circumstances, but also confirm that I am somehow entangled with the history of these lands. I will never understand the full scope of this history. I too have developed my own myths, biases, and blind spots along this journey.

The first gotyk was the two antique German reichsmark notes that Augustyn had kept after his parents found them stashed away in a barn when they were renovating it. He and Stanisława gave me two "as a memory" (*na pamiątkę*) of them and also of their ongoing custodianship of the German property. This gift represented a common appreciation of the postwar history and a sense of historical understanding over a mutual "hidden transcript" that we shared during the visit, unfortunately at Anke's expense.

The second gotyk came from hundred-year-old Silesian photographer Arkadiusz and his wife, Leokadia, a former ballet dancer, who had witnessed the transformation of German Breslau into Polish Wrocław. It is a 1962 signed photograph of the thirteenth-century Gothic Wrocław town hall—Stary Ratusz—with an astronomical clock. To me, it represents the cosmic timelessness of the issues I had been addressing for the past eight years. It represented our mutual interest in capturing the past, however raw and ugly.

The third gotyk came from Piero, the seventy-four-year-old Italian owner of the German Junker estate where we stayed in Silesia. He and his wife, Anastazja (from Słupsk), truly understood the situation I was in, for they too had hyphenated identities and had experienced their share of German Heimat tourists. We three sought some refuge in vodka. Piero and Anastazja were my home away from home. On the last day, Anke started buying the not-for-sale paintings off the walls of the mansion for thousands of złoty for her daughter and her real estate clients back in New York who might want to buy the struggling estate. While Anke was laying out money on the table, Piero disappeared into the kitchen and returned with the gift of a painting by a local Czech artist of a single rose on the edge of the Sudeten Mountains. He handed it to me as a gift. I cried, Piero cried, and we left for Berlin.

The fourth gotyk came from my mother, who traveled to Poland around the same time in late July 2015. She brought back a red brick from Zofia's barn, which was in the process of being taken apart, and she told me that if I build my own house one day, it should be incorporated into it. Roman was in rehabilitation following his stroke; Zofia had fallen and broken her hip and was being taken care of by my aunt in another village. The farm is in ruins. Roman never finished taking apart the barn, so Uncle Kuba has been taking it apart and selling off the bricks. My mother brought me back one of those German gotyk bricks, a building block of my life, to remember what was once there. Like many other objects in the Recovered Territories, there are only memories of what was and is slowly being disassembled and eroded with time. This gotyk represents an intergenerational passing of the baton of our mutual peasant history. Or does it? Could it instead signify my successful indoctrination into the arts of kombinacja? My transformation into a nationalistic kombinatorka who protects the past from outsiders? My ability to see, feel, and perceive the world through a mystical dimension of kombinacja that outsiders cannot detect?

Searching for fragments of my father's world, I stumbled into the labyrinthine region of the Polish imagination that is ruled by kombinacja. Nearly a decade later, I am not convinced that I have found my way out. Perhaps there is no exit. As my mother says, corrupt states penetrate and corrupt states of mind. Kombinacja controls me more than I control it. It is not something that time, space, or political transformation can exorcise from the mind. Like the alienated Bursztynians, I carry it in me and search for ways that it can bring me closer to some kind of collective. This is why dystopia is important to me and to them, why we must do whatever it takes to provoke and propagate it. We are addicted to its magical properties, whatever their price. Is this comfort in dystopia the "empowerment" I was searching for after my father's death? Is this the fossilized past I came to excavate? Or might this book be nothing more than a physical product of my own kombinacja? Rather than providing a portal for lonely souls to escape from dystopia, have I simply reinforced the suspicion that the whole world is one big kombinacja?

There are no clear answers. Many of the village elders who first exposed me to kombinacja have since passed away. Zofia has been laid to rest next to Konrad in Bursztyn's cemetery, among the broken shards of German tombstones. What I have described has already been encased in amber. It is already a border memory.

Notes

1. Demshuk, *Lost German East*, 2.
2. Ibid., 85.
3. Snyder, *Bloodlands*, 405.
4. Applebaum, *Iron Curtain*, 124.
5. Kate Connolly, "Germans Greet Influx of Refugees with Free Food and Firebombings, *The Guardian*, July 30, 2015, https://www.theguardian.com/world/2015/jul/30/germans-greet-influx-of-refugees-free-food-fire-bombings.
6. Gatehouse, "Germany's Open-Door Policy," 04:49–05:50 (video report).
7. Snyder, *Bloodlands*, 16–17.
8. Tokarczuk, *House of Day*, 91–92.

Bibliography

Abrahamian, Levon. "Lenin as a Trickster." *Anthropology and Archeology of Eurasia* 38, no. 2 (1999): 8–26.

Ahonen, Pertti, and Tamas Stark. *People on the Move: Forced Population Movements in Europe in the Second World War and Its Aftermath.* Oxford, UK: Berg, 2008.

AlSayyad, Nezar, and Ananya Roy. "Urban Informality: Crossing Borders." In *Urban Informality: Transnational Perspectives from the Middle East, Latin America, and South Asia*, edited by Ananya Roy and Nezar AlSayyad, 1–6. Lanham, MD: Lexington Books, 2004.

Applebaum, Anne. *Iron Curtain: The Crushing of Eastern Europe, 1944–1956.* New York: Doubleday, 2012.

Ball, Alan M. *Russia's Last Capitalists: The Nepmen, 1921–1929.* Berkeley: University of California Press, 1987.

Bammer, Angelika. "When Poland Was Home: Nostalgic Returns in Grass and Wolf." In *Germany, Poland and Postmemorial Relations: In Search of a Livable Past*, edited by Kristin Kopp and Joanna Niżyńska, 109–30. New York: Palgrave Macmillan, 2012.

Barcikowski, Wacław. Introduction to *Odzyskane Ziemie-Odzyskani Ludzie* (Recovered Territories, Recovered People). Poznań: Wydawnictwo Zachodnie, 1946.

Bergmann, Theodor. "Change Processes in Farming and Political Consciousness and Attitudes of Peasants and Worker-Peasants." *Sociologia Ruralis* 15, nos. 1–2 (1975): 73–89.

Bevir, Mark. *The Making of British Socialism.* Princeton, NJ: Princeton University Press, 2011.

Bierut, Bolesław. "We Are Building the Structure of Socialist Poland." In *The Six-Year Plan of Economic Development and Building the Foundations of Socialism in Poland*, 5–18. Warsaw: Książka i Wiedza, 1950.

Blum, Jerome. "The Rise of Serfdom in Eastern Europe." *American Historical Review* 62, no. 4 (1957): 807–36.

Bourdieu, Pierre. *The Field of Cultural Production.* Edited by Randal Johnson. New York: Columbia University Press, 1993.

Boy-Żeleński, Tadeusz. *Flirt z Melpomeną* (Flirt with Melpomena). Warsaw: Biblioteka Polska, 1920. Available at Wolne Lektury, http://wolnelektury.pl/katalog/lektura/flirt-z-melpomena.html.

———. *Jak skończyć z piekłem kobiet? Świadome macierzyństwo* (How to end women's hell? Conscious motherhood) Warsaw: Państwowy Instytut Wydawniczy, 1932. Available at Wolne Lektury, http://wolnelektury.pl/katalog/lektura/jak-skonczyc-z-pieklem-kobiet.html.

Brown, Kate. *A Biography of No Place: From Ethnic Borderland to Soviet Heartland.* Cambridge, MA: Harvard University Press, 2004.

Bücher, Karl. *Industrial Evolution.* Translated by S. Morley Wickett. New York: Henry Holt, 1901.

Buchli, Victor. *An Archaeology of Socialism.* Oxford, UK: Berg, 1999.

Cain, Peter J. "Railway Combination and Government, 1900–1914." *Economic History Review* 25, no. 4 (1972): 623–41.

Chan, Anita, and Jonathan Unger. "Grey and Black: The Hidden Economy of Rural China." *Pacific Affairs* 55, no. 3 (1982): 452–71.

Chari, Sharad. *Fraternal Capital: Peasant-Workers, Self-Made Men, and Globalization in Provincial India.* Stanford: Stanford University Press, 2004.

Chmarzyński, Gwido. *Pomorze Zachodnie* (West Pomerania). Poznań: Instytut Zachodni, 1949.

Chodakiewicz, Marek Jan. *Between Nazis and Soviets: Occupation Politics in Poland, 1939–1947.* Lanham, MD: Lexington Books, 2004.

Chojanski, Władysław. *Słownik Polskich Nazw Miejscowości W B. Prusach Wschodnich I Na Obszarze B. Wolnego Miasta Gdańska, Według Stanu Z 1941 G.* (A dictionary of Polish places in Eastern Prussia and the periphery of the former Free City of Gdańsk, as of the 1941 borders). Poznań: Instytut Zachodni, 1946.

Cinnirella, Francesco, and Erik Hornung. "Landownership Concentration and the Expansion of Education." *Journal of Development Economics* 121 (2016): 135–52.

Clark, Anna. *The Struggle for the Breeches: Gender and the Making of the British Working Class.* Berkeley: University of California Press, 1995.

Czeszko, Bohdan. *Pokolenie* (A generation). 2nd ed. Warsaw: Czytelnik, 1951.

Davies, Norman. *God's Playground: A History of Poland*, vol. 2, *1795 to the Present.* New York: Columbia University Press, 2005.

Davis, Eric. *Memories of State: Politics, History, and Collective Identity in Modern Iraq.* Berkeley: University of California Press, 2005.

Demshuk, Andrew. *Lost German East: Forced Migration and the Politics of Memory, 1945–1970.* New York: Cambridge University Press, 2014.

Dicey, Albert Venn. "The Combination Laws as Illustrating the Relation Between Law and Opinion in England during the Nineteenth Century." *Harvard Law Review* 17, no. 8 (1904): 511–32.

Dobrzycki, Wiesław. *Granica zachodnia w polityce Polskiej, 1944–1947* (The western border in Polish politics, 1944–1947). Warsaw: Państwowe Wydawnictwo Naukowe, 1974.

Dulczewski, Zygmunt, and Andrzej Kwilecki. "Wstęp" (Introduction). *Pamiętniki Osadników Ziem Odzyskanych* (*Diaries of Recovered Territories settlers*), 7–26. Poznań: Wydawnictwo Poznańskie, 1963.

Dylik, Jan. *Geografia Ziem Odzyskanych w zarysie* (A cursory geography of the Recovered Territories). Warsaw: Książka, 1946.

Dziedzic, Franciszek. *Rolnictwo Pomorskie w Zarysie Geograficzno-Gospodarczym* (Polish agriculture in a geographic-agricultural framework). Toruń: Instutyt Bałtycki, 1934.

Erdmans, Mary Patrice. *Opposite Poles: Immigrants and Ethnics in Polish Chicago, 1976–1990.* University Park: Pennsylvania State University Press, 1998.

Felski, Rita. *The Gender of Modernity.* Cambridge, MA: Harvard University Press, 1995.

Fidelis, Małgorzata. *Women, Communism, and Industrialisation in Postwar Poland.* New York: Cambridge University Press, 2010.

Firlit, Elżbieta, and Jerzy Chłopecki. "When Theft Is Not Theft." In *The Unplanned Society: Poland during and after Communism*, edited by Janine R. Wedel, 95–109. New York: Columbia University Press, 1992.

Fitzpatrick, Sheila. *Tear off the Masks! Identity and Imposture in Twentieth-Century Russia*. Princeton, NJ: Princeton University Press, 2005.

Friedmann, Ryszard. "Szlak obozowy" (The concentration camp trail). *Ośrodek Karta* 73 (2012): 48–85.

Gatehouse, Gabriel. "Is Germany's open-door policy fuelling the far right?" *BBC News*, October 8, 2015 (video report).

Gatrell, Peter. "Trajectories of Population Displacement in the Aftermaths of Two World Wars." In *The Disentanglement of Populations: Migration, Expulsion and Displacement in Postwar Europe, 1944–1949*, edited by Jessica Reinisch and Elizabeth White, 3–26. New York: Palgrave Macmillan, 2011.

George, M. Dorothy. "Revisions in Economic History: IV. The Combination Laws." *Economic History Review* 6, no. 2 (1936): 172–78.

Gibney, Frank. *The Frozen Revolution—Poland: A Study in Communist Decay*. New York: Farrar, Straus & Cudahy, 1959.

Gibson-Graham, J. K. *A Postcapitalist Politics*. Minneapolis: University of Minnesota Press, 2006.

Gliński, Piotr. "Acapulco Near Konstancin." In *The Unplanned Society: Poland during and after Communism*, edited by Janine R. Wedel, 144–52. New York: Columbia University Press, 1992.

Gombrowicz, Witold. *Ferdydurke*. Translated by Danuta Borchardt. New Haven, CT: Yale University Press, 1937.

———. *Iwona, Księżniczka Burgunda* (Iwona, Princess of Burgundy). 1938. Warsaw: Państwowy Instytut Wydawniczy, 1958.

Grass, Günter. *Peeling the Onion: A Memoir*. Translated by Michael Henry Heim. New York: Harcourt, 2006.

Gray, J. L. "The Law of Combination in Scotland." *Economica*, no. 24 (December 1928): 332–50.

Gross, Jan. *Fear: Anti-Semitism in Poland After Auschwitz*. New York: Random House, 2007.

Gross, Jan, and Grudzińska-Gross, Irena. *Golden Harvest: Events at the Periphery of the Holocaust*. New York: Oxford University Press, 2012.

Grossman, Alyssa. "Memory Objects, Memory Dialogues: Common-Sense Experiments in Visual Anthropology." In *Experimental Film and Anthropology*, edited by Arnd Schneider and Caterina Pasqualino, 131–46. New York: Bloomsbury, 2014.

Grossman, Gregory. "The 'Second Economy' of the USSR." *Problems of Communism* 26, no. 5 (1977): 25–40.

Hann, Chris. *A Village without Solidarity: Polish Peasants in Years of Crisis*. New Haven, CT: Yale University Press, 1985.

Hardy, Jane, and Al Rainnie. *Restructuring Krakow: Desperately Seeking Capitalism*. London: Thomson Learning, 1996.

Hart, Keith. "Small-Scale Entrepreneurs in Ghana and Development Planning." *Journal of Development Studies* 6, no. 4 (1970): 104–20.

Hašek, Jaroslav. *The Good Soldier Švejk and His Fortunes in the World War*. Translated by Cecil Parrott. London: Penguin Books, 1973.

Henare, Amiria, Martin Holbraad, and Sari Wastell. "Introduction: Thinking through Things." *Thinking through Things: Theorising Artefacts Ethnographically*, edited by Amiria Henare, Martin Holbraad, and Sari Wastell, 1–31. London: Routledge, 2007.

Holmes, Douglas R. "A Peasant-Worker Model in a Northern Italian Context." *American Ethnologi*st 10, no. 4 (1983): 734–48.

Holmgren, Beth. *Rewriting Capitalism: Literature and the Market in Late Tsarist Russia and the Kingdom of Poland.* Pittsburgh, PA: University of Pittsburgh Press, 1998.

Hulewicz, Wacław, and Stanisław Manthey. "Rolnicza spółdzielczość niemiecka i polska na Pomorzu" (German and Polish agricultural cooperation in Pomerania). *Pamiętnik Instytutu Bałtyckiego.* Toruń: Instytut Bałtycki, 1934.

Humphrey, Caroline. "Ideology of Infrastructure: Architecture and Soviet Imagination." *Journal of the Royal Anthropological Institute* 11, no.1 (2005): 39–58.

———. *Marx Went Away: But Karl Stayed Behind.* Ann Arbor: University of Michigan Press, 1998.

Ilf, Ilya, and Evgeny Petrov. *The Golden Calf: A Novel.* Translated by Helen Anderson and Konstantin Gurevich. 1931. Rochester, NY: Open Letter, 2009.

———. *The Twelve Chairs: A Novel.* Translated by Anne O. Fisher. 1928. Evanston, IL: Northwestern University Press, 2011.

Ingbrant, Renata. "In Search of the New Man: Changing Masculinities in Late Nineteenth-Century Polish Novels." *Polish Review* 59, no. 1 (2014): 35–52.

Jauregui, Beatrice. "Dirty Anthropology: Epistemologies of Violence and Ethical Entanglements in Police Ethnography." In *Policing and Contemporary Governance: The Anthropology of Police in Practice*, edited by William Garriott, 125–53. New York: Palgrave Macmillan, 2013.

Jędrychowski, Stefan. *The Recovered Territories, An Integral Part of Poland.* Warsaw: Książka i Wiedza, 1952.

Kelen, Andras. "Reciprocity." In *International Encyclopedia of Civil Society*, edited by Helmut K. Anheier, Regina List, and Stefan Toepler, 1296–1300. New York: Springer Reference, 2010.

Kenney, Padraic. *Rebuilding Poland: Workers and Communists, 1945–1950.* Ithaca, NY: Cornell University Press, 1997.

Kiełczewska, Maria. "Rodzaje i Typy Osiedli Wiejskich na Pomorzu" (Types of rural settlements in Pomerania). *Pamiętnik Instytutu Bałtyckiego.* Toruń: Instutyt Bałtycki, 1934.

Kiełczewska, Maria, and Andrzej Grodek. *Odra-Nysa Najlepsza Granica Polski* (The Oder-Neisse is the best Polish border). Poznań: Instytut Zachodni, 1946.

Kieniewicz, Stefan. *The Emancipation of the Polish Peasantry.* Chicago: University of Chicago Press, 1969.

Kligman, Gail, and Katherine Verdery. *Peasants under Siege: The Collectivization of Romanian Agriculture, 1949–1962.* Princeton, NJ: Princeton University Press, 2011.

Kochanowski, Jerzy. *Tylnymi dzwiami: Czarny rynek w Polsce, 1944–1989* (Through the back door: the black market in Poland, 1944–1989). Warsaw: Neriton and Instytut Historyczny Uniwersytetu, 2010.

Kolchin, Peter. *Unfree Labor: American Slavery and Russian Serfdom.* Cambridge, MA: Belknap Press of Harvard University Press, 1987.

Kolipiński, Juliusz. "The Economic Problems of the Western Territories." In *Polish Western Territories.* Translated by Wanda Libicka. Edited by Bohdan Gruchman,

Edward Serwański, Alfons Klafkowski et al., 159–216. Poznań: Instytut Zachodni, 1959.

Korbonski, Andrzej. *Politics of Socialist Agriculture in Poland, 1945–1960*. New York: Columbia University Press, 1965.

———. "The 'Second Economy' in Poland." *Journal of International Affairs* 35, no. 1 (1981): 1–13.

Kornai, János. "The Reproduction of Shortage." In *Contradictions and Dilemmas: Studies on the Socialist Economy and Society*, 6–32. Cambridge, MA: MIT Press, 1986.

Kotkin, Stephen. *Magnetic Mountain: Stalinism as a Civilization*. Berkeley: University of California Press, 1997.

Kruszewski, Zbigniew Anthony. *The Oder-Neisse Boundary and Poland's Modernization*. New York: Praeger Publishers, 1972.

Kubik, Jan. "From Transitology to Contextual Holism: A Theoretical Trajectory of Postcommunist Studies." In *Postcommunism from Within: Social Justice, Mobilization, and Hegemony*, edited by Jan Kubik and Amy Linch, 27–94. New York: New York University Press, 2013.

———. *The Power of Symbols against the Symbols of Power: The Rise of Solidarity and the Fall of State Socialism in Poland*. University Park, PA: Penn State University Press, 1994.

Kulczycki, John J. *Belonging to the Nation: Inclusion and Exclusion in the Polish-German Borderlands, 1939–1951*. Cambridge, MA: Harvard University Press, 2016.

Kurczewski, Jacek. *The Resurrection of Rights in Poland*. Oxford, UK: Clarendon Press, 1993.

Lampland, Martha. "Corvée, Maps, and Contracts: Agricultural Policy and the Rise of the Modern State in Hungary during the Nineteenth Century." *Irish Journal of Anthropology* 3 (1998): 7–41.

———. *The Object of Labor: Commodification in Socialist Hungary*. Chicago: University of Chicago Press, 1995.

LaPierre, Brian. *Hooligans in Khrushchev's Russia: Defining, Policing, and Producing Deviance during the Thaw*. Madison: University of Wisconsin Press, 2012.

Ledeneva, Alena. "Economies of Favors or Corrupt Societies?" *Baltic Worlds* 1 (2014): 13–21.

———. *Russia's Economy of Favours: Blat, Networking and Informal Exchange*. Cambridge: Cambridge University Press, 1998.

Lekan, Thomas. "German Landscape: Local Promotion of the *Heimat* Abroad." In *The Heimat Abroad: The Boundaries of Germanness*, edited by Krista O'Donnell, Renate Bridenthal, and Nancy Reagin, 141–66. Ann Arbor: University of Michigan Press, 2005.

Lenin, Vladimir Ilyich. *State and Revolution*. New York: International Publishers, 1932.

Levi, Primo. *Survival in Auschwitz*. New York: Simon & Schuster, 1958.

Lewis, Paul. "The Peasantry." In *Social Groups in Polish Society*, edited by David Lane and George Kolankiewicz, 29–87. New York: Columbia University Press, 1973.

Lipovetsky, Mark. *Charms of the Cynical Reason: The Trickster's Transformation in Soviet and Post-Soviet Culture*. Boston: Academic Studies Press, 2011.

Lomnitz, Larissa Adler. "Informal Exchange Networks in Formal Systems: A Theoretical Model." *American Anthropologist* 90, no. 1 (1988): 42–55.

Łoś, Maria. "The Dynamics of the Second Economy in Poland." In *The Second Economy in Marxist States*, edited by Maria Łoś, 27–49. London: Macmillan Press, 1990.

Ludowski, Jerzy, and Hubert Zawadzki. *A Concise History of Poland*. 2nd ed. Cambridge: Cambridge University Press, 2006.

Mach, Zdzisław. *Symbols, Conflict, and Identity: Essays in Political Anthropology*. Albany: State University of New York Press, 1993.

Malinowski, Bronisław. *A Diary in the Strict Sense of the Term*. Stanford, CA: Stanford University Press, 1989.

Marx, Karl. "Chartism." *New-York Daily Tribune*, July 14, 1853. https://www.marxists .org/archive/marx/works/1853/07/14.htm.

———. *The Poverty of Philosophy*. 1847. New York: International Publishers, 1992.

Materka, Edyta. "Hybridizing Postsocialist Trajectories: Investigating the *Biznes* of the US missile base in Rędzikowo and Urbanization of Villages in Provincial Poland." *Anthropology of East Europe Review* 30, no. 1 (2012): 141–83.

———. "Poland's Quiet Revolution: The Unfolding of Shale Gas Exploration and Its Discontents in Pomerania." *Central European Journal of International and Security Studies* 6, no. 1 (2012): 189–218.

———. "Women in 1848, Poland." In *The International Encyclopedia of Revolution and Protest: 1500 to the Present*, edited by Immanuel Ness, 3544–45. Oxford, UK: Wiley-Blackwell, 2009.

Mazurek, Małgorzata. "Keeping It Close to Home: Resourcefulness and Scarcity in Late Socialist and Postsocialist Poland." *Communism Unwrapped: Consumption in Cold War Eastern Europe*, edited by Paulina Bren and Mary Neuburger, 298–324. New York: Oxford University Press, 2012.

Męclewski, Edmund. "Repolonizacja-programem politycznym i realizacyjnym" (The political and realistic program of re-Polonisation). In *Odzyskane Ziemie-Odzyskani Ludzie* (Recovered Territories, Recovered People). Poznań: Wydawnictwo Zachodnie, 1946.

Mikołajczyk, Stanisław. *The Rape of Poland: Pattern of Soviet Aggression*. Westport, CT: Greenwood Press, 1948.

Mill, John Stuart. *On Liberty and Other Essays*. Edited by John Gray. 1859. New York: Oxford World's Classics, 1991.

Miłosz, Czesław. *Native Realm: A Search for Self-Definition*. Translated by Catherine S. Leach. 1968. New York: Farrar, Straus & Giroux, 2002.

Minc, Hilary. "The Recovery of the Regained Territories." In *Industrial Reconstruction in the Polish Regained Territories*, 14–20. Warsaw: Ingos Publishing, 1947.

———. "The Six-Year Plan of Economic Development and Building the Foundations of Socialism in Poland." In *The Six-Year Plan of Economic Development and Building the Foundations of Socialism in Poland*, 19–66. Warsaw: Książka i Wiedza, 1950.

Mitkowski, Józef. *Pomorze Zachodnie W Stosunku do Polski* (Western Pomerania in Relation to Poland). Poznań: Wydawnictwo Instytutu Zachodniego, 1946.

Murat, Leszek. "Promiscuous Pioneers of Morality: The Code of Ethics of a Secret Service Functionary in Communist Poland as Set by Law and Practice, 1944–1989." PhD diss., State University of New York, Albany, 2010.

Myant, Martin. *Transforming Socialist Economies: The Case of Poland and Czechoslovakia*. Hants, UK: Edward Elgar, 1993.

Nafisi, Azar. *The Republic of Imagination: America in Three Books*. New York: Viking Press, 2014.

Napierała, Joanna, and Paulina Trevena. "Patterns and Determinants of Sub-Regional Migration: A Case Study of Polish Construction Workers in Norway." In *A Continent Moving West? EU Enlargement and Labor Migration from Central and Eastern Europe*, edited by Richard Black, Cristina Pantîru, Godfried Engbersen, and Marek Okólski, 51–72. Amsterdam: Amsterdam University Press, 2010.

Onesti, Sally Joanna. "Portrait of a Generation. Soviet Interpretations of Soviet Foreign Policy and Détente: The Brezhnev-Nixon Years, 1969–74." PhD diss., Columbia University, 1991.

Ortner, Sherry B. "Dark Anthropology and Its Others: Theory since the Eighties." *HAU: Journal of Ethnographic Theory* 6, no. 1 (2016): 47–73.

Orwell, George. *1984*. New York: Signet Classics, 1950.

Ost, David. *The Defeat of Solidarity: Anger and Politics in Postcommunist Europe*. Ithaca, NY: Cornell University Press, 2005.

Paczkowski, Andrzej. "Poland, the 'Enemy Nation.'" In *The Black Book of Communism*, edited by Mark Kramer. Translated by Jonathan Murphy and Mark Kramer, 363–93. Cambridge, MA: Harvard University Press, 1999.

Pagel, Karl Heinz. "Rathsdamnitz." In *Der Landkreis Stolp in Pommern: Zeugnisse seiner deutschen Vergangenheit*, 800–11. Lübeck: Heimatkreises Stolp, 1989.

Paine, Thomas. "Rights of Man." 1791. In *Rights of Man, Common Sense and Other Political Writings*, edited by Mark Philp, 83–332. New York: Oxford World's Classics, 1995.

Parrott, Cecil. Introduction to *The Good Soldier Švejk and His Fortunes in the World War*, by Jaroslav Hašek, translated by Cecil Parrott, vii–xxii. London: Penguin Books, 1973.

Pawlik, Wojciech. "Intimate Commerce." In *The Unplanned Society: Poland during and after Communism*, edited by Janine R. Wedel, 78–94. New York: Columbia University Press, 1992.

Penn, Shana. *Solidarity's Secret: The Women Who Defeated Communism in Poland*. Ann Arbor: University of Michigan Press, 2005.

Pesmen, Dale. *Russia and Soul: An Exploration*. Ithaca, NY: Cornell University Press, 2000.

Phillips, Ursula. Introduction to *The Heathen*, by Narcyza Żmichowska. Translated by Ursula Phillips, ix–xlviii. DeKalb, IL: Northern Illinois University Press, 2012.

Pine, Frances. "Dangerous Modernities? Innovative Technologies and the Unsettling of Agriculture in Rural Poland." *Critique of Anthropology* 27, no. 2 (2007): 183–201.

Polian, Pavel. *Against Their Will: The History and Geography of Forced Migrations in the USSR*. Budapest: Central European University Press, 2004.

Polish Socialist Party. "From Narodism to Marxism." *Przedświt* 8 (October 10, 1905): 83–89. http://www.marxists.org/archive/lenin/works/1905/oct/10.htm.

Pollak, Roman. *Rola Ziem Zachodnich w Polskiej Kulturze* (The role of western lands in Polish culture). Poznań: Wydawnictwo Polskiego Związku Zachodniego, 1946.

Polonsky, Antony, and Bolesław Drukier. *The Beginnings of Communist Rule in Poland*. London: Routledge & Kegan Paul, 1980.

Prus, Bolesław. *The Doll*. 1890. Translated by David Welsh. New York: New York Review Books, 2011.

———. *Lalka, tom pierwszy* (The Doll, Volume 1). 1890. Warsaw: Państwowy Instytut Wydawniczy, 1975. Available at Wolne Lektury, http://wolnelektury.pl/katalog /lektura/lalka-tom-pierwszy.html#info.

———. *Lalka, tom drugi* (The Doll, Volume 2). 1890. Warsaw: Państwowy Instytut Wydawniczy, 1975. Available at Wolne Lektury, http://wolnelektury.pl/katalog /lektura/lalka-tom-drugi.html.

———. *Powracająca fala* (The Returning Wave). 1880. Warsaw: Państwowy Instytut Wydawniczy, 1976. Available at Wolne Lektury, http://wolnelektury.pl/katalog /lektura/powracajaca-fala.html.

"Rebellious Compromiser." *Time Magazine*. December 10, 1956, 29–34.

Reymont, Władysław. *Ziemia Obiecana, tom pierwszy* (The Promised Land, Volume 1). 1899. Warsaw: Gebethnera i Wolffa, 1920. Available at Wolne Lektury, http:// wolnelektury.pl/katalog/lektura/ziemia-obiecana-tom-pierwszy.html.

———. *Ziemia Obiecana, tom drugi* (The Promised Land, Volume 2). 1899. Warsaw: Gebethnera i Wolffa, 1920. Available at Wolne Lektury, http://wolnelektury.pl/katalog /lektura/ziemia-obiecana-tom-drugi.html.

Roll, Erich. "Review: Industrial Combination." *Economic History Review* 6, no. 1 (1935): 107–9.

Sachs, Jeffrey. *Poland's Jump to the Market Economy*. Cambridge, MA: MIT Press, 1993.

Sampson, Steven. "The Second Economy of the Soviet Union and Eastern Europe." *Annals of the American Academy of Political and Social Science* 493 (1987): 120–36.

Santos, Daniel. "The Second Economy in Agola: Esquema and Candonga." In *The Second Economy in Marxist States*, edited by Maria Łoś, 157–74. London: Macmillan, 1990.

Schneider, Deborah Cahalen. *Being Góral: Identity Politics and Globalization in Postsocialist Poland*. Albany: State University of New York Press, 2006.

Schneider, Jason. "Inventing Home: Movement, Place, and the Rhetorics of Polish Chicago." PhD diss., University of Illinois at Chicago, 2012.

Scott, James C. *Domination and the Arts of Resistance: Hidden Transcripts*. New Haven, CT: Yale University Press, 1990.

Siegelbaum, Lewis. Introduction to *Stalinism as a Way of Life: A Narrative in Documents*, edited by Lewis Siegelbaum and Andrei Sokolov. Translated by Thomas Hoisington and Steven Shabad, 1–27. New Haven, CT: Yale University Press, 2000.

Skultans, Vieda. *The Testimony of Lives: Narrative and Memory in Post-Soviet Latvia*. London: Routledge, 1998.

Śmigielska, Joanna. "There's the Beef." In *The Unplanned Society: Poland during and after Communism*, edited by Janine R. Wedel, 110–22. New York: Columbia University Press, 1992.

Smith, Adam. *The Wealth of Nations*. 1776. Edited by Edwin Cannan. New York: Bantam Classic, 2003.

Snyder, Timothy. *Bloodlands: Europe between Hitler and Stalin*. New York: Basic Books, 2010.

Spiegelman, Art. *Maus: A Survivor's Tale*. New York: Pantheon Books, 1973.

Stauter-Halsted, Keely. *The Nation in the Village: The Genesis of Peasant National Identity in Austrian Poland, 1848–1914*. Ithaca, NY: Cornell University Press, 2001.

Stenning, Alison, Adrian Smith, Alena Rochovská, and Dariusz Świątek. *Domesticating Neo-Liberalism: Spaces of Economic Practice and Social Reproduction in Postsocialist Cities*. West Sussex, UK: Wiley-Blackwell, 2010.

Steven, Stewart. *The Poles.* New York: Macmillan, 1982.

Szaz, Michael Z. *Germany's Eastern Frontiers: The Problem of the Oder-Neisse Line.* Chicago: Regnery, 1960.

Szelenyi, Ivan. *Socialist Entrepreneurs: Embourgeoisement in Rural Hungary.* Madison: University of Wisconsin Press, 1988.

Telgarsky, Jeffrey P., and Reymond J. Struyk. *Toward a Market-Oriented Housing Sector in Eastern Europe: Developments in Bulgaria, Czechoslovakia, Hungary, Poland, Romania, and Yugoslavia.* Washington, DC: Urban Institute Press, 1990.

Thomas, William I., and Florian Znaniecki. *The Polish Peasant in Europe and America,* edited by Eli Zaretsky. 1918. Urbana: University of Illinois Press, 1996.

Thompson, E. P. *The Making of the English Working Class.* New York: Vintage Books, 1963.

Thum, Gregor. *Uprooted: How Breslau became Wrocław during the Century of Expulsion.* Princeton, NJ: Princeton University Press, 2011.

Tokarczuk, Olga. *House of Day, House of Night.* Translated by Antonia Lloyd-Jones. Evanston, IL: Northwestern University Press, 2003.

Tucker, Erica L. "Conspiring with Memory: Remembering World War II in Post-Communist Poland." PhD diss., University of Wisconsin–Madison, 2005.

Tucker, Robert C. *Stalin in Power: Revolution from Above, 1928–1941.* New York: W. W. Norton, 1992.

Verdery, Katherine. *The Vanishing Hectare: Property and Value in Postsocialist Transylvania.* Ithaca, NY: Cornell University Press, 2003.

Weber, Max. *The Agrarian Sociology of Ancient Civilizations.* 1909. Translated by R. I. Frank. London: Verso, 2013.

———. *From Max Weber: Essays in Sociology.* 1946. Translated by H. H. Gerth and Wright Mills. New York: Oxford University Press, 1958.

Wedel, Janine. *The Private Poland.* New York: Facts on File, 1986.

Whatley, Christopher. "'The Fettering Bonds of Brotherhood': Combination and Labor Relations in the Scottish Coal-Mining Industry c. 1690–1775." *Social History* 12, no. 2 (1987): 139–54.

Wisse, Ruth R. *The Modern Jewish Canon: A Journey Through Language and Culture.* Chicago: University of Chicago Press, 2001.

Witkiewicz, Ignacy Stanisław. *Narkotyki* (Narcotics). 1932. Warsaw: Państwowy Instytut Wydawniczy, 1993. Available at Wolne Lektury, https://wolnelektury.pl/katalog/lektura/witkacy-narkotyki.html.

Yoshioka, Jun. "Imagining Their Lands as Ours: Place Name Changes on Ex-German Territories in Poland after World War II." *Acta Slavica Iaponica* 15 (2008): 273–87.

Zaretsky, Eli. Epilogue to *The Polish Peasant in Europe and America,* edited by Eli Zaretsky, 123–27. Urbana: University of Illinois Press, 1996.

Zbierski-Salameh, Suava. *Bitter Harvest: Antecedents and Consequences of Property Reforms in Postsocialist Poland.* Lanham, MD: Lexington Books, 2013.

Żeromski, Stefan. *Syzyfowe prace* (Labors of Sisyphus). 1897. Available at Wolne Lektury, http://wolnelektury.pl/katalog/lektura/syzyfowe-prace/.

Zholkovsky, Alexander. *Text Counter Text: Rereadings in Russian Literary History.* Stanford, CA: Stanford University Press, 1996.

Zielinski, Konrad. "To Pacify, Populate and Polonise: Territorial Transformations and the Displacement of Ethnic Minorities in Communist Poland, 1944–49." In *Warlands: Population Resettlement and State Reconstruction in the Soviet–East*

European Borderlands, 1945–50, edited by Peter Gatrell and Nick Baron, 188–209. New York: Palgrave Macmillan, 2009.

Ziółkowski, Janusz. "The Population of the Western Territories." In *Polish Western Territories*. Translated by Wanda Libicka. Edited by Bohdan Gruchman, Edward Serwański, Alfons Klafkowski et al., 115–58. Poznań: Instytut Zachodi, 1959.

Żmichowska, Narcyza. *Narcyssa i Wanda: Listy Narcyzy Żmichowskiej do Wandy Grabowskiej (Żeleńskiej)*. (Narcyssa and Wanda: Letters of Narcyza Żmichowska to Wanda Grabowska [Żeleński]). 1930. Available at Wolne Lektury, https://wolnelektury.pl/katalog/lektura/narcyssa-i-wanda.html.

Żukrowski, Wojciech. *Kamienne tablice* (Stone tablets). Warsaw: Wydawnicto Ministerstwa Obrony Narodowej, 1966.

Index

Page numbers in *italics* refer to figures.

Accra, informal sector practices in, 10. *See also* Hart, Keith

activists: gay rights activists, 68; Party activists, 5, 43, 45–46, 130–33, 142; peasant activists, 87; Soviet activists, 71; trade union activists, 167. *See also* persuasion

agency, 1; dystopian form of, 43–44; in hunt for resources, 71; kombinacja as a form of, 20–22; liminality as form of, 43–44; patriotic trickster as a form of, 65; Polish masculinity as a form of, 65; postsocialist agency, 183; Soviet agency, 70; state as platform to enact, 60

Agrarian Sociology of Ancient Civilizations, The (Weber), 101. *See also* obligatory labor

agricultural circles (*kółka rolnicze*): as backdoor collectivization, 149; bridging agro-industrial divide, 152–53; Catholic-run, 61; centralization, 149, 155; courts, 61; demographic shifts, 158; family networks in, 17, 39; First National Conference of Agricultural Circles, 149; kombinacja within, 150–52; national identity, 66; nomenklatura privatization, 169, 188; organic work, 61; paper contract (*umowa*), 150; Polish October reforms, 148; Polish schoolhouses, 61; postsocialist corruption of, 176–77; quota production, 152; self-governance, 149; worker-peasant class, 150–53

agricultural production cooperative (*rolnicza spółdzielnia produkcyjna*), 41, 118, 130–33; collective farm workers (*kołchoźnik*), 133, 135; enemy work (*wroga robota*), 139; as enlightenment project, 130; and feudal debts, 134–35; kombinacja, 131–32, 139–41; persuasion (*namawianie*) during collectivization, 45; politics of Soviet and Polish terms, 144; postsocialist variants, 202; quota production, 136–38; self-liquidation and abandonment, 133; as Soviet kolkhoz (*kołchoz*), 41; worker-peasant alliance, 130

agricultural quota production (*kontyngenty*), 17, 23, 45; in the agricultural circles, 148–52, 154; in the agricultural production cooperative,

131–34; and collapse of socialism, 24, 39–40; collective farm workers resistance against, 137–38; as dekulakization, 119–22; as encounter with occupation, 121, 123, 143; and feudal obligations, 34, 122–23, 125, 134–36; formal structure of, 118, 120, 123–24, 127; kombinacja against, 120–21, 126–27, 133, 136–37, 139–43, 149, 156–58, 167; in late socialist period, 148–51, 155–57, 169; memories of, 6, 17, 121, 129; during Nazi occupation, 6–7, 76–77, 121; peasant complaints against, 125–26; as response to failed collectivization, 122; in Russia (*prodrazvyorstka*), 68; state records of, 124–29, 136–37. *See also* obligatory labor

Akt nadania land titles, 92, 101, 119, 122, 143

alcoholism, 24, 173–74, 178; alcohol money, 24–25, 174–76; and collective identity, 25–26, 52n10, 158, 173–74, 181, 190–93, 205; and corruption, 169, 178; during fieldwork, 39; illegal moonshine (*bimber*), 163; illegal pubs, (*meliny*), 163; and kombinators, 174–75; nationalization of production (socialism), 163; and Polish People's Army, 173; rituals, 162–63

allotment gardens (*działki*), 26

AlSayyad, Nezar, 10–11

anti-combination laws, 3; Act to Prevent the Unlawful Combinations of Workmen (1800), 54, 79n2; Combinations of Workmen Act of 1825, 55; overturn of, 60. *See also* Conspiracy and Protection of Property Act of 1875; Trade Union Act of 1871

archives, 6–7, 22, 120; bodies as, 40; "domestication" of, 35–36, 201, 209; during fieldwork, 15–16n5; fragments of, 30, 102, 104; kombinator as term used in, 47, 49–50, 143–44; as obfuscation of history, 38, 41, 45, 95, 120–21, 124–25, 129, 195; and peasant memories, 121; as record of feudal obligations, 95, 98; as record of peasants' plight, 128, 141; as socialist performance, 129; Third Reich administrative papers in, 30, 31

EDYTA MATERKA received her PhD from the London School of Economics and Political Science and is a Leverhulme Trust Early Career Fellow in the School of Geography, Queen Mary University of London.

CPSIA information can be obtained
at www.ICGtesting.com
Printed in the USA
LVOW13s0516200218
567139LV00015B/176/P